Oil and Gas Law in the UK

Oil and Gas Law in the UK

Mohammad Alramahi

Lecturer in Law at the University of Hull
Consultant in Oil and Gas Law, KENA Consultants Ltd

Bloomsbury Professional

Bloomsbury Professional Ltd, Maxwelton House, 41–43 Boltro Road, Haywards Heath, West Sussex, RH16 1BJ

© Bloomsbury Professional Ltd 2013

Bloomsbury Professional, an imprint of Bloomsbury Publishing plc

A CIP Catalogue record for this book is available from the British Library.

ISBN: 978 1 84766 555 3

Typeset by Phoenix Photosetting, Chatham, Kent
Printed in Great Britain by Hobbs the Printers Ltd, Totton, Hampshire.

Preface

This book is an essential foundation text for Oil and Gas Law as an area that has developed over the last decade, and considers its relevance to the UK oil and gas industry. It initially considers the general framework of the International Oil and Gas industry and then examines in detail the UK Oil and Gas industry, based primarily on the UK Continental Shelf (UKCS).

In **Part 1** the relevant key terms, definitions and applicable principles common to this area of the law are introduced. In **Part 2** the book offers practical information on the overall UKCS framework from an operational point of view. **Part 3** focuses on relevant commercial issues and current contractual arrangements common in the UKCS. It also provide some useful guidance on how to negotiate and review oil and gas contracts, how to assess and manage risks in oil and gas contracts, how to avoid common contract pitfalls and how to make effective use of the alternative dispute resolution option. In **Part 4** the future of the UKCS Oil and Gas industry is assessed, and the important future role of renewable energy is analysed in some detail.

It is suggested that the reading list at the end of each part is examined carefully by the reader. It has two sections: Essential Reading; and Suggested Reading. The reader should, at the minimum, read and assimilate the Essential Reading section. For those with particular interest in individual sections of the previous part, the relevant works in the Suggested Reading section should be consulted.

Mohammad Alramahi

July 2013

Contents

Contents

Contents

Table of Statutes

[All references are to paragraph numbers]

Table of Statutes

Table of Statutory Instruments

[All references are to paragraph numbers]

Table of Cases

[All references are to paragraph numbers]

Part 1

Overview of the UKCS

1.1   This Part acts as the foundation to an introductory insight into the general structure of the oil and gas industry and legal relationships encountered therein. The maturing nature of the United Kingdom Continental Shelf (UKCS) is highlighted in this section, and the changing nature of the regulatory regime is examined. Key terms and abbreviations, which act as reference points throughout this Part, are defined.

A   BACKGROUND OF OIL AND GAS LAW

1.2   Oil and gas law is the legal regime that governs various aspects of oil and gas business, exploration, drilling, transportation and commercial transactions in an oil and gas province. An understanding of oil and gas law equips the individual with the awareness and skills necessary to succeed in the ever-changing global commercial oil and gas environment. Oil and gas commercial advisors and legal practitioners acting on behalf of oil companies require this basic skill-set in order to be efficient legal personnel, negotiators, contractual draftsmen and successful individuals possessing up to date information, resulting in the overall efficiency of the organisation they represent.

1.3   Generally, oil and gas law refers to the wide range of legal processes and regulations fundamental to the industry, such as the many contractual arrangements used on a daily basis between its many players. These are used to advance the key stages of hydrocarbon operations, particularly the exploration, exploitation, collection and distribution of oil and gas resources. These arrangements are based on agreements between a wide range of players such as individuals or corporate entities or a mixture of both; citizens and foreign investors; and local companies and international companies, which create legally binding rights and obligations. These different relationships are by and large influenced by the contract law of the country concerned. However, this book will examine those arrangements specifically related to the international oil and gas industry.

1.4   Another key issue is that oil and gas law is generally influenced by the manner in which the rights to explore and exploit the natural resources of a particular country are dealt with. In a number of countries the starting point for determining this is to look its constitution, which clarifies the position of the ownership of the natural (oil and gas) resources. Usually the constitution would bestow the ownership of the oil and gas resources on the state, or would affirm that the state has sovereign rights over the resources within the boundaries of the country, including the continental shelf, on behalf of the people of the country. This implies that anyone who wants to explore and exploit these resources will have to apply to the state, usually through the government, for permission (usually through a licence or contract) to do so. Such permission may also depend on the degree of involvement by government, which differs widely from jurisdiction to jurisdiction. In some countries, because of the highly technical nature of the industry, a national oil company (NOC) is established to act as an agent of government in awarding the right to undertake this activity; in other countries the NOC would carry out the activity itself, and merely invite the international oil company (IOC) to deliver a particular service on a contractual basis. In other jurisdictions, because of the highly capital-intensive nature of the industry, the IOC is invited to apply for a licence and undertake this activity on its own account. The successful IOC will then enter into a number of different contracts with a number of different entities and players in the oil and gas industry, in order to undertake this activity. Oil and gas law is therefore the law that regulates the relationships between the various players in the oil and gas industry.

This section provides a general overview of the international industry, including an examination of the various types of legal arrangements that are used internationally. It also considers those arrangements currently used in the oil and gas industry in the UKCS.

Key oil and gas terminology

1.5   This is an overview of some of the key concepts of oil and gas law, including some of the most common oil and gas industry terms, to provide the reader with an understanding of the general background of the industry. These terms and definitions (some of them are very technical in nature) are utilised throughout the industry on a daily basis, and will constantly recur throughout this book. Thus one should have some degree of understanding of these key concepts.

ASSIGNMENT/ ASSIGNATION	The legal name for the process by which a party's rights and obligations under a contract are transferred to a third party.
BID	This is the process by which an operator makes an offer for a licence; it also describes the process by which contractors will bid for work from the operators or from the lead contractors.

BLOCK	Subdivision of sea area for the purpose of licensing to a company or companies for exploration/production rights. A UK block is 1/30 of a quadrant and is approximately 200–250 sq km (a quadrant is one degree by one degree).
BLOW OUT PREVENTER	The equipment installed at the wellhead to control pressures in the space between the casing and drill pipe or tubing during drilling and other operations.
CHRISTMAS TREE	The assembly of valves, pipes, and fittings used to control the flow of oil and gas from a well.
CONCESSION	The right to drill for oil or gas on a block obtained under licence from the state.
CRINE/LOGIC (see abbreviation section below)	Both are (in the case of CRINE, were) supply chain organisations supported by and supporting the UK oil and gas industry. CRINE put in place a standard contracting structure which is widely used now the UK industry and which is now managed by LOGIC, as the successor to CRINE. The Industry Mutual Hold Harmless Agreement is administered by LOGIC.
DECOMMISSIONING	The process by which production facilities are removed from depleted fields.
DOWNHOLE	This is the term used to describe tools, equipment, and instruments used in the borehole for the drilling and extraction process.
DRILLING CONTRACTOR	A person or company whose business is drilling wells. Wells are drilled on several contract specifications: per foot, day rate, or turnkey (that is, upon completion). Most major oil companies do not own drilling rigs. Exploration and development drilling is contracted. Personnel manning the rigs work for the contractor.
DRILLING MUD	A special mixture of clay, water, or refined oil, and chemical additives pumped downhole. The mud cools the drillbit and lubricates the drill pipe as it turns in the well bore. Mud also carries rock cuttings to the surface and prevents the wall of the borehole from crumbling or collapsing.
DOWNSTREAM	Usually refining and the marketing and distribution operations that occur after refining as opposed to upstream.
FABRIC MAINTENANCE	The process by which the fabric of the topsides is maintained. This may be as simple as painting or may involve specialised cleaning and coating processes.

FLOATER	An offshore drilling platform without a fixed base.
FPSO	Floating Production Storage and Offloading facilities.
GOOD OIL FIELD PRACTICE	The technical matters within the disciplines of geology and reservoir, petroleum and facilities engineering, and with attention to the impact of the development on the environment. The company is required to follow good practice in formulating plans for the development and management of a field. When considering what constitutes good practice, the company's proposals will be compared with the practice adopted in similar, successful developments.
INDUSTRY MUTUAL HOLD HARMLESS	This is an agreement which the oil and gas industry in the UK is encouraged to sign up to in order to allow every contactor and operator to be safe from the claims of other contractors for injury or death to their employees or subcontractors and for claims for loss of or damage to equipment. It interacts with the CRINE contract system.
INSPECTION	The process by which a regular system of inspection is used to identify whether equipment is still serviceable; whether it is safe and whether it is compliant with the various regulations on safety and usage.
JACKET	Supporting structure for an offshore platform.
JACKUP	Mobile offshore drilling platform with retractable legs, on which the platform rests on the seabed when operational.
LICENCE	An exploration licence permits only geological and geophysical surveying and the drilling of shallow wells; a production licence confers exclusive rights on the licensee to search and bore for and get petroleum.
LNG	Liquefied Natural Gas: Gas, mainly methane, liquefied under pressure and low temperature.
LOG	Logging is to collect information about the drilling and extraction process; a log is the results of such a survey. The equipment used to collect such information is usually highly specialised.
LPG	Liquefied Petroleum Gas: Propane and butane, liquefied under pressure or refrigeration. Often known as bottled gas.

NOVATION	Often confused with assignation/assignment, this is a process by which a party's rights and obligations under a contract are replaced with a new set of rights and obligations. A novation replaces the former obligations/rights by new ones and may take place between the two original parties, whereas an assignation brings in at least one new party.
OPERATOR	The individual, partnership, firm or corporation having control or management of operations on a leased area or a portion thereof. The operator may be a lessee, designated agent of the lessee, holder of rights under an approved operation agreement, or an agent of an operating rights holder.
OUTER CONTINENTAL SHELF (OCS)	All submerged lands seaward and outside the area of lands beneath navigable waters. In the USA, lands beneath navigable waters are interpreted as extending from the coastline three nautical miles into the Atlantic Ocean, the Pacific Ocean, the Arctic Ocean and the Gulf of Mexico, excluding the coastal waters off Texas and western Florida. Lands beneath navigable waters are interpreted as extending from the coastline three marine leagues into the Gulf of Mexico off Texas and western Florida. Most countries have their own definition of the OCS.
PLATFORM	A fixed structure resting on the seabed or piled into it from which development wells are drilled, using directional drilling, to exploit an oil or gas field. To date, these platforms are of two kinds, although several novel designs are in existence: gravity structures, either concrete or hybrid with concrete base and steel legs and superstructure, which rest on the seabed by virtue of their own weight, or steel, which are piled into the seabed.
RESERVOIR	A subsurface, porous, permeable rock formation in which oil and gas are found.
RIG	A term for a mobile drilling unit, sometimes used to refer to a platform, usually used to describe the entire structure.
ROTATING EQUIPMENT	Any mechanical equipment that rotates, eg vertical pumps and gas turbine engines. Oil platforms use rotating equipment to drill for and extract oil.

ROYALTY	Payment of a percentage of gross income from the production of minerals, including hydrocarbons, by the company licensed to produce, to the state. A step-scale royalty rate increases by steps as the average production on the lease increases. A sliding-scale royalty rate is based on average production and applies to all production from the lease.
SEMI-SUBMERSIBLE	Mobile offshore drilling platform with floats or pontoons submerged to give stability while operating, kept in position by anchors or dynamic positioning.
SUBSEA	The equipment or structures which are below the surface of the sea in offshore structures. The subsea industry is specialised inasmuch as equipment has to be able to withstand use in water (saline or fresh), often with cold temperatures; the personnel require diving skills; the safety profiles of such operations are specialised.
TOPSIDES	The top part of a platform positioned on the jacket.

Key abbreviations

1.6

AFE	Authorisation For Expenditure
AIPN	Association of International Petroleum Negotiators
AMI	Area of Mutual Interest
BNOC	British National Oil Company
CRINE	Cost Reduction Initiative for the New Era
DCPD	Decommissioning Cost Provision Deed
DECC	Department of Energy and Climate Change
DSA	Decommissioning Security Agreement
EEA	European Economic Area
EEC	European Economic Community
ERRES	Economically Recoverable Reserves
EU	European Union
FPAL	First Point Assessment Limited
HCIP	Hydrocarbons Initially in Place
HCPV	Hydrocarbon Pore Volume
IMHH	Indemnity Mutual Hold Harmless deed
IMO	International Maritime Authority
IOC	International Oil Company

IRRES	Initial Recoverable Reserves
JBA	Joint Bidding Agreement
JOA	Joint Operating Agreement
JOC	Joint Operating Committee
LOGIC	Leading Oil and Gas Industry Competitiveness
MHCIIP	Moveable Hydrocarbons Initially in Place
OPCOM	Joint Operating Committee
OPOL	Offshore Pollution Liability Agreement
PRT	Petroleum Revenue Tax
RFCT	Ring Fence Corporation Tax
STOOIP	The Stock Tank Oil Originally in Place
UKCS	United Kingdom Continental Shelf
UUOA	Unitisation and Unit Operating Agreement

Main production areas

1.7   Globally, the main production areas are:

- Gulf of Mexico: USA (and onshore in Texas and Oklahoma), Mexico;
- Trinidad and Tobago; The Americas: Venezuela; Brazil; Canada;
- Russia: Sakhalin and Siberia;
- Middle East: Azerbaijan; Iran, Iraq, Kuwait, Saudi Arabia, Bahrain, Qatar, UAE, Kazakhstan;
- North Africa: Libya; Algeria;
- West Africa: Nigeria; Ghana; Equatorial Guinea;
- Asia: India, Malaysia, Indonesia; Vietnam;
- Europe: Norway, UK (northern North Sea), Netherlands.

This is not an exhaustive list, but sets out the main areas where oil and gas are produced. Some of these areas have been producing oil and gas for a very long time, eg Trinidad and Tobago, Indonesia and Azerbaijan have been producing for well over a century.

1.8   This Part will take the reader through the basic structure of oil and gas law from the ownership of the mineral rights, through rights to exploit these, the contractual matrix in which such rights are exploited; the structure of the industry, the contractual relationship between the owners of the mineral rights, the oil and gas production companies and their contractors and sub-contractors.

The North Sea will be used as the model for this, but different jurisdictions will be referred to where useful comparisons can be made. The standard contracting model for the North Sea will be used as the contract model for the Part.

Contracting structure: UK

1.9

State
Award
Decree
Licencee

Government Regulator
Ministry of Oil and Gas/
Petroleum/Other
Departments
Permission to carry out E&P

National Oil Company (NOC)
Advisor/Regulator/Promoter
Commercial Partner in:
Joint Venture/Production Sharing
Contract/Licence/Service Contract

International Oil Company (IOC)
Investor
Licensee
Contractor
Service Provider
Technical Advisor

B   RELATIONSHIPS OF DIFFERENT PLAYERS IN THE OIL AND GAS INDUSTRY

Phases of the oil and gas industry

1.10   The oil and gas industry is generally divided into four major phases:

- **Upstream:** The upstream oil sector is a term commonly used to refer to the searching for and the recovery and production of crude oil and natural gas. The upstream oil sector is also known as the exploration and production (E&P) sector. The upstream sector includes searching for potential underground or underwater oil and gas fields (reconnaissance), drilling of exploratory wells (exploration), and subsequently operating the wells that recover and bring the crude oil and/or raw natural gas to the surface (production);

- **Midstream:** Midstream is used to describe the processing, storage and transportation sectors within the oil and gas industry. Midstream defines the industry processes that occur between the upstream and downstream sectors;

- **Downstream:** The downstream oil sector is a term commonly used to refer to the refining of crude oil and the selling and distribution of natural gas and products derived from crude oil. Such products include liquefied petroleum gas (LPG), gasoline or petrol, jet fuel, diesel oil, other fuel oils, asphalt and petroleum coke. The downstream sector includes oil refineries, petrochemical plants, petroleum product distribution, retail outlets and natural gas distribution companies. The downstream industry touches consumers through thousands of products such as petrol, diesel, jet fuel, heating oil, asphalt, lubricants, synthetic rubber, plastics, fertilizers, antifreeze, pesticides, pharmaceuticals, natural gas and propane;

- **Decommissioning:** The abandonment/decommissioning of offshore installations involves the taking out of service, dismantling and making safe of an installation after the end of a production field life or the operational life of an installation.

Activities

1.11   For this introductory section, undertake the following exercise to enhance your own understanding of the industry.

- In advising an IOC to obtain the right to explore and exploit the oil and gas resources of a particular country, think about the key issues that you would include in the contract that will be concluded with the national partner (ie government or NOC).

- Find a copy of your country's national law relating to oil and gas activities (upstream) (eg oil and gas act/decree; petroleum legislation), read and summarise the following provisions:
  — the award of a licence or contract to the IOC and the nature of these rights;
  — the role and relationship of the government/NOC and that of the IOC;
  — the procedure for obtaining a contract;
  — any procedures for negotiation;
  — the type of contract (ie model petroleum agreement).

9

Suggested reading

1.12   Useful websites

- Leading Oil & Gas Industry Competitiveness (LOGIC): www.logic-oil. com
- Industry Mutual Hold Harmless (IMHH): www.imhh.com
- Pilot: www.pilottaskforce.co.uk
- Department of Energy and Climate Change (DECC): www.og.decc.gov. uk
- Oil and Gas UK (OGUK): www.ukooa.co.uk
- Organization of the Petroleum Producing Countries (OPEC): www.opec. org/home
- The Petroleum Act 1998 can be found at www.opsi.gov.uk/acts/acts1998/ ukpga_19980017_en_1.

Some useful information which will give an overview of the UKCS:

- www.oilandgasuk.co.uk/issues/economic/econ09/economic_report_09. pdf
- UK Oil and Gas Industry statistics (DECC): https://www.og.decc.gov. uk/information/statistics.htm
- Guide to the North Sea Fiscal Regime at www.hmrc.gov.uk/international/ ns-fiscal.htm.

International petroleum industry

1.13   This section provides an overview of the international oil and gas industry; discussion of ownership of oil and gas and sovereignty of natural resources, including the law of the sea regime and the continental shelf; and main international petroleum arrangements, including a summary of the UK licensing system.

World oil markets

1.14   Crude oil, also known as petroleum, is the world's most actively traded commodity. The largest markets are in London, New York and Singapore but crude oil and refined products—such as gasoline (petrol) and heating oil—are bought and sold all over the world.

Crude oil comes in many varieties and qualities, depending on its specific gravity and sulphur content, which depend on where it has been pumped from.

If no other information is given, an oil price appearing in UK and other European media reports will probably refer to the price of a barrel of Brent blend crude oil from the North Sea sold at London's International Petroleum Exchange (IPE).

The North Sea's Brent is used to price most other crudes. The recent rise in the price of oil has focused attention on the markets where the 'black gold' is traded. But what exactly is being traded, where and how?

Futures contract

1.15 This would commonly be in a futures contract for delivery in the following month. In this type of transaction, the buyer agrees to take delivery and the seller agrees to provide a fixed amount of oil at a pre-arranged price at a specified location. Futures contracts are traded only on regulated exchanges and are settled (paid) daily, based on their current value in the marketplace. The minimum purchase is 1,000 barrels.

Who's who in the oil and gas industry

Governments

1.16 Governments write the laws and regulations which control the oil and gas industry within a country. Occasionally, they get together and enter into international agreements which affect oil and gas companies (commonly agreements which define the boundaries between offshore jurisdictions such as the UK–Norway–Denmark–Germany–Netherlands boundaries in the North Sea).

Generally, governments compete to attract oil and gas companies and their investment money to ensure the development of oil and gas in their country.

In some circumstances, countries are 'over-subscribed' and actively manage to limit oil and gas developments. An example is Norway, which produces vastly more oil and gas than it needs, and is choosing to limit the pace of development to ensure a long-term benefit to the country as a whole.

Oil companies

National oil companies (NOCs)

1.17 Around the world most countries with an oil and gas industry have a national oil company.

In some countries they are given a monopoly on oil and gas developments, eg in Saudi Arabia, Saudi Aramco is **the** oil and gas company and is also the largest oil and gas company in the world.

In some countries the national oil company is a passive participant in the industry, taking revenues but not contributing capital, eg Sonangol in Angola.

In a small number of countries the national oil company is a full commercial player in the oil and gas industry, paying its full share of capital costs and taking its share of revenues, eg Statoil in Norway.

International oil companies (IOCs)

1.18   These are the commercial oil companies that are well known globally: Exxon (known as Esso in some countries), Shell, Total, BP, Chevron, ConocoPhillips, Marathon Oil and the like.

There is no strict definition of these companies, but they tend to be vertically integrated: involved in oil and gas exploration, production, refining and sale to the end consumer.

Independent oil companies (independents)

1.19   These are the smaller commercial oil companies that tend to have a tight geographical focus.

Again there is no strict definition of these companies, but they tend not to be vertically integrated: usually only involved in oil and gas exploration and production.

Examples include:

- in the USA: Devon Energy, Hunt Oil;
- in the UK: Tullow Energy, Sterling Resources, Ithica Energy;
- in Africa: Afren, SNEPCO, PetroSA.

Service companies

1.20   This expression generally applies to specialist companies which provide highly specialised equipment, operating personnel and design engineers who deliver one niche service.

Examples might include:

- cementing companies that provide the high-pressure pumps and specialised cements to cement the steel casing in the well to isolate the oil production from the surrounding rock, eg Halliburton, BJ Services, Schlumberger;
- jet engine maintenance companies that service and maintain the huge fleets of gas turbine engines that drive power generators and gas compressors offshore, eg Solar Turbines, Rolls Royce and Wood Group Turbines.

Contractors

1.21   In oil industry parlance, the 'contractors' are the companies that design, build and install offshore platforms.

The major contractors—companies such as McDermotts, Brown and Root and Aker—can do all aspects of such work. They will do the detailed engineering design, manage the whole project, own yards where platforms are fabricated and own the crane barges which install the platforms.

Increasingly, this business has fragmented, so there are many companies that deliver component parts of this process, such as:

- Saipem and Heerema, which specialise in heavy lift cranes and barges;
- Subsea 7, Technip and Acergy, which specialise in sub-sea construction.

Vendors

1.22   The expression vendors refers to all companies that supply pieces of equipment such as compressors, separators, storage tanks pumps, valves. There are thousands of these companies around the world.

Regulators

1.23   These are the government agencies that actually implement and enforce the regulations and laws in a particular country.

In some countries the 'regulator' is also the government agency that creates the laws, and may also be the national oil company.

In the more mature oil and gas provinces, these three functions are separated. For example, in the UK and Norway:

- legislation and regulation is proposed by a government department but approved by parliament;
- the award of licences and policy matters such as depletion rates are set by a regulating government department. In the UK this is the Oil and Gas Department within the Department for Business, Enterprise and Regulatory Reform (formerly the Department of Trade and Industry). In Norway the agency is the Norwegian Petroleum Directorate (NPD);
- following a major offshore disaster (the Piper Alpha disaster in 1989), oil and gas safety matters are overseen by a separate regulatory agency to avoid conflicts of interest. In the UK this is the Offshore Safety Division of the Health and Safety Executive. In Norway it is the Petroleum Safety Authority.

Others: mainly lobbyists

1.24   A number of other entities—manly lobby groups—help to shape and govern oil and gas industry activity.

Best known is Greenpeace, which mounted a very visible campaign to dissuade the UK government from allowing Shell to dump a disused facility ('Brent Spar') in a deep gorge under the North Atlantic. That campaign substantially changed public attitudes, and hence political attitudes. As a result, oil and gas installation disposal is now generally dismantling and disposal/recycling onshore.

Overview of industry

1.25   There are many arrangements that are used today to regulate the contractual relationship between the host country government and the oil industry for the exploration and exploitation of the oil and gas resources. These arrangements exist within well-established legislative frameworks around the world. The following arrangements will be examined in this section: production sharing contracts, concessions, service contracts and licences. Note: the licensing regime as it applies in particular to the UK and some other countries in the world is examined at Part 2 below.

The following is an overview of the legal framework and the types of contracts found within the industry.

> **Note:** An understanding of the different arrangements will be an advantage for working within an international oil industry.

1.26   For any company wishing to explore and exploit oil and gas it is important to have access to the lands or subsea areas. The oil company must therefore obtain the necessary permissions and approvals to enable it to have uninterrupted access to the licence areas. The consents that the company will require from the government will usually include the grant of a concession in the form of a licence or lease or by way of a production sharing contract. The obtaining of the licence or the contract is usually by way of a tender or negotiation process between the company (IOC) and the host government, in most cases represented by the NOC. This will involve co-operation of the host government and compliance by the company with whatever consents are necessary.

1.27   An important aspect to be considered by an IOC before investing in any country's natural resources sector is the relevant legislative framework. The framework, amongst other things, should provide the basic context for and the rules governing petroleum operations in the host country; regulate the operations carried out by both the IOC and the domestic industry; and define the key administrative, economic and fiscal guidelines for investment in the sector.

> **Think:** What other aspects should an effective legislative framework for oil and gas provide for?

1.28   The main elements of the petroleum law are usually very broad and generic, complemented by enabling regulations and a model contract (as the basis for negotiations) that would regulate the relationship between the IOC and the host government. These three main elements are important to both the host government and the IOC in providing a clear legal and contractual context within which to negotiate a petroleum arrangement which is both mutually advantageous and developmental of the petroleum resources of the host country.

1.29   The fiscal, tax and environmental aspects of the complete legislative framework may either be detailed in the petroleum law itself or it could be set out separately in a supplementary document (eg a 'petroleum taxation law' and an 'environmental law').

The following discussion highlights some of the above aspects of the petroleum framework.

> **Note:** The essential elements of a petroleum law include the following:
>
> - state ownership over the petroleum resources;
> - administrative body (usually ministry of oil and gas) that administers the law;
> - application procedures for permission/award/licence to carry out petroleum operations;
> - national regulatory authority to monitor the health, safety and environmental aspects;
> - petroleum operations (reconnaissance, exploration and production);
> - petroleum agreements (model agreement used in negotiations);
> - regulations (administrative and technical);
> - qualifications, duties and rights of right holder or contractor;
> - taxation of profits;
> - other taxes duties and exchange controls;
> - fiscal stabilisation;
> - environmental protection and safety considerations;
> - miscellaneous provisions (penalties for breach of law);
> - unitisation;
> - jurisdiction of national courts;
> - international arbitration.

Ownership over oil and gas resources

1.30   Generally, the state asserts and confirms through the national constitution or relevant legislation that all oil and gas resources (also referred to as hydrocarbons or petroleum) found within its territory, both onshore and offshore, are the exclusive property of the state:

- in the United States the right to minerals (including petroleum) in the ground belongs to the landowner. Therefore, access to petroleum depends on owning land, or on purchasing or (more commonly) leasing those rights from the landowner, usually in return for a royalty. An important figure in the US oil industry is the 'landsman', who is responsible for obtaining and maintaining petroleum leases from landowners.

  The petroleum rights in the US are governed by the 'rule of capture' which entitles the holder to get whatever petroleum he can from the wells on his land, irrespective where the oil migrated from.

  Note that offshore petroleum rights are not subject to private ownership in the United States;

- in the rest of the world, the petroleum rights belong to the state itself, or to a nominal figure such as the British Crown, or else they may be vested in a state-owned entity such as the state oil company;

- in respect of petroleum rights deposits found on the continental shelf of coastal states, the United Nations Convention on the Continental Shelf 1958[1] and the United Nations Convention on the Law of the Sea 1982[2], the state is vested with its sovereignty and control. Thus, the state administers the oil and gas which is within its geographical territory and territorial sea as it deems fit. Since this is the case, it is then up to the state/coastal state to select and adopt how it wants to go about extracting its natural resource (in this case oil and gas).

1   Article   2,   http://untreaty.un.org/ilc/texts/instruments/english/conventions/8_1_1958_ continental_shelf.pdf
2   Article 77, www.un.org/Depts/los/convention_agreements/texts/unclos/closindx.htm.

1.31   State property in petroleum relates to the ownership of the resources and the jurisdiction (or the control) over the activities to exploit them. This issue is based on the concept of sovereignty, which plays an important part in the law and stems from the internationally recognised principle of permanent sovereignty over natural resources. Generally speaking, the principle is the basis upon which states assert their ownership and jurisdiction or control over the resources and their exploitation within their territorial boundaries, and is an important aspect in the territorial claims by coastal states over their oil and gas resources.

> **Think:** What is the meaning of sovereignty? What degree of sovereignty does the host state have over the oil and gas resources in terms of international law and national law?

1.32   A state's sovereignty is based on a proprietary right over its territory (*dominium*) and the right to exercise therein, to the exclusion of any other state, the functions of a state (*imperium*). The rights appertaining to a state in this regard include the right to create rules of law, by legislation or administrative act, and the right to enforce these laws in courts. Within the context of international law, the main elements of sovereignty can be distinguished from the outset.

> **Note:** 'internal sovereignty' means the government is the ultimate authority within its borders and jurisdiction; 'external sovereignty' means the state has the right to freely determine its relations with other states or other entities without the restraint or control of another state.

1.33   The sovereign rights of states over oil and gas resources include the ownership of the resources and the jurisdiction or control over the activities to exploit them. A transfer of ownership of the petroleum resource takes place from the state as the owner *in situ* to the licensee or company at the moment the petroleum enters the licensee or company's well. The ownership of petroleum at this point depends on the commercial arrangements that exist between the government and the oil company. In some countries, the company exploits the resource based on a licence, which requires the payment of a royalty (and/ or other taxes) at point of production to the government in exchange for the oil extracted. In other countries, the Production Sharing Contract requires the payment of a royalty to government, the award of the 'cost oil' to the company and the division of the 'profit oil' between the company and national oil company (NOC) according to an agreed structure. In these countries the legislation for petroleum and mining vest any right in mining or petroleum operations in the state.

> **Note:** Control means the power to give orders or to restrain something. It also includes regulating or having power to regulate the activities of companies in the exploitation of the oil and gas resources in the country. In terms of offshore oil and gas activities, the concept of control includes the jurisdiction of coastal states over activities to exploit the offshore resources on the seabed, including jurisdiction over installations, vessels, and pipelines.

Permanent sovereignty over natural resources

1.34   The rights and duties of states concerning the exploitation of natural resources require an examination of the principle of permanent sovereignty, which is normally regarded as the basic right of states to explore and exploit their natural resources. This principle also provides for rights: to dispose freely of natural resources; to explore and exploit natural resources freely; to regain effective control; to compensation for damage caused by third states or enterprises; and for the right to expropriate.

> **Note:** For text of the principle please see the UNGA Resolution 1803 (xvii), Permanent Sovereignty over Natural Resources, 1194th plenary meeting, 14 December 1962, in Rauschning, et al, Key Resolutions of the United Nations General Assembly 1946–1966 (1997), p 318. See also Brownlie (ed), *Basic Documents in International Law* (4th edn, 1995), pp 235–239; see also www.koteka.net/undres1803.htm.

1.35   The principle of international law which has been recognised as the basis of ownership of states over their natural resources is set out in the principle of permanent sovereignty over natural resources (PSONR). The creation of this principle was spearheaded by former colonies and developing countries which gained their independence in order to take control of the exploitation of natural resources within their boundaries, a privilege historically available only to foreign investors, mainly from developed countries.

1.36   Initial demands to limit foreign control of national resources were made by Latin American states in terms of the '*Calvo doctrine*' by which the alien agrees not to seek diplomatic protection of his own state and to submit to the jurisdiction of the host state. These attempts were supported by the eastern European socialist countries, and further demands were made by newly-independent states in Asia and Africa, which resulted in the great 'north-south' confrontation over the issue of permanent sovereignty over natural resources. In addition, the main factors that shaped this principle into international recognition include the following: concerns about the scarcity and optimum utilisation of natural resources; deteriorating terms of trade of developing countries; promotion and protection of foreign investment; state succession; nationalisation; Cold War rivalry; the demand for economic independence and strengthening of sovereignty; and the formulation of human rights.

1.37   The principle was formulated and debated in the United Nations under the auspices of the Commission on Permanent Sovereignty over Natural Resources which, together with the Economic and Social Council, produced the text for Resolution 1803 (XVII). It was adopted by the UN General Assembly on 14 December 1962. After its adoption, the principle became linked with efforts to promote the economic development of developing countries and to establish a New International Economic Order (NIEO).

1.38   The Commission on Permanent Sovereignty over Natural Resources was set up in 1958 by the UN to conduct a full survey with recommendations of the status of permanent sovereignty over 'natural wealth and resources' as a basic constituent of the right to self-determination. The Commission was instructed to consider the rights and duties of states under international law and the importance of encouraging international co-operation in the economic development of developing countries[1]. The focus of the principle shifted after 1975 to the promotion of exploration and exploitation of natural resources in developing countries and the role played by the international institutions on foreign investment.

1   UNGA Resolution 1314 (XIII) of 12 December 1958.

1.39   Today permanent sovereignty remains an important concern for the UN in any discussion on sustainable development. The whole debate on permanent sovereignty has been influenced by the rights and duties of developing countries and the attempt to create a balance between the main interests of all parties (including developed and developing countries) involved in order to promote economic development mainly in the developing countries.

1.40   The main objective of the Principle was to:

'underscore the claim of colonial peoples and developing countries to the right to enjoy the benefits of resource exploitation and in order to allow "inequitable" legal arrangements, under which foreign investors had obtained title to exploit resources in the past, to be altered or even to be annulled *ab initio*, because they conflict with the concept of permanent sovereignty. Industrialised countries opposed this by reference to *pacta sunt servanda* and respect for acquired rights'.

Note: The maxim *Pacta sunt servanda* means that agreements are binding and are to be observed in good faith.

1.41   The purpose of the Principle is mainly to emphasise the importance of sovereignty over natural resources and to encourage international cooperation in the economic development of developing countries. It also emphasises the recognition and respect of the sovereign right of every state to freely dispose of its wealth and its natural resources in accordance with national interests, and respect for the economic independence of states. The Principle stipulates a duty on states to exercise their right to permanent sovereignty over their natural wealth and resources in the interest of their national development, for the well-being of the people of the state concerned. Another duty is that the exploration, development and disposition of such resources as well as the import of foreign capital required for these purposes, should be in conformity with the national rules and conditions which authorise, restrict or prohibit such activities.

1.42   Generally, the above Resolutions on permanent sovereignty are viewed as recommendations only, with no legislative effect and are merely regarded as informal prescriptions of legal principles. However in certain cases they may become legally binding. In the case of the above Principle, many scholars have viewed it in different ways. Some have regarded it as *opinio juris*, while others have described it as a peremptory norm or *jus cogens* of international law, which prevails over contrary treaties and agreements. Some have regarded it as a mere political conception, supported by a majority of states with the same authority as any UNGA Resolution. For developed western countries the concept was a 'comfortable … expression of the powers inhering in the territorial sovereign in accordance with existing rules of international law'[1]. However, for many developing countries, this principle is the ultimate foundation on which the exploitation of natural resources is undertaken within the national boundaries.

1   Brownlie (ed), *Basic Documents in International Law* (4th edn, 1995).

Regulation of oil and gas activities

1.43   In many cases, the petroleum law identifies a single government agency as the competent regulatory authority vested with the exclusive mandate to implement government policy for hydrocarbon development. The competent authority usually represents the state in contacting and negotiating with the IOC and in regulating and administering the implementation of the contractual framework. The petroleum law in most cases names the competent authority so that international investors will know who will be their single point of contact with the government. In most countries, the role of the competent authority is played by the Ministry of Petroleum or oil and gas/energy which also has the responsibility for petroleum exploration, development and production.

1.44   In some countries, the national oil company (NOC) will have varying degrees of experience and responsibilities including the excusive authority over the sector as the de facto competent authority. This role would allow the NOC to allocate acreage by direct negotiation or tender, contract on behalf of the state with the selected licensees or participate as state partner in joint ventures; and administer the petroleum contract and act as technical interface for the state with the licensees.

> **Think:** What role should the NOC play in the development of the oil and gas resources?

Oil and gas legislative framework

1.45   The framework for oil and gas exploration and exploitation is mainly based on government policy, petroleum law/act, petroleum regulations (including guidelines and standards) and the contract/agreement.

Oil and gas law

1.46   The petroleum law is the basic instrument that regulates the activities to explore and exploit the oil and gas resources in the country. The key issues that would be included in a typical oil and gas law are the following:

- role of government, national regulator;
- creation of a national oil company;
- method and application procedures for licences/contracts;
- different stages of the operations;
- environmental requirements;
- financial aspects;
- dispute resolution;
- role of national courts;
- fines and penalties.

Oil and gas regulations

1.47 In most countries, regulations are usually issued in conjunction with the petroleum law to address the detailed technical nature of the requirements of the industry. They are regarded as subsidiary instruments. It is generally accepted that they should not be enacted as law in order to allow for sufficient flexibility and adaption. The petroleum law usually contains a general provision authorising the competent authority to make regulations from time to time, consistent with the policy objectives of the petroleum law. This allows for greater flexibility to the regime allowing for changes to be in line with the current developments, without the need for a lengthy legislative process to have them changed. Some regulations may be very cumbersome, detailed and very specific to the industry and some may be very general and allow the industry some freedom to adhere to their industry regulation. The key areas that the regulations include are: the establishment of the regulatory authority; health, safety and environment; technical aspects; financial considerations; application procedure; etc. The successful implementation of the regulations in most cases depends on the capability of the regulatory authority itself (including trained and experienced staff to carry out their regulatory functions).

> **Task:** Examine the difference between prescriptive and goal-setting regulations.

Petroleum exploration and production operations

1.48 The petroleum law provides that the operations are conducted only under a duly issued permit or licence from the competent authority in such form and on such terms as are prescribed in the petroleum law, the regulations and the petroleum agreement. It also provides the maximum flexibility to the state as regards its means of conducting petroleum operations through a NOC, a private entity or in any manner which it may deem appropriate.

> **Think:** What level of control should the government have over the operations of the IOC?

21

Oil and gas/petroleum agreements

1.49 The petroleum law usually introduces the concept and the possible contents of a model contract. It authorises the competent authority to prepare and provide model contracts to potential applicants at the commencement of the negotiation of an exploration and production petroleum agreement.

1.50 In the next section the main petroleum arrangements will be examined in detail:

- concession;
- production sharing contract;
- service contract;
- joint venture;
- licence.

Bp is concession (handwritten)

> **Think:** What is the best type of contractual relationship that should dictate the relationship between the IOC and the host government?

Concession

1.51 A concession is a civil agreement under which the state provides on a compensated basis and the investor purchases the exclusive right to the use of a subsoil area for agreed purposes including prospecting, exploration and extraction of oil and gas (and other minerals). The company bears all the expenses and risks, including payments to the state for the use of the subsoil, taxes and other mandatory payments as required by the law. A concession is a type of lease agreement.

1.52 In the early part of the last century, concessions were granted mainly to the large US and British oil companies in various parts of the world. Seven major international oil companies (IOCs), known as 'the Seven Sisters' dominated the oil and gas production in these countries through the concession arrangement.

> **Note:** The original Seven Sisters were the following companies:
> - Standard Oil of New Jersey (Esso), which merged with Mobil: ExxonMobil;
> - Royal Dutch Shell (60% Dutch/40% British);
> - Anglo Arabian Oil Company (APOC)/Anglo-Iranian Oil Company (AIOC)/British Petroleum /BP Amoco: now known solely by the initials BP;
> - Standard Oil Company of New York ('Socony')/Mobil/ExxonMobil;
> - Standard Oil of California ('Socal')/Chevron/ChevronTexaco known as Chevron;

- Gulf Oil;
- Texaco, which merged with Chevron in 2001.

Note: The new Seven Sisters are the national oil companies:

- Saudi Aramco (Saudi Arabia);
- Gazprom (Russia);
- CNPC (China);
- NIOC (Iran);
- PDVSA (Venezuela);
- Petrobras (Brazil);
- Petronas (Malaysia).

1.53   After one-sided negotiation processes, the original concessions were granted for very long periods and over large areas in favour of the IOCs. The concession involved the granting of exclusive rights to exploit the oil and gas resources of the host country with few regulatory controls and minimal state intervention. The host government did not reserve a right to participate in the process of exploitation and operation of any field developed.

This practical arrangement was perceived, mainly by the developed countries, to be the best option because the IOC possessed all financial resources and technical expertise. However over a period of time, the concessions were seen as too generous in nature and the host governments wanted to introduce changes in the arrangement that would give them more control over their resources.

1.54   As political complexities changed over time, a growing resentment became obvious on the part of host governments, since it appeared that the extent of the rights granted was seen as a direct challenge to their territorial sovereignty. After some countries that were previously under the control of colonial powers gained their independence, in some cases through political revolution or liberation wars, newly independent governments started to assert their state ownership over their natural resources.

The international principle on permanent sovereignty over natural resources was adopted by many developing countries and established as the most important instrument in designing new oil and gas laws.

Most governments asserted control over their oil and gas resources through programmes of 'nationalisation'. However, the new rights in many cases did not sit well with the existing concession agreements in place between the oil company and the host government. In other cases the concession agreements were abruptly ended despite the fact that there were provisions for renegotiation, etc.

Note: A brief chronology of events concerning the nationalisation of oil and gas industries in oil-producing countries:

- in 1938 Mexico nationalised the foreign oil companies in the country and placed all assets under the control of Pemex, the national oil company;
- in 1951 Iran nationalised the Anglo-Iranian Oil Company;
- in 1959 the Arab Oil Congress in Cairo adopted a 'gentleman's agreement' for oil-producing countries to have a greater influence on oil production and marketing;
- the OPEC countries began nationalising the oil industries within their boundaries: Libya nationalised the BP concession (1971); Iraq nationalised the Iraq Petroleum Concession (1972); Iran nationalised the industry (1973); Saudi Arabia acquired a 25% interest in Aramco (1973); Venezuela nationalised the oil industry (1975); etc.

Example: Saudi/Chevron concession:

- One of the very few traditional oil production concessions that survived the Saudi nationalisation of the oil industry in the 1970s was extended in 2008 by the Saudi Arabian cabinet. The concession is held by the US major Chevron in the Neutral Zone of Saudi shared with Kuwait. The 60-year deal was first granted in 1949 to a company founded by the US industrialist Jean Paul Getty. 'The council of ministers has decided to approve the extension and amendment agreement between Saudi Arabia and Chevron Saudi Arabia at the Neutral Zone,' a report said. In July 2008, the Saudi cabinet authorised the oil minister to sign an extension.
- Saudi Arabia and Kuwait share the estimated 550,000 bpd output from the Neutral Zone. The zone is a region between Saudi Arabia and Kuwait that dates back to 1920s treaties to establish regional borders. Chevron acquired the concession when it bought Texaco in 2001. Texaco had acquired it from Getty Oil in 1984.

Production sharing agreement/contract

1.55   The production sharing agreement (PSA), also referred to as a production sharing contract (PSC), has evolved as the most prevalent instrument for controlling the relationship between the government and the IOCs in the petroleum-rich areas in the Middle East, west Africa and Asia Pacific region. The PSC is now widely used in more than 45 countries worldwide.

1.56   PSCs came to prominence in the 1970s in countries such as Indonesia, Egypt, Syria, Peru and Nigeria. As they have matured, the PSCs evolved and the methods of calculating the government revenue also changed over the years. Revenues could, for example, be based on an agreed share of the actual production so that the share increases as the production also increases; or they could be based on the company's return on investment (a proportion of the yield as a percentage of the capital employed). The PSC proved very attractive to developing countries and in particular the economies in transition, as a form of cooperation between the investor and the state in the process of the use of the subsoil.

Indonesia

1.57   It is widely accepted that the first concept of the PSC for the extraction of useful minerals (oil) was applied in Indonesia in the 1960s and this model was gradually adopted by the international oil industry and governments worldwide. In Indonesia the PSC was introduced as a replacement of the exclusive licence agreements that existed in the country which were terminated by Government Decree No 44 of 26 October 1960.

> **Note:** Some trace the concept of production sharing back to the 1899 Netherlands–Indies Mining Law (amended in 1919) whereby the minister was allowed, on the basis of a special law, to enter into the contract with an oil enterprise which granted the contractor the exclusive right to search for and produce petroleum within a certain territory and for a certain number of years. The contractor was obliged to pay a royalty and a proportional part of the gross profit (revenues less costs and losses carried forward). The proportion was connected to the annual capital expenditures. The government had the right to demand the royalty and profit share be paid in oil or oil products, provided the oil or oil products so received would be used by the government for its own needs.
>
> Note also that some refer to Bolivia as the first country to use the concept of production sharing in 1950.

1.58   In terms of the Indonesian Decree No 44 of 1960, oil and gas were deemed to be part of the national riches, under the control of the state. Exploration and exploitation were regarded as the sole responsibility of the state, which could delegate this function to the national state enterprise as established by the national law. The national state enterprise of Indonesia was Perusahaan Pertambangan Minyak dan Gas Bumi Negara (Pertamina) established under Law No 8 of 1971. Its main objective was to develop and carry out the exploitation of oil and natural gas for the maximum prosperity of the people and the state, as well as creating national strength, and to supply and serve the domestic demand.

1.59   The law allows Petramina to cooperate with a third party in a production sharing contract, to be approved by the President with notification to the Parliament. The terms and conditions of the production sharing were set out in a special government regulation. From the earliest contracts awarded there was an element of mandatory state participation which entitled Pertamina to require a foreign contractor to offer (within three months after first declaration of commercial discovery) a 5% (later increased to 10%) interest in the contact to an Indonesian enterprise designated by Pertamina. If the contractor's offer was accepted, the ensuing cooperation between the contractor and the Indonesian partner was governed by the rules of an agreement of co-operation, the main principles of which were then attached to the PSC.

Egypt

1.60   In 1970 Egypt was one of the first countries to follow the example of Indonesia, and adopt the concept of production sharing with an Indonesian-style PSC between the national oil company, Egyptian General Petroleum Corporation (EGPC), and a Japanese company. Since then the PSC became generally applied throughout the whole of Egypt. The PSC regime has gone through changes in recent years and the 2006 Model Concession Agreement for petroleum exploration and exploitation is now the basis for the agreement between the government, EGPC and the contractor.

1.61   The preamble narrates that all minerals, including petroleum existing in mines and quarries in Egypt including the territorial waters and the seabed subject to its jurisdiction and extending beyond the territorial waters, are the property of the state. It further states that EGPC has applied for an exclusive concession for the exploration and exploitation of petroleum in and throughout the area referred to in Article II attached to the Agreement. It further narrates that The Law N 86 of 1956 provides that the Minister of Petroleum with EGPC enter into the concession agreement with the contractor in the said area.

Peru

1.62   Based on the experiences in Indonesia and Egypt, Peru adopted a simple form PSC in 1971 mainly on the recommendation of one of the international oil companies operating in the country, Occidental Petroleum Corporation. In the Peruvian PSC, the production was mainly divided into two equal shares between the national state oil company (Petroperu) and the contractor. The contractor was responsible for the payment of income tax. The PSC was replaced in 1985 by the risk-bearing service contract.

Philippines

1.63   The Indonesian-style PSC was introduced in the Philippines in 1972 through the adoption of Presidential Decree of 22 December 1972, which dealt with the 'promotion of petroleum exploration and production in the Philippines and the publication of new conditions for service contracts'. The service contract appears to be similar to the Indonesian-style PSC, but with 'proceeds sharing' instead of 'production sharing' whereby the total production is sold by the contractor and the sales proceeds shared between the parties in the same way as any production would have been shared between them. The contracts are made between the foreign oil company (contractor) and the state company.

Libya

1.64   Libya adopted the PSC in 1974 as the basis of an agreement between Occidental and the Libyan National Oil Corporation (LNOC). Before then, the Petroleum Law of 1955 provided for exclusive petroleum rights in the form of concessions. With the introduction of the PSC the 1955 Petroleum Law was not abolished, but its scope was restricted to the activities of the LNOC in that all the exclusive rights were reserved for and only granted to the LNOC. LNOC was then authorised to enter into a PSC with interested international oil companies, provided that the proposed negotiated agreement was submitted to the governmental authorities for approval.

Malaysia

1.65   The Malaysian Petroleum Development Act of 1974 was adopted to regulate all the petroleum operations in the country. The Act cancelled all existing petroleum agreements, from 1 April 1975, and vested the ownership in and the exclusive right of exploring for, exploiting, winning and obtaining petroleum in the state oil company, Petronas.

1.66   Petronas was given the mandate to agree the new terms and conditions of any new contracts, including those that were meant to replace the agreements which were cancelled by the Act. Again, the Malaysian PSC was similar to the Indonesian PSC in the concept of production sharing as the standard for all new agreements. The recent PSC provides for further state participation through the subsidiary of Petronas, Carigali, on the contractor's side of the contract.

Angola

1.67   Angola became independent in November 1975 and adopted the Petroleum Law of 1978[1]. The framework law declared all onshore and offshore petroleum resources to be the property of the people of Angola and all the exploration and exploitation rights to be transferred to the national oil company, Sonangol. Sonangol is the national concessionaire of the mining rights for exploration, development and production of liquid and gaseous hydrocarbons in Angola. Sonangol is allowed under the law to carry out bidding rounds and to invite pre-qualified oil companies to submit their bids for joint venture with Sonangol under PSCs.

1   Law 13/78 of 26 August 1978.

China

1.68   China started inviting international oil companies from 1982 to apply for PSCs for exploration and production operations on the Chinese part of the continental shelf. The basis for the PSCs was laid down in Regulations for the exploitation of offshore petroleum resources in cooperation with foreign enterprises. The new regulations were based on the Indonesian model that vested ownership of petroleum on the continental shelf in the state. The Chinese National Offshore Oil Corporation (CNOOC) was given exclusive rights to search for and exploit the resources in cooperation with foreign oil companies.

Nigeria

1.69   Soon after Nigeria became a member of OPEC in 1971 the OPEC Conference adopted a resolution calling on all members to enter into negotiations with their respective concessionaries and licence holders on the acquisition of a state interest in the traditional concessions in their respective countries. Consequently, Nigeria acquired 35% interest in the petroleum rights by means of an agreement signed on 11 June 1973 with the concessionaire. The state interest was subsequently increased to 60%.

Russia

1.70   Russia adopted the Federal Law 'On Agreements about Production Sharing' in 1995 and since then several companies have been conducting their business on the basis of the PSC. Between 1994 and 1995 Russia signed several PSCs as a way of attracting foreign investment in geologically isolated and technologically challenging hydrocarbon projects and boosting its oil and gas production.

Service contract

1.71   The service contract is an arrangement whereby the state would grant contractual, but not proprietary, rights to an oil company. Under this arrangement the government retains the majority control over the operations and the contractor provides the necessary services required to carry out the project. The contractor does not gain any title to production except under a separate sale and purchase agreement.

1.72   There are basically two types of service contracts: the buy back contract and the technical assistance contract:

- *Buy back contract:* Here the company takes the risk in relation to exploration, similar to the PSC, but in consideration of a fee. Under this arrangement, the company has the right to purchase any production, usually at a discount (ie buy back contract). These arrangements do not entitle the IOCs to any claims on the crude oil produced. Usually the scope of work that the IOC would carry out is set out in a development plan, which normally forms part of the technical bids for the project. The development phase is the period from the effective date to the final commissioning, which ends when all the development operations have been completed by the contractor in accordance with the buy back contract and all wells and facilities have been installed, commissioned, started up, tested and handed over to the NOC. The contractor acts as the field operator during the development operations, under the control and direction of a joint management committee comprising representatives from the contractor and the NOC. The contractor funds all the developmental operations and non-capital expenditures and all operating costs incurred in the performance of the development operations. After the successful completion of the operations the operatorship of the field is transferred back to the NOC for production operations. The buy back contract may offer the IOC an exploration contract, however it will not necessarily be converted into a development contract even if commercial discovery is declared.

- *Technical Assistance Contracts* (TAC): This type of contract is where the company simply provides a service to the government in return for a service fee. That service may, for example, simply be the overall management of the oil field in question on behalf of the government— the so called Technical Assistance Contracts (TAC) or the Technical Service Agreements (TSA). These contracts are usually referred to as rehabilitation, redevelopment or enhanced oil recovery projects. They are associated with existing fields of production, including abandoned fields. The contractor is responsible for the capital or technical knowhow and the operations, including equipment and personnel. These types of contract are used in countries where the government has enough money but only seeks the expertise of the IOC for specialised projects. These arrangements are suitable for the service industry where the contractor is paid a fee for performing a service, such as drilling, development or medium-risk exploration services. These contracts are not favoured by the IOCs and their track record is one of very limited success. The short-term nature of these contracts and the lack of access to project risks/ upside materially diminish the appetite of IOCs to invest and deploy their resources in such projects. An IOC is unlikely to deploy leading-edge technology or assign significant numbers of experts to a project with no long-term leverage

1.73 It is worth noting that in exceptional circumstances the payments could be in the form of oil, for example the recent Rumaila oil field one-year service contracts made between the Iraqi government Ministry of Oil and four major IOCs.

Countries that use the service contract arrangement include Iran and Iraq, although early versions of service contracts were used in the 1950s by the Mexican National Oil Company (PEMEX).

> **Note:** See 'Iraq to outline oil contracts to companies', Upstream, 9 October 2008 www.upstreamonline.com/live/article164512.ece.

Joint ventures

1.74 In order to address the local content requirement, most regimes also provide for and encourage the setting up of joint ventures between foreign investors and national enterprises. For oil and gas operations, the joint venture between the IOC and the NOC is a commercial arrangement between two economically independent entities which can take a number of legal forms. The objective of the joint venture is to execute the particular business undertaking of oil and gas including a number of activities such as the registration of the local company, the application of the right for petroleum exploration and production, the management of the operations, decision making, financing of activities, employment of nationals, etc.

Joint ventures are discussed in detail at para **3.16**.

Licences

1.75 In oil and gas terms, a licence generally grants the investor the right to exploit a defined area in consideration of a fee and/or royalty payment. In most cases, it also contains a work programme commitment. The right to exploit the land is usually associated with a 'profit a pendre'/a proprietary right and not just a right of use. However the term licence does not mean that the proprietary rights are automatically granted. It all depends on the nature of the grant, which differs from country to country.

1.76 Sometimes a licence is granted in combination with the PSC. The contractor's rights, however, arise from the PSC. The licence is a mere confirmation of the rights derived from the PSC and the licence does not confer a separate set of rights or obligations. Usually the full proprietary licence is given to the NOC and the licence is simply an instrument to give the NOC the status to contract with the IOC under the PSC.

1.77   A licence could be issued for the exploration and exploitation of oil and gas resources, for the acquisition of data, and may be exclusive or non-exclusive. Most licences granted by governments to exploration operators are exclusive. A non-exclusive licence would leave the government free to grant further licences over the same area to third parties, but generally operators are not keen on other parties having equal rights over areas they have paid large sums of money to exploit.

1.78   Under the licensing system the IOC purchases the exclusive right to use the subsoil area for the extraction of mineral resources. The investor is also the owner of the minerals extracted, bears all the risks and expenses, and makes payments to the state for the use of the subsoil and other taxes. The licence is the permission of the state for the IOC to use the land on conditions and the state may withdraw its decisions, limit the rights of the investor or completely withdraw the investor's rights and revoke the licence.

Countries with licensing regimes include Trinidad and Tobago, the UK, and most Commonwealth countries.

The UK licensing regime is discussed in detail at Part 2 below, but first it is necessary to understand the background and development of the UK oil and gas industry.

Trinidad and Tobago: The legal and fiscal regime for gas (and oil) development in Trinidad and Tobago is governed primarily by the petroleum legislation. The regime allows for the granting of exploration and production licences and PSCs.

The Petroleum Act establishes a framework for the grant of licences/ contracts for the conduct of petroleum operations, including exploration and production activities, onshore and offshore in the country's territorial waters. Under the Act, the Minister of Energy and Energy Industries is responsible for determining the areas to be made available for petroleum operations, and may elect to invite applications for the rights to explore and produce hydrocarbons from these areas, via competitive bidding. Exploration and production licences, and PSCs are awarded depending on the particular circumstance of the acreage up for bid. Several variations of these granting instruments currently exist between the government and numerous operators. At present the fiscal system is biased toward large gas fields (typically around 1tcf gas in place or larger) as attractive development targets. However, the fiscal regime is currently being reviewed by the government to make small and marginal accumulations more attractive.

Activities

Issues for discussion

1.79
- What are the host country's main objectives for petroleum development?
- What are the IOC's objectives for petroleum investment?
- Which key aspects should be included in an effective legislative framework for oil and gas exploration and production?
- What are the key types of contractual arrangements that you would encounter in the oil industry?

Tasks

1.80
- Find out which type of petroleum arrangement is used in your country for exploration and productions operations and obtain a copy of the model contract to familiarise yourself with it. In not more than 500 words, briefly describe the main features. AND/OR
- Find out which type of contractual arrangement was recently proposed and adopted by Iraq for the exploitation of the oil and gas resources in the country and summarise the key aspects in not more than 500 words.

Further reading

1.81
- B Taverne, *Petroleum, Industry and Governments: A Study of the Involvement of Industry and Governments in the Production and Use of Petroleum* (2nd edn, 2008, Kluwer), Ch 1.
- D Yergin and M Stoppard, 'The Next Prize' (2003) 82 Foreign Affairs Journal, pp 103–114 (available on Heninonline at www.heinonline.org/HOL/Page?handle=hein.journals/fora82&id=1&size=2&collection=journals&index=journals/fora).
- D Yergin, *The Prize: The Epic Quest for Oil, Money and Power* (2009, Simon & Schuster).
- E Smith, et al, *International Petroleum Transactions* (2nd edn, 2000), Ch 1.
- A Sampson, *The Seven Sisters: The Great Oil Companies and the World They Shaped* (1975, Viking Press).
- I Brownlie, *The Legal Status of Natural Resources in International Law* (1979, Recueil des Cours, Academie de Droit International).
- N Schrijver, *Sovereignty Over Natural Resources* (1997, Cambridge University Press), Ch 1.

- See 'Iraq to outline oil contracts to companies', Upstream, 9 October 2008 www.upstreamonline.com/live/article164512.ece.
- B Taverne, 'Production Sharing Agreements in Principle and in Practice' in M David, *Upstream Oil and Gas Agreements* (1996, Sweet and Maxwell), pp 43–96.
- Angolan oil and gas regime see SONANGOL website: www.sonangol.co.ao/wps/portal/ep.
- Libyan oil and gas regime see LNOC website: http://en.noclibya.com.ly/index.php?option=com_docman&task=cat_view&gid=23&Itemid=34.
- Example of a PSC: 2006 Model Concession Agreement for the exploration and exploitation of oil and gas between the Government of Egypt, EGPC and the company: see www.egpc.com.eg/2006/Agreement_N.pdf.
- For further reading on the Trinidad and Tobago regime see: Petroleum Act at http://rgd.legalaffairs.gov.tt/Laws/Chs.%2061-62/62.01/62.01%20 aos.htm; The Petroleum Taxes Act at http://rgd.legalaffairs.gov.tt/Laws/Chs.%2074-78/75.04/75.04%20aos.htm and the Income Tax Act at http://rgd.legalaffairs.gov.tt/Laws/Chs.%2074-78/75.01/75.01%20aos.htm.

C   THE UK OIL AND GAS INDUSTRY

1.82   The previous section dealt with the most common international petroleum arrangements in the industry and discussed the issues of ownership and sovereignty over oil and gas resources. This section provides an overview of the United Kingdom Continental Shelf including an in-depth historical account of oil and gas exploration and exploitation in the UK. It sets out the regulatory framework and aspects of ownership that have been established in the UK from the first oil discovery to the current situation. This part is followed by a more specific discussion on the UKCS licensing regime.

> **Note:** The United Kingdom Continental Shelf is also referred to as the UKCS.

1.83   The main producing areas in the UK are located on the seabed of the Atlantic Ocean that surrounds the mainland of Great Britain, known as the 'North Sea'. Part 2 deals directly with the licensing of oil and gas operations on the UK continental shelf (UKCS). It is therefore useful to have an understanding of the nature of the continental shelf to fully comprehend the importance of the UKCS offshore oil and gas activities. Thus, the following brief discussion highlights the concept of the continental shelf and its importance to the exploration and exploitation of oil and gas resources. It is followed by a discussion on the historical development of the oil and gas industry in the UK.

The UK Continental Shelf (UKCS)

1.84   The seabed and the maritime areas have been used by states for various economic activities. However, formal attempts to exercise certain rights over the seabed or shelf and to define the concept of the continental shelf started in 1945 and 1958 with the Geneva Convention on the Continental Shelf and also the adoption by the international community of states, under the umbrella of the United Nations, of a revised concept which is now embodied in the 1982 United Nations Convention on the Law of the Sea (UNLCOS)[1].

1   Find a copy of the Convention (and read through the provisions concerning the continental shelf) at Oceans and Law of the Sea, Division for Ocean Affairs and the Law of the Sea at http://www.un.org/Depts/los/convention_agreements/convention_overview_convention.htm. See also AV Lowe and SAG Talmon, *Basic Documents on the Law of the Sea, The Legal Order of the Oceans* (2009, Hart Publishing).

1.85   Article 76 stipulates that:

'The continental shelf of a coastal state comprises the sea-bed and subsoil of the submarine areas that extends beyond its territorial sea throughout the natural prolongation of its land territory to the outer edge of the continental margin, or to a distance of 200 nautical miles from the baselines from which the breadth of the territorial sea is measured where the outer edge of the continental margin does not extend up to that distance'.

Note: One of the first official claims of jurisdiction by a coastal state over the resources of the continental shelf was made by the US President Truman on 28 September 1945. The Truman Proclamation stated that 'the United States regards the natural resources of the subsoil and sea-bed of the continental shelf beneath the high seas but contiguous to the coasts of the United States as appertaining to the United States, subject to its jurisdiction and control'.

In addition, on the same day President Truman issued an 'Executive Order of the President' reserving and placing the natural resources of the subsoil and the sea-bed of the continental shelf under the control and jurisdiction of the Secretary of the Interior. It is noteworthy that jurisdiction was only claimed over the natural resources and not the continental shelf *per se*.

Other coastal states, particularly the Latin American states, followed with 'patrimonial and matrimonial' claims over the resources, the continental shelf, superjacent waters, airspace above and 200 mile territorial seas.

See text of the 'Truman Proclamation' in (1946) 40 AJIL and AV Lowe and SAG Talmon, *Basic Documents on the Law of the Sea, The Legal Order of the Oceans* (2009, Hart Publishing), pp 19–20.

> See the Mexican Presidential Statement of 29 October 1945 and the Argentinean 'Declaration proclaiming sovereignty over the epicontinental sea and continental shelf' of 9 October 1946: in (1947) 41 AJIL.

1.86   The concept of the continental shelf was further developed in the *North Sea Continental Shelf case of 1969*[1], when the International Court of Justice (ICJ) underscored the firm status of coastal states' rights with respect to the continental shelf by stating that:

> '… the rights of the coastal state in respect of the area of the continental shelf that constitutes a natural prolongation of its land territory into and under the sea exist *ipso facto* and *ab initio*, by virtue of its sovereignty over the land, and as an extension of it in an exercise of sovereign rights for the purpose of exploring the seabed and exploiting its natural resources. In short, there is here an inherent right …'

> **Note:** Find a copy of the ICJ judgment for an understanding of the agreements regarding the maritime boundaries between the countries in the North Sea.

1   The 1969 North Sea Continental Shelf cases involved the delimitation of the continental shelf between Germany and Netherlands, and Germany and Denmark respectively, where the ICJ considered the applicable principles and rules of international law on delimitation between the North Sea states (ICJ Reports, 1969).

1.87   Since the 1970s revenues from offshore production have been a major source of government income and are therefore highly important to the national economy of countries like the United States, United Kingdom, Norway, and the OPEC member states[1]. Most crude oil recovered from the UKCS offshore fields comes from the North Sea. It is estimated that:

- between 1975 and 2002 over 2.5 billion tonnes were recovered from the UKCS offshore oil fields;
- there are an estimated 920 million tonnes of recoverable crude oil remaining in the UKCS;
- the current UKCS production makes the UK the third largest gas and second largest oil producer in Europe, and 19th largest in the world for both oil and gas (BP's Statistical Review of World Energy 2012). However the situation will change as the UKCS production declined to 1.8 million boepd in 2011.
- it is estimated that the UKCS will only provide 12% of the nation's oil and gas supply in 2020.

> **Think:** Can the continental shelf be owned by the coastal state?
>
> On what basis does the coastal state issue licences for the exploitation of its offshore oil and gas resources?

1   See Organization of Petroleum Exporting Countries (OPEC) website at www.opec.org.

Development of the UK oil and gas industry

1.88   For ease of reference, the following brief historical overview of the development of the UK's offshore oil and gas industry is divided into the following three phases.

Phase 1: Establishment of an oil and gas industry in the UK

1.89   The desire to own oil for energy independence (for securing supplies for the Royal Navy Fleet) during the First World War and a reduction on reliance of other states can be said to be the main influence for the evolution of the UK oil and gas law[1]. After the outbreak of the First World War in 1914, the UK government thought it wise to acquire a controlling interest of 51.7% in the then Anglo Persian Oil Company (later to become British Petroleum). The Anglo-Persian Oil Company had only recently acquired the D'Arcy Concession (the first Middle East concession of oil acquired by William Knox D'Arcy covering the whole of Persia with the exclusion of five northern states). The Concession had struck oil on 25 May 1908; thus the acquisition of shares by the UK government provided it with the power to nominate members unto the Anglo-Persian board, control its activities and also control the disposition of the oil and gas produced. In addition this influence gave the UK government an advantage in accessing information about operations of other concessions granted in the Middle East[2].

1   See D Yergin, *The Prize: The Epic Quest for Oil, Money and Power* (2009, Simon & Schuster).
2   See Daintith, T, & Hewitt, G (2012) *United Kingdom Oil and Gas Law.* London, Sweet & Maxwell at p 1017.

1.90   In 1917, the idea of encouraging exploration and exploitation of oil and gas within the UK was abandoned by the government because of the resistance against the setting up of royalties' funds for the owners of the lands which overlay reservoirs. However with the adoption of the 1918 Petroleum (Production) Act the government obtained the right to enter any land for the purpose of exploring and exploiting petroleum reserves, and preventing others from doing so (guarding against unnecessary competitive drilling and capture)[1].

1   See Daintith, T, & Hewitt, G (2012) *United Kingdom Oil and Gas Law.*

1.91   The Petroleum (Production) Act 1918, although avoiding the question of who owned petroleum *in situ,* confronted the competitive drilling problem by establishing and restricting the class of persons entitled to search or bore for or get petroleum to only persons acting on behalf of the government. In terms of the Act, anyone caught violating this regulation was liable to forfeit any petroleum gained and in addition pay a penalty of three times the value of the petroleum obtained.

1.92   Oil was subsequently found in May 1919 in Hardsoft in Derbyshire on the property of the Duke of Devonshire by S Pearson and Sons Ltd (an American firm with substantial experience in exploring American oil fields). Lord Cowdray, Chairman of Pearson, had been instrumental to the abolition of competitive drilling and through his company acted on behalf of the government in searching for and getting petroleum. The quantity of petroleum found at Hardsoft was found to be of no commercial interest, resulting in the eventual abandoning of the prospects of a province at that time[1]. This was the case until 1934.

1   See Daintith, T, & Hewitt, G (2012) *United Kingdom Oil and Gas Law*.

1.93   At the end of the First World War, supplies from abroad became available again and further exploration in the UK was virtually abandoned. However one lasting result was that the Anglo-Iranian Oil Company suggested that the British government simplify the legal and administrative aspects for prospecting. The search for petroleum had been unduly fraught with uncertainties as to who owned the petroleum underlying lands. The resulting Petroleum (Production) Act 1934 vested Crown ownership of all mineral oil, in effect vesting in the Crown all property rights in petroleum *in situ* in Great Britain and giving the Crown 'exclusive right of searching and boring for and getting such petroleum'[1]. It was therefore possible for a company to acquire exploration licences in the UK for the first time. The 1934 Act authorised the UK government to grant licences to explore for and exploit the petroleum resources of the UK and its territorial waters (the Continental Shelf Act 1964 extended these rights to the UKCS). Regulations made under the Petroleum (Production) Act 1934 set out how and by whom applications for these licences can be made. The 1934 Act, unlike the 1918 Act, did not stipulate any penalties for breach of these provisions, but it is inferred that as owner of the petroleum *in situ* the Crown had the power to take legal action for breach[2].

1   Petroleum (Production) Act 1934, s 1(1).
2   Gordon, G, Paterson, J and Usenmez, E (2011), *Oil and Gas Law: Current Practice and Emerging Trends*. (2nd edn) Dundee, Dundee University Press.

Phase 2: Discovery of offshore oil and gas resources on the continental shelf

1.94   During the late 1950s it became quite clear that gas deposits found in the north west of the Netherlands (the Groningen gas field) might extend into its continental shelf and beyond, even into the shelves of neighbouring countries. This prompted governments with continental shelves on the North Sea to devise a legal framework to control the exploration, exploitation and production of offshore oil and gas. The continental shelf had been defined by the Geneva Convention on the Continental Shelf 1958, thus setting the stage for any legal framework pertaining to the continental shelf.

1.95   The UK government, in seeking to provide an appropriate legal framework, imported the largely untested and untried landward regime, ie from the Petroleum (Production) Act 1934, although it was clear that operational conditions might differ. The result was the Continental Shelf Act (CSA) 1964, applying to areas outside territorial waters with respect to the seabed and subsoil and natural resources.

1.96   The CSA 1964 contained provisions that extended the application of most of the key licensing provisions of the Petroleum (Production) Act 1934, although the provision vesting property in petroleum in the Crown could not be applied, as only a sovereign right may be held in respect of the continental shelf. The CSA 1964 and its ensuing regulations constituted the legal regime of the UKCS until 1975. It is worthy of note that the UK's first major oil discovery in the northern North Sea (BP Forties) occurred under this regime, in 1970.

1.97   In 1975, the British National Oil Company (BNOC) was created by the Petroleum and Pipelines Act (PPA) 1975 to, amongst other functions, control the government's participatory and regulatory role in the oil and gas industry. Unilateral changes to the terms of existing licences which had been granted in previous rounds and similar changes to be incorporated into future licences were introduced by the PPA 1975. During this period it became a condition precedent to the granting of a licence, for the BNOC to acquire 51% participation in the licence; in respect of existing licences the BNOC was enabled to take up at market price, up to 51% of the oil attributable to the licensees under a licence and to have a vote on the operating committee of the joint venture for that licence. However, during the 1980s and as a result of a change of government from Labour to Conservative, which favoured the privatisation of public corporations, the participatory powers of the government through BNOC and its descendant corporations dwindled and eventually died[1].

1   For a list of the key dates of the UKCS oil and gas production see OGUK website at www. oilandgas.org.uk/education/dates/v0000091.cfm

Phase 3: The development of the UK legal regime for the oil and gas industry

1.98   The provisions of the Petroleum (Production) Act 1934, with all other statutory provisions relating to oil and gas licensing, were consolidated and re-enacted in the Petroleum Act (PA) 1998[1]. The PA 1998 is the main regulatory legal framework for exploration, exploitation and production of oil and gas in the UK. Although very little had been changed by the introduction of the Act, it sought to consolidate the legal framework for the UK oil and gas industry as the single reference point for the granting of licences.

1   Available at www.opsi.gov.uk/acts/acts1998/ukpga_19980017_en_1.

1.99   Similar to the Petroleum (Production) Act 1934, Part I of the PA 1998 vests all rights to petroleum in the Crown, including the rights to search for, bore for and get the petroleum (oil and gas). The Act empowers the Secretary of State to grant licences to search for and bore for and get petroleum to such persons as he thinks fit. Part III of the Act deals with submarine pipelines and Part IV deals with abandonment of offshore installations.

1.100   The PA 1998 does not operate entirely in isolation in the regulation of oil and gas licences. The government department entrusted with the regulation of the industry, the Department of Energy and Climate Change (DECC, previously known as the Department of Business, Enterprise and Regulatory Reform or DBERR), developed a set of guidance notes that set out the information required concerning licences in the UK[1].

1   See www.decc.gov.uk.

1.101   In addition, regulations containing licence model clauses are released and updated from time to time and these are attached as conditions to the licences. The PA 1998 requires the Model Clauses to be published in order to avoid any uncertainties. The government's practice up to the 19th Round was that the model clauses were incorporated into licences by means of a single short paragraph, but from the 20th round onwards they have been incorporated in full in the licence itself to clarify the rules. It is therefore the responsibility of the licensee to read through the model clauses to understand the conditions and ensure compliance with all the rules.

> **Note:** The Model Clauses currently in use for Seaward Production Licences can be inspected on the OPSI website at the Petroleum Licensing (Production) (Seaward Areas) Regulations 2008, SI 2008/225. Those used for the Landward Production Licences and for the Seaward Exploration Licences are at the Petroleum Licensing (Exploration and Production) (Seaward and Landward Areas) Regulations 2004, SI 2004/352. The latest piece of petroleum related legislation is the Energy Act 2008, which introduced some minor changes relating to the decommissioning of offshore installations.

1.102   An important aspect of oil and gas regulation in the UK context is the impact of the European Union. As a result of the UK's accession to the European Communities on 1 January 1973, European Directives have to be complied with. Certain Directives that affect the oil and gas regulatory regime have to be made law (by way of Regulations). In 1994, the EU laid down strict rules under the Hydrocarbon Licensing Directive that member states have to follow when issuing petroleum licences, covering such things as the factors that may (and may not) be taken into account when deciding whether or not to issue a licence, and the minimum amount of public consultation[1].

1 Directive 94/22/EC of the European Parliament and of the Council of 30 May 1994 at http://
eur-lex.europa.eu/smartapi/cgi/sga_doc?smartapi!celexapi!prod!CELEXnumdoc&lg=EN&nu
mdoc=31994L0022&model=guichett

1.103 The Hydrocarbons Licensing Directive Regulations[1] has restricted the type of terms that can be put into a licence; it has also widened the scope, for granting of licences, and stipulates publication in the Official Journal of the European Union as necessary for applications for licences. This ensures that companies located within the European Union get a fair opportunity to compete in applications for acreage.

1 Hydrocarbon Licensing Directive Regulations 1995, SI 1995/1434: see text at www.opsi.gov.
uk/SI/si1995/Uksi_19951434_en_1.htm.

1.104 Other important EU Directives relevant to the UK's oil and gas industry include the Habitats Directive[1] and the Strategic Environmental Assessment Directive[2], which have been transposed into domestic law. These Directives are geared towards the protection of the environment, which is of paramount importance when considering areas within the UKCS to be offered for exploration.

1 Council Directive 92/43/EEC on the Conservation of natural habitats and of wild fauna and
flora of 21 May 1993: see www.jncc.gov.uk/page-1374.
2 Directive 2001/42/EC of the European Parliament and of the Council of 27 June 2001: for
further information please see ec.europa.eu/environment/eia/home.htm.

1.105 There are three types of production licences available for prospective licensees (promote, traditional/standard and frontier licences). This current mature province licensing style, coupled with the impact of accession to the European Union, international obligations, Regulations and guidance notes issued by the government relating to oil and gas activities, make up the UK petroleum regime. The UKCS licensing regime is discussed in greater detail after the brief overview of operating on the UKCS.

Activities

1.106
- Read through the latest Model Clauses and summarise the key aspects of the conditions that concern the production of offshore oil and gas resources and also the changes that were introduced from the 2004 Model Clauses.
- Find out the main objectives of BNOC and the key reasons for its eventual privatisation.

Further reading

1.107
- D Yergin, *The Prize: The Epic Quest for Oil, Money and Power* (2009, Simon & Schuster).

- T Daintith & G Hewitt (2012), *United Kingdom Oil and Gas Law* (Sweet & Maxwell), Ch 1.
- A Lowe and SAG Talmon (eds), *The Legal Order of the Oceans* (2009, Hart Publishing).
- B Taverne (2008). Petroleum, industry and governments. International energy and resources law and policy series, 15. Alphen aan den Rijn, Kluwer Law International, Chapter 6. 11.1.
- Continental Shelf Act 1964 (c 29), s 1(1): www.legislation.gov.uk/ukpga/1964/29/contents.
- The Petroleum Licensing (Production) (Seaward Areas) Regulations 2008 (SI 2008/225): www.legislation.gov.uk/uksi/2008/225/contents/made.
- For a detailed historical background of the UK oil industry consult the websites of DECC at: og.decc.gov.uk and the Oil and Gas UK at: www.oilandgasuk.co.uk.

Part 2

Operations in the UKCS

2.1   This section considers the current contractual, legal and regulatory framework under which the UKCS operations are performed. It examines various contractual, legal and regulatory issues of relevance to the key UKCS players.

A   OPERATING ON THE UKCS

The licensing regime

2.2   In this section the UKCS licensing regime is looked at in more detail in terms of regulating exploration and production. The correlation between ownership/sovereignty of natural resources and the right to explore for these resources, in this context offshore oil and gas, is set out in Part 1 of the Petroleum Act (PA) 1998. The PA 1998 consolidates the Petroleum (Production) Act 1934 and its application and extension offshore on the basis of the Continental Shelf Act 1964. The Energy Act 2008 introduced changes to offshore oil and gas licensing by improving the licensing regime in response to changes in the commercial environment and enabling DECC to carry out its regulatory functions more effectively.

2.3   The current UKCS licensing regime inherited an important feature of the Petroleum (Production) Act 1934, in that the proprietary rights in petroleum remain radically unchanged. The rights/licences to search and bore for and get petroleum within Great Britain, its territorial sea and the UKCS are granted by the Crown by virtue of powers conferred under the Petroleum Act 1998, s 3(1).

2.4   Strictly speaking, any person or group of persons wishing to explore, exploit or produce oil and gas within this jurisdiction has/have to obtain a licence from the UK government. The position on ownership of onshore resources is quite clear, however that of offshore natural resources is debatable, as the Crown, by virtue of the Continental Shelf 1964 and UN Law of the Sea 1982, is only conferred exclusive 'sovereign' rights over its continental shelf.

2.5   The Crown (represented by the government department, DECC) is free to decide on the form, mode or style employed to explore and produce its natural resources. Section 3 of the PA 1998 empowers the Secretary of State[1] to grant to such persons as he thinks fit licences to search and bore for petroleum in Great Britain under the territorial sea and under the continental shelf for such consideration as he shall with the consent of the Treasury determine, and on such other terms and conditions as he thinks fit. This is a wide discretionary power conferred upon the Secretary of State, albeit subject to EU Directives, regulations, guidance issued by the department and model clauses incorporated into the licence.

1 The generic title given to senior Ministers of government departments, in this case the Secretary of State for the DECC.

European Union dimension

2.6   As a result of the accession of the UK to the European Community in 1973, the Secretary of State, in his exercise of licensing powers cannot lawfully discriminate on grounds of nationality against member states of the Community[1]. The Secretary is constrained from restricting the freedom of nationals of member states to establish or provide services under the same conditions as UK nationals which include conditions of access to petroleum licences, removal of landing requirements, removal of policies encouraging procurement from UK companies, etc.

1 The Treaty establishing the European Community, Article 12.

2.7   The Hydrocarbon Licensing Directive[1] serves as the framework for the granting of petroleum licences in all member states of the EU. The Directive, through the establishment of uniform rules, aims at achieving uniformity of procedures in the grant of licences for exploring, exploiting and production of hydrocarbons. The right to apply for licences is open to all nationals of the EU who possess the necessary expertise, and obligations are imposed on governments to assess and authorise such applications in a non-discriminatory manner based on criteria published in the Official Journal of the European Communities, inviting applications and to be published at least 90 days before the closing date for applications[2].

1 Directive 94/22/EC of the European Parliament and of the Council of 30 May 1994.
2 Article 3(2).

2.8   The Hydrocarbon Licensing Directive was implemented in the UK by the Hydrocarbons Licensing Directive Regulations 1995[1]. All applications shall be determined under the criteria set out in reg 3(1) of Regulations:

(a)   the technical and financial capability of the applicant;
(b)   the way in which the applicant proposes to carry out the activities that would be permitted by the licence;
(c)   in a case where tenders are invited, the price the applicant is prepared to pay in order to obtain the licence; and

(d)   where the applicant holds, or has held a licence of any description under the Petroleum (Production) Act 1934, any lack of efficiency and responsibility displayed by the applicant in operations under that licence.

1   SI 1995/1434.

Application procedure for a licence

2.9   Anyone who wants to explore for, drill for or extract oil or gas in the UK must hold a licence issued under the PA 1998 by the Secretary of State for Energy and Climate Change. The government department responsible for the licensing of oil and gas upstream activities is now called the Department of Energy and Climate Change (DECC), for which a government minister is responsible.

2.10   Applications for such licences can only be made in response to a formal invitation from DECC. An application must be made on the approved application form, with supporting information including a proposed work programme, which describes the minimum amount of exploration work that the applicant would carry out during the initial term if awarded a licence, operating competence (technical and environmental) and financial capacity to carry out the work programme.

Assessing applications

2.11   Where two or more applications have equal merit, the Secretary of State has the discretion to apply other relevant criteria, although the other relevant criteria cannot be applied in a discriminatory manner[1]. The Secretary of State also has the discretion to refuse an application where he is of the opinion that such denial is in the interest of national security where the applicant is effectively controlled by, or by nationals of, a state other than a member state[2].

1   Hydrocarbons Licensing Directive Regulations 1995, reg 3(2).
2   Regulation 3(4).

2.12   Apart from the consideration of EU law when assessing competing applications, the Oil and Gas Industry Taskforce (now PILOT) in its report A Template for Change (published in 1999) identified a need to improve the licence administration[1]. The taskforce recommended the use of a marking scheme to be published in advance of every licensing round, against which all applications would be assessed. The marks awarded to successful applicants in respect of acreage where there has been competition are published together with a short summary of the work programme connected to such application[2]. It is important to note that no marks are awarded in respect of the technical and financial capabilities of the applicants as these are basic criterion which must be attained by all applicants.

1 Available at http://webarchive.nationalarchives.gov.uk/20101227132010/http:/www.pilottask force.co.uk/docs/aboutpilot/atemplateforchange.pdf.
2 See Applications for Production Licences: Guidance, Annex 2: The Marks Scheme, available at https://og.decc.gov.uk/assets/og/licences/rounds/4228-guidance-technical.pdf.

Applicant

2.13   An application may be made by a single company or by a group of companies (provided they have the same equity interests throughout). References to 'the applicant' cover both situations unless clearly stated otherwise, and references to 'the company' refer to a single company making an application, whether on its own or as part of an applicant group. A company must be registered in the UK, either as a company or as a branch of a foreign company.

2.14   The application must include the registered name, address and number of each company that is to hold the licence. The applicant should clearly indicate which companies they want to hold the licence, and ensure that those are the companies that apply in the first place. DECC will not consider any request to award a licence to a company unrelated to the applicant.

2.15   A single application should contain the list of companies and their proposed equity interests and it must be the same throughout any single application; and may only seek a single type of licence (landward, traditional, promote or frontier).

Note: An application can combine geographically separate areas, even if those areas could not be covered by a single licence.

For instance, suppose Company A and Company B want to make a joint application, each proposing to take a 50% interest in any licences awarded; and they seek a traditional licence over one block in the northern North Sea and another over a block in the southern Basin.

They can combine the two blocks in a single application (because both licences would be of the same type and the companies would have the same equity interests in both).

However, if they wanted a third traditional licence but with a 70:30 equity split, they would have to make a separate application; as they would if they also wanted to apply for a promote licence.

2.16   Traditional, frontier and landward applicants must demonstrate to DECC that, if awarded a licence, they will have the technical and environmental competence to operate to the necessary standards.

2.17 All companies must demonstrate financial viability. In addition, companies applying for traditional, frontier and landward licences must demonstrate the financial capacity to carry out the licence's work programme. That capacity must be clearly available to the applicant at the time of application, and not be subject to uncertain future events like share issues.

2.18 DECC accepts that some elements of the applicant's competence may not be in place at the application stage. For example, some posts may not be filled at the moment of application, which may occur months or even years ahead of any need for them. Nevertheless, the applicant will have to convince DECC that it knows what structure and skills are needed and that it has a management team capable of delivering it.

2.19 Companies applying for promote licences do not have to demonstrate a minimum level of technical, environmental or financial capacity, but they have to demonstrate financial viability. However a 'promote licensee' will not be allowed to drill until it has demonstrated that it meets those criteria, and the licence will expire at its second anniversary if the licensee has not done so by then.

Financial capacity

2.20 There are two types of financial check that DECC may apply in a licensing round:

- a Financial Viability Assessment, which will be applied to all applications to ensure that a licence is likely to continue in sound financial health for the foreseeable future; and
- a Financial Capacity Assessment, which will be applied to all applicants (except applicants for promote licences) to demonstrate that the applicant has access to sufficient funds to pay for its share of all the elements of the proposed work programme (including firm, contingent or 'drill-or-drop' commitments).

DECC applies all these financial checks to individual companies within an applicant group, so each company must provide its own set of financial/corporate information.

Technical capacity

2.21 The applicant is required to include its technical understanding of the acreage and its plans for exploitation, including information to:

- demonstrate the quality and understanding of its technical evaluation;
- identify prospectivity;
- explain the exploration (and/or exploitation) rationale;

- propose a detailed work programme;
- (in all cases except promote applications) operatorship competence;
- (for promote applicants only) present its plans and approach to secure the resources necessary to complete the work programme.

Acreage selection

2.22   The Secretary of State has the discretion to prescribe the area and size of the area to be offered under every licence and so also the number of blocks offered. It is usual practice on the UKCS that blocks are offered in standard measurements of 10km by 25km although this size reduces over the life of the licence as relinquishment of part of the area occurs at different phases of the licence. Note that the discretion as to which area within the UKCS can be made available for exploration and production of oil and gas has been curtailed by two important EU environmental protection measures: the Habitats Directive[1] and the Strategic Environmental Assessment Directive[2]. The former guards against the granting of a licence without proper assessment of the conservation implications for the site, whilst the latter guards against the granting of a licence without the proper consideration of the environmental effects of the proposed project:

- the Habitats Directive has been subsumed into domestic law by the Conservation (Natural Habitats, etc) Regulations 1994[3] and Offshore Petroleum Activities (Conservation of Habitats) Regulations 2001[4]. It is important to note that although these Regulations enjoin the minister to consider as paramount the adverse effect a proposed project might have on a site, where there is no satisfactory alternative and where the minister is satisfied that the project should be carried out for imperative reasons of overriding public interest, he is entitled to grant the licence[5];
- the Strategic Environmental Assessment (SEA) Directive is included in the Environmental Assessment of Plans and Programmes Regulations 2004[6], Environmental Assessment of Plans and Programmes (Northern Ireland) Regulations 2004[7]; Environmental Assessment of Plans and Programmes (Wales) Regulations 2004[8]; and Environmental Assessment (Scotland) Act 2005[9]. The SEA is documented on a dedicated website Offshore SEA[10] and encourages public consultation on the Environmental Impact Assessment.

The sponsoring department has the usual practice of advertising available acreage for exploration and production; this practice is further strengthened by the obligation imposed upon it by the Hydrocarbons Licensing Directive.

1   European Council Directive 92/43/EEC of 21 May 1992 on the Conservation of Natural Habitats and of Wild Fauna and Flora.
2   Directive 2001/42/EC of the European Parliament and of the Council of 27 June 2001 on the Assessment of the Effects of Certain Plans and Programmes on the Environment available at http://ec.europa.eu/environment/eia/full-legal-text/0142_en.pdf.
3   SI 1994/2716.

4   SI 2001/1754.
5   Offshore Petroleum Activities (Conservation of Habitats) Regulations 2001, reg 6.
6   SI 2004/1663.
7   SR 2004/280.
8   WSI 2004/1656 (W 170).
9   asp 2005/15.
10 At www.offshore-sea.org.uk/site.

Licensing rounds

2.23   Licences are issued within licensing rounds. In 2012 the 27th offshore oil and gas licensing round saw a total of 224 applications covering 418 blocks of the UKCS. It is the largest number since offshore licensing began in 1964 and is 37 more than the previous high total received in the last licensing round[1]. On the UKCS there have been 27 such licensing rounds, whereby applications are invited via a notice specifying the acreage available, and a closing date stipulated for such interest. As a result of the Hydrocarbons Licensing Directive (discussed above), such invitation to bid should also be made in the *Official Journal of the European Union* at least 90 days before the closing date for interested applicants.

1   For further information on the 27th Oil and Gas Offshore Licensing Round, visit http://og.decc.gov.uk.

2.24   It is not unusual for licences to be granted by the department outside regular licensing rounds. These out of round applications (as they are known by) must be presented with compelling reasons for their grant. The department states that an applicant for an out of round bid must show grounds of urgency (it had in the past accepted the basis of the availability of a drilling rig); it would also be inclined to consider an out of round bid where there is no prospect of competition (where acreage is only of interest to a company owning a contiguous or adjoining acreage).

Note: Please consult the DECC website for detailed information on all the UKCS licensing rounds.

Types of licences

2.25   There are two broad types of licence that can be obtained for exploration and production of oil and gas in the UK. There are the seaward (UKCS) licences and the landward (Onshore) licences. Seaward licences can be further divided into exploration licences and production licences:

- an exploration licence is a non-exclusive licence to search for petroleum in the strata in the islands and in the seabed and subsoil in any seaward area and in those parts of any landward area which are below the low-water line. This right does not extend or interfere with rights held under a production licence by another, unless both agree otherwise[1]. The exploration licence runs for a period of three years renewable for a further period of three years, subject to the provision of a three-month written request. The exploration licence permits the holder to conduct non-intrusive surveys such as seismic data-gathering or other geological prospecting. The exploratory licence does not allow for any significant drilling, as the licence holder can only drill to a maximum depth of 350m below the seabed (this is for purely exploratory purposes);

- a production licence is the main form of licence. It confers exclusive rights to search or bore for or get petroleum in the seabed and subsoil under the seaward area. In the first rounds of UKCS licensing standard production licences were granted, but as the province matured, and in a bid to sustain its attractiveness, changes were made to the standard production licences.

All seaward production licences run for three successive terms:
— the Initial term: after which, if the agreed work programme has been completed and if a minimum amount of acreage has been relinquished, the licence may continue into a second term;
— the second term: after which, if a development plan has been approved and if all of the acreage outside that development has been relinquished, the licence may continue into a third term;
— the third term: for any continuation of work.

The terms are of different lengths according to the licence type. The terms of the standard licences are contained in the model clauses of the Petroleum Licensing (Production) (Seaward Areas) Regulations 2008[2]. These terms have evolved over time and are not retroactive in nature; the model clauses governing the licence at its time of grant continue to govern it.

1   The department and Oil and Gas UK have encouraged this through the open access system, whereby seismic data can be obtained for exploration companies. See Oil and Gas UK, Guidelines for Permitting Open Access over Licensed Acreage for Seismic Acquisition.
2   SI 2008/225.

Traditional/standard licences

2.26   This is the original type of seaward production licence. The standard production licence is by far the most common form of licence issued over the life of the UKCS. In the last licensing round (ie the 27th round) there were 192 applications for traditional licences out of a total 224 applications. Applicants must prove technical, environmental and financial capacity before being offered a standard (traditional) licence:

- the initial term lasts for four years. This period is usually for exploration and the gathering of geological information;

- the second term lasts for four years. This is usually the period where the project is appraised and the production of the licensed area is prepared and anticipated;
- the third term lasts for 18 years. This is the final and last stage of the project, it is the production stage.

The mandatory relinquishment at the end of the initial term is of 50%.

Frontier licences

2.27 Certain areas of the UKCS (eg the deep waters west of the Shetlands) are particularly technically challenging and lack proper infrastructure. In recognising this, the DECC offers frontier licences that are adapted to suit these conditions. In the last licensing round (ie the 27th round) there were seven applications for frontier licences out of a total 224 applications. The objective of this variant is to allow companies to screen large areas, potentially with greater materiality, so they can look for a wider range of prospects; therefore the time allowed for exploration, appraisal and development is greater:

- the initial term lasts for six years;
- the second term lasts for six years;
- the third term lasts for 18 years.

2.28 The rental rate in the first three years is low so that such licences are not prohibitively expensive even when they cover large areas. However, by the end of the initial three years the licensee must have surrendered 75% of the acreage. After that, the rental rates are the same as those for a standard licence. As with other licence types, there is a 50% relinquishment at the end of the initial term, though coming on top of the 75% relinquishment at three years, on a frontier licence this amounts to seven-eighths of the original area.

2.29 The DECC recognised that there might be occasions where the licensee is able to demonstrate prospects over more than 25% of the licence. In such exceptional circumstances the government has made it clear that it may consider requests to accept only a 50% relinquishment after three years (as opposed to the 75%). This is at DECC's discretion. It is also important to note that the second relinquishment would still have to bring the area down to one-eighth of its original value.

2.30 Frontier licences issued previously had a more complicated format, with the initial term being split at the time of the 75% relinquishment into an initial term and a second term. Therefore neither of these terms corresponded to the initial term of other licence types, and the third term on an old frontier licence corresponds to the second term on other licence types.

Promote licences

2.31   The 'promote' licence is similar to the traditional licence. The initial, second and third terms are of the same length. The last licensing round (ie the 27th round) saw 25 applications for promote licences out of a total 224 applications. The origin of this licence goes back to 2002, when the government observed demand for a new licensing opportunity for companies that were not able to compete in traditional licensing rounds. This demand saw the creation of the promote licence type in 2003, in the 21st seaward licensing round.

2.32   The promote licence allows up to two years for a company to hold the licence before it has to meet DECC's financial, technical and environmental checks. The checks are deferred, not waived, and invariably the promote licensees will not be allowed to drill until they have met the appropriate criteria.

2.33   The licensee therefore has two years after award to attract the technical, environmental and financial capacity to complete the agreed work programme. To implement this, each promote licence carries a 'drill-or-drop' initial term work programme. The licence will expire after two years if the licensee has not satisfied DECC of its technical, environmental and financial capacity to complete the work programme (ie to drill a well), and made a firm commitment to DECC to do so.

2.34   Assuming the licence continues into years 3 and 4, the work programme must be carried out before the end of the initial term (ie within four years). One possible course of events is set out here to illustrate the general idea of the promote licence: The DECC envisages that the first year in the promote licence would be for data purchase and evaluation, the second being for attracting a new co-venturer, who would acquire an interest in the licence subject to DECC's approval and whose presence as a licensee seeks to satisfy the financial and technical requirements. Towards the end of the second year, a report would be submitted to DECC making a firm drilling commitment and providing evidence of its technical and financial competence; and by the third and fourth year complete its work programme by drilling a well.

UKCS fiscal regime

2.35   The fiscal regime of companies operating on the UKCS, for purposes of petroleum exploration, exploitation, production and all oil and gas activities, is administered by the Large Business Service Oil and Gas Sector (LBSOG), an arm of HM Revenue & Customs (formerly the Oil Taxation Office). Over the course of the last 33 years, the UK has developed into one of the world's major producing oil countries. To cope with changing conditions, economies, and fluctuating oil prices, successive governments have had to develop a fiscal regime providing sufficient incentive to companies to explore and produce petroleum, whilst at the same time ensuing that the benefit of such great natural resources accrues to the UK coffers[1].

1   See HM Revenue & Customs: A Guide to UK and UK Continental Shelf, Oil and Gas Taxation 2008, available at www.hmrc.gov.uk/international/ns-fiscal3.htm. Furthermore, on the UK oil and gas tax regime: statistics and information see www.oilandgasuk.co.uk/taxation.cfm.

2.36   Apart from the primary oil and gas extractive industry, a series of dependent industries, which support and supply exploration and production activities, have evolved. These industries stem from ancillary activities, and also rely to some extent on the fiscal regime in place[1].

The tax regime which applies to exploration for, and production of, oil and gas in the UK and on the UKCS currently comprises three elements[2]: Petroleum Revenue Tax (PRT); Supplementary Charge (SC); and Ring Fence Corporation Tax (RFCT).

1   Para 1.4.
2   Further information on government revenues from UK oil and gas production see www.gov.uk/government/uploads/system/uploads/attachment_data/file/203892/UKCS_Tax_Table_May_2013.pdf and www.gov.uk/government/uploads/system/uploads/attachment_data/file/203893/UKCS_Tax_Charts_May_2013.pdf.

Petroleum Revenue Tax (PRT)

2.37   **PRT** is a special tax on oil and gas production directed at taxing a higher proportion of the economic rent from the UKCS[1]. The PRT was introduced under the Oil Taxation Act 1975[2]. It is a field-based tax charged on profits arising from individual oil fields[3] and not charged on cumulative profits from all oil fields owned by each company. The PRT in the UK was formerly 75% but that rate was reduced to 50% by the Finance Act 1993[4]. With effect from 16 March 1993, the Finance Act 2003 abolished PRT for all fields given development consent on or after that date; thus only fields which obtained development consent before this date are charged with PRT.

1   PRT and Government revenues from UK oil and gas production on the HMRC website at www.hmrc.gov.uk/statistics/prt.htm.
2   Oil Taxation Act 1975, s 1.
3   Although there are quite a number of reliefs and allowances that can be set off against the PRT, see HM Revenue & Customs: A Guide to UK and UK Continental Shelf, Oil and Gas Taxation 2008, Ch 4.
4   Finance Act 1993, s 186.

2.38   PRT is assessed and chargeable on each participator (in this instance the whole joint venture and then divided according to each co-venturer's percentage interest) in each field; the assessments are raised for six-month chargeable periods ending on 30 June and 31 December of each year[1].

1   HM Revenue & Customs: A Guide to UK and UK Continental Shelf, Oil and Gas Taxation 2008, para 2.6.

2.39   The PRT taxable income is computed by adding recognised incomings[1] and deducting allowed reliefs and allowances[2]. The responsible person, for each taxable field, has to submit a return of the total amount of oil and gas produced from the field within one month of the end of the chargeable periods (30 June and 31 December). This gives details of each joint venture company's percentage interest in the field and thus each joint venture's percentage share of total oil and gas produced[3].

1   These include three main items: the gross profit arising from disposals of oil and gas produced by each joint venture company in each chargeable period (equity); tariff receipts (consideration received from the leasing out of assets or provision of services to other participators in other fields) and disposal receipts (consideration received from sale of certain assets). See HM Revenue & Customs: A Guide to UK and UK Continental Shelf, Oil and Gas Taxation 2008, Ch 3.
2   Allowed field-related expenditure relief and supplement; oil allowance and safeguard; tariff receipts allowance; and cross field allowance. See HM Revenue & Customs: A Guide to UK and UK Continental Shelf, Oil and Gas Taxation 2008, Ch 3.
3   HM Revenue & Customs: A Guide to UK and UK Continental Shelf, Oil and Gas Taxation 2008, para 5.2.

2.40   The joint venture company has two months after the end of the chargeable periods (ie until 31 August and 28 February) to submit a return of its incomings from each taxable field in which it has an interest. In addition it has to submit details of actual sale and purchases of crude oil to aid the regulator in the computation of the statutory market value[1].

1   HM Revenue & Customs: A Guide to UK and UK Continental Shelf, Oil and Gas Taxation 2008, para 5.3.

2.41   Payments for each chargeable period are due two months after the end of the period (ie by 31 August and 28 February)[1]. Assessments are usually issued by LBSOG five months after the end of each chargeable period (ie 31 May and 30 November). Where there is need for further PRT payment the joint venture company is obliged to make such payment within the six months after the end of the relevant chargeable period (or 30 days after issue of the assessment, if later). Where the participator has overpaid, the excess is repaid[2].

1   HM Revenue & Customs: A Guide to UK and UK Continental Shelf, Oil and Gas Taxation 2008, para 5.8.
2   Para 5.11.

Supplementary Charge (SC)

2.42   **SC** in respect of ring fence activities is very similar to the ring fence corporation tax. It is a creation of the Finance Act 2002[1], and only applies to oil and gas production (contractors do not have to pay this tax). All oil producing companies pay a supplementary charge of 20% on production profits in addition to the 30% RFCT. The RFCT and SC are payable in three instalments on 14 July, 14 October and 14 January of each year[2].

1 Finance Act 2002, s 91.
2 HM Revenue & Customs: A Guide to UK and UK Continental Shelf, Oil and Gas Taxation 2008.

Ring Fence Corporation Tax (RFCT)

2.43   **RFCT** is corporation tax charged on 'oil extraction activities' undiluted by any losses or any other form of allowance arising out of any other form of business activities[1]. The RFCT is paid by all companies operating on the UKCS; it is 30% of an 'undiluted' ring fence profit.

1 HM Revenue & Customs: A Guide to UK and UK Continental Shelf, Oil and Gas Taxation 2008, para 6.1.

2.44   Oil extraction activities are activities carried on the UKCS in exploring, producing, transporting, treating and storing oil and gas; profits made from these activities are ring fenced.

2.45   In computing the ring fence profits, capital losses from other business activities are precluded from being set off against gains accruing within the ring fence[1] (although losses from oil extraction may be carried back and forth against the ring fence profits). This, however, does not preclude RFCT losses from being set off against other business activities of the company[2].

1 HM Revenue & Customs: A Guide to UK and UK Continental Shelf, Oil and Gas Taxation 2008, para 6.2.
2 The ring fence only works in one direction (para 6.4).

2.46   Although the RFCT is a strict tier in the regime and very little can be set off against the ring fence profits, PRT paid, capital expenditure on oil extraction[1], plant and machinery expenditure[2], exploration and appraisal activities, mineral extraction, industrial buildings and decommissioning costs are allowed to be set off against ring fence profits.

1 From 17 April 2002 first year allowance is available for all ring fence capital expenditure (para 6.9).
2 For expenditure incurred before 17 April 2002, a 25% relief was available on writing down allowance basis, after this date (not including long life assets) expenditure qualifies for a 100% allowance (para 6.10).

Ring Fence Expenditure Supplement (RFES)[1]

2.47   RFES assists companies that do not yet have sufficient taxable income for ring fence corporation tax purposes against which fully to set their exploration, appraisal and development costs. The RFES increases the value of losses carried forward from one accounting period to the next by a compound 10% a year (6% a year for accounting periods beginning before 1 January 2012)– for a maximum of six years, not necessarily consecutively.

1 Further details available at www.hmrc.gov.uk/manuals/otmanual/OT26105.htm.

Brown Field Allowances

2.48   Following the announcement on 7 September 2012 that the government would introduce a Brown Field Allowance (BFA), HM Treasury has circulated a guidance note[1], giving further information on the BFA qualification criteria and the process for BFA cost verification. Companies undertaking incremental projects that might be eligible for a BFA are advised to ensure they are familiar with this process if they wish those projects to qualify for the allowance.

1   Further details available at www.hmrc.gov.uk/manuals/otmanual/OT26105.htm.

Oil and gas decommissioning tax relief[1]

2.49   Legislation was introduced in Finance Act 2012[2] to restrict tax relief for decommissioning expenses for Supplementary Charge purposes to 20%. There will be no restrictions to decommissioning relief beyond this level for the lifetime of the current Parliament. The government is currently consulting on proposals to give further, longer-term certainty on decommissioning[3].

1   See Budget 2012: Upstream Oil and Gas Taxation ('North Sea Tax') available at www.gov. uk/government/uploads/system/uploads/attachment_data/file/15754/4812-budget-2012-tax-changes.pdf.
2   Finance Act 2012 Available at www.legislation.gov.uk/ukpga/2012/14/section/183/enacted.
3   Decommissioning Relief Deeds: Summary of Responses (December 2012) available at www. gov.uk/government/uploads/system/uploads/attachment_data/file/190266/consult_responses_ decommissioning_relief_deeds_111112.pdf. Further details are available at www.gov.uk/ government/consultations/decommissioning-relief-deeds-increasing-tax-certainty-for-oil-and-gas-investment-in-the-uk-continental-shelf.

2.50   In conclusion, the above paragraphs have considered the requirements for the application of a UKCS licence by a single company or by a group of companies. The following section examines the situation where more than one company decide to share their interests and liabilities in the execution of the required licence obligations (ie work programme and financial commitment) through a joint operating agreement.

Activities

2.51
- The UK licensing regime has been described as a contractual and regulatory hybrid arrangement. Do you think this is a fair description?
- Comment on whether the EU Directives, which were highlighted in this part, make any difference to the UKCS licensing regime?
- In advising an international oil company to obtain an exploration licence in the UK, what are the key criteria that should be included in the application?

B   FURTHER READING

Suggested reading

2.52

- G Gordon, J Paterson & E Usenmez (2011), *Oil and Gas Law: Current Practice and Emerging Trends* (2nd edn, Dundee University Press), Licensing and Regulation.
- J Wils & EC Neilson, *The Technical and Legal Guide to the UK Oil and Gas Industry* (2007, Aberlour), Ch 2.
- D Martyn, *Upstream Oil and Gas Agreements* (1996, Sweet & Maxwell).
- The UK Government Department of Energy and Climate Change (DECC), formerly known as Business Enterprise and Regulatory Reform (BERR) and formerly Department of Trade and Industry (DTI) at: www.gov.uk/browse/business/licences/oil-and-gas-licensing.
- Licensing: Legislative background: http://og.decc.gov.uk/en/olgs/cms/licences/licensing_guid/legislative_ba/legislative_ba.aspx.
- The Oil and Gas UK Ltd (OGUK) formerly United Kingdom Offshore Operators Association (UKOOA): the voice of the offshore industry, keeps useful and up to date information on industry issues. See www.oilandgasuk.co.uk.
- Offshore Strategic Environmental Assessment: UK public consultation for offshore energy licensing www.offshore-sea.org.uk/site/index.php.
- Conservation (Natural Habitats, &c) Regulations 1994, SI 1994/2716: www.legislation.gov.uk/uksi/1994/2716/contents/made.
- Hydrocarbons Licensing Directive Regulations 1995, SI 1995/1434: www.legislation.gov.uk/uksi/1995/1434/contents/made.
- Petroleum Act 1998 (c 17): www.legislation.gov.uk/ukpga/1998/17/contents.
- Petroleum Licensing (Exploration and Production) (Seaward and Landward Areas) Regulations 2004, SI 2004/352: www.legislation.gov.uk/uksi/2004/352/contents/made.
- Petroleum Licensing (Exploration and Production) (Seaward and Landward Areas) (Amendment) Regulations 2006, SI 2006/784: www.legislation.gov.uk/uksi/2006/784/contents/made.
- Petroleum Licensing (Production) (Seaward Areas) Regulations 2008, SI 2008/225.

Part 3

Contracting in the UKCS

3.1   This part focuses on the key contractual and commercial issues used by most of the key players working on the UKCS, and includes the contracting arrangements of the contractors in various forms. It will highlight key contractual issues that have proved to be problematic over the years to the many contractors operating on the UKCS. It also provides some guidance on how to negotiate and manage oil and gas contracts more profitably.

3.2   This part also identifies how to assess and manage the common contractual risks in the oil and gas industry, and provide guidance on how to avoid common contract pitfalls. Finally it examines the effective use of alternative dispute resolution options.

A   STANDARD AGREEMENTS

CRINE/LOGIC contracts

3.3   The standard contracts for the UK offshore oil and gas industry (formerly CRINE contracts) have been developed by the Standard Contracts Committee and are issued by LOGIC (hereinafter referred to as LOGIC contracts) for use within the industry between the major oil companies and their contractors, including subcontractors.

3.4   The contracts are structured on similar terms. There are a range of model contracts that cover different aspects of the industry, including the following:

- offshore services;
- onshore services;
- on and offshore services;
- well services;
- construction;
- marine construction;
- design;
- SME services;
- subcontracts;
- supply of mobile drilling rigs;

- purchase orders;
- supply of major items of plant and equipment.

All LOGIC contracts are available in PDF format, and may be downloaded free of charge, on the LOGIC website at www.logic-oil.com/standard-contracts.

3.5 LOGIC contracts have a number of recognised sections, which generally include the following:

- Section I: Form of contract, including Appendix 1;
- Section II:
  (a) standard contract terms
  (b) special conditions of contract;
- Section III: Remuneration;
- Section IV: Scope of work;
- Section V: Health, safety and environment (SH&E);
- Section VI: Company's general obligations.

Other sections may be added, depending on the contract, and some contracts may have nine or more sections.

3.6 The structure can be explained by breaking it down as follows:

— Section I is the simplest section and creates the contractual relationship. This section also sets out what the other sections are and how they are to be used. This is the section which is signed by the parties to create the contractual relationship. There is an appendix to Section I.
— Section II contains the main contractual sections. Section II(a) contains the general terms, which are those published by LOGIC. These terms are not set out in full here, but should be downloaded from the LOGIC website at www.logic-oil.com. The general terms in Section II(a) are modified by the special terms in Section II(b).

3.7 All contracts which have several sections should have an interpretation section, which explains which sections are to have precedence over the others. This can be important in deciding how to interpret a contract. Generally, where there is one section which has precedence over another, then if there is any conflict in terms, the section having precedence will govern how the contract is to be read. For instance, in LOGIC contracts the general rule is that the earlier sections will have precedence over the later. There is one exception to this rule: Section II(b) has precedence over Section II(a). This clearly makes sense since Section II(b) comprises the special terms which the parties agree will apply to any particular contract. The contract will be used to govern work which will be instructed from time to time by purchase orders (POs). It would be possible to allow the contract terms to be modified by special terms on the face of a PO. However this practice is generally not followed, since it would allow anyone issuing a PO to modify the contract, which could result in differences in warranties and insurance issues under the same contract, leading to a lack of uniformity and potential uncertainty.

3.8   The general conditions are the model contract conditions. The special conditions are those agreed upon by the parties themselves (though almost always imposed by the operator), which in turn modify the general conditions.

3.9   It is important to realise that the legal terms of the contract in Section II can often be affected by Section III, Remuneration and Section IV, Workscope. The other sections are generally for specialist review. In addition, the terms will always be amended in important ways by the Appendix which is part of Section I, and which contains important statements on liability.

Review of LOGIC General Conditions

3.10–3.12   The LOGIC General Conditions for Services (On- and Off-Shore) (Edition 2, October 2003) document is not set out here, but what follows is a detailed analysis of the conditions, with particular emphasis on areas which may prove problematic. All references are to clauses of the aforementioned LOGIC contract. The reader is strongly recommended to download it free of charge from the LOGIC website in order to follow the discussion below.

- Clause 1 (Definitions): The definition of 'affiliates' (clause 1.1) defines third parties associated with the parties to the contract horizontally. Similar considerations apply to the contractor; if the contractor is part of a joint venture then the company may require that all the members of the joint venture are included as affiliates of the contractor.

  The definition of 'company group' (clause 1.2) and 'contractor group' (clause 1.6) define the vertical relationships with third parties. The Guidance Notes to the General Conditions suggest that the reason the General Terms do not include contractors and subcontractors of the company as a matter of course is due to the difficulty of creating such a regime given the English doctrine of privity of contract. The view of most contractors and some production companies operating in the North Sea is to provide such indemnities in any case and it is arguable that a sufficiently widely drafted indemnity could give protection. Notice that the same limitation does not apply to the definition contractor group, which suggests there is some confusion over the extent of such indemnities. 'Contractor group' includes subcontractors.

  The definition of 'Co-venturers' (clause 1.8) also clarifies horizontal relationships. Whereas 'affiliates' is taken to refer to what may be termed as members of the group of companies to which the company belongs, 'co-venturers' refers to third party entities who are not part of that group. It is quite usual that the company contracts as operator of the joint venture on behalf of its co-venturers. It is good practice, therefore, that if (for example) the company is one of a number of companies working in alliance that all the members of the alliance are included as co-venturers.

This does not usually apply to joint venture companies where a separate joint venture company has been incorporated, though it may sometimes be necessary to do so and thought should be given to this in every case. Co-venturers are part of the company group.

The definition of 'work' (clause 1.13) should be checked against the Workscope.

The definition of 'worksite' (clause 1.14) is important, as it can affect indemnities. Contractors need to ensure that the worksite as defined is one which will be covered by their insurance. To give one example, if the worksite includes a ship, contractors may need to ensure they have insurance cover for damage to vessels. This may require special marine cover and can be expensive.

- Clause 4 (Contractor's General Conditions): Clause 4.2 is essentially the contractor's warranty. If the level of skill required is lower than this, then this clause should be amended.
- Clause 5 (Offshore Transportation) has important issues for insurance cover. Normally contractors would not be expected to have cover for offshore transport, therefore since the operators (usually the company) have cover for this, it is customary for the operator to organise and pay for the transport. This can be expensive, especially if equipment is being transported. If there is any unusual requirement for transport then this clause should be amended to cover this. In addition, the contractor should check the location of the company-designated heliport and supply base, since the company's obligations only begin there.
- Clause 8 (Assignment and Sub-contracting): Clause 8.2 sets out the contractor's right to sub-contract. As may be expected, the whole of the contract may not be subcontracted. However, it is not unknown for this to be the case under certain arrangements and where this happens amendments would need to be made to this clause.

  The company normally reserves the right to review sub-contracts. This is taken seriously by oil and gas companies. There are normally risk issues and supply chain issues which they would need to address. It is therefore customary to advise subcontractors of this requirement. Generally, insofar as possible, the terms of the contact would be passed down to subcontractors, but it would be fair to say that, although this might be desirable as a matter of law, it may not be appropriate as a matter of practice. In a small sub-contract the LOGIC terms would generally not be backed down, though it may be more likely in a subcontract which was a material part of the overall contract. The contractor needs to bear in mind they are responsible for the sub-contractor's performance of the work and also have a responsibility under the Indemnities.
- Clause 9 (Contractor Personnel): Clause 9.2 is another warrant clause as to the quality of the workmanship. The term 'Key personnel' in clause 9.3 is taken seriously and any such personnel need to be identified and

managed. Clauses 9.4 and 9.7 have become more important, due to an increasing number of overseas workers in the industry. Clauses 9.5 and 9.6 are important in many contracts where the contractor's workforce is composed of short-term contracted staff. This is common, for instance, in fabric maintenance contracts where there will be a continuing low level of maintenance all the time on platforms. During the summer, there are often campaigns or special projects to carry out larger repair or maintenance programmes which require, often at short notice, a very large number of workers to be brought offshore. These conditions make it clear that it is the contractor who is responsible for these workers. Clause 9.8 means that the employment contracts of employees need to be flexible enough to allow this; it is less of a problem for contracted workers whose contracts can usually be terminated at short notice with no repercussions.

- Clause 10 (Examination and Defects Correction) is the corollary to the warranties mentioned in clauses 4.2 and 9.2. It would be fair to say that the LOGIC warranty terms are very favourable to the Company. This can present problems for Contractors who normally prefer to use their own warranty terms which are usually much tighter. The parties could agree a modification in the Special Terms to modify the General Terms. The problem is that it is unclear from the General Terms how far the requirement to correct defects goes – is it just the defective part; or is it the defective part and the further damage caused by it?

The Contractor should try and ensure that they will be liable only to repair or replace the defective part and nothing more. The risk of further damage remains with the Company and their insurance arrangements.

The defects correction clause also extends to any remedial work carried out or replacement part provided while correcting defects. This could be seen as an evergreen warranty, but generally attempts to cap this are resisted by the Company. In a sense this is not unfair since it is up to the Contractor to do a good job. There is provision that the Company can have the work carried out by another party if they wish. There is usually some amendment of this since the power is unfettered in the General Terms (although it only arises if the Company decides that that it will be prejudicial to the Company's interests to have the Contractor carry out the corrective work). There is usually a requirement agreed that the Contractor will be given the first opportunity to remedy the defect, unless there is an urgent requirement. This can be the case offshore when it may be impracticable to wait for the Contractor to send out a repair team when there is someone on the platform who can carry out the work.

In clause 10.2(d), while the Contractor is not liable for the expenses of personnel, there is no such exclusion for parts and equipment. It is recommended that these are also excluded, though it is arguable that Clause 5 already deals with this.

- Clause 12 (Force Majeure): Unless the parties agree otherwise, then such events as are outlined in this clause could, if not otherwise dealt with, result in a termination of the contract as a matter of law or in the frustration of the contract. Frustration is a difficult and imprecise concept in contract law and requires a court decision to operate. Therefore it is generally better for parties to agree in advance what events may create problems in the performance of the contract and to agree how these will be dealt with should they occur. This clause should be carefully reviewed in each case.

- Clause 13 (Suspension): The contractors should consider if it is likely that additional expense could be incurred by termination. For instance, if there are subcontractors, is there a possibility that early termination could trigger penalty payments? Or if raw materials are bought and allocated in advance which cannot be re-used, then some factor for these should be included in the Remuneration Section III. The reference in clause 13.8 to clause 11 is somewhat obscure, but it is suggested that this means that the omission is to be treated as a variation and the Work priced accordingly.

- Clause 17 (Patents and Other Proprietary Rights) is not usually the subject of much discussion. Sometimes the Company will state that any rights arising out of the Work will vest in it and not in the Contractor. In most cases this is not a major cause for concern since it is unlikely that such rights will arise. Where they may arise, however, then they could be valuable. The rights to use them in connection with the work may be critical, and should be the subject of discussion and agreement between the parties.

- Clauses 19, 20 and 21 (on indemnity, insurance and consequential loss, respectively) are discussed below in various sections. However, these three areas require extensive explanation beyond the scope of this book.

- Clause 22 (Confidentiality): note that while the Contractor's obligation is for five years from the termination of the Contract, that of the Company is for five years from the commencement of the Contract. This is generally not a problem, but could be an issue where the Contractor is passing confidential information to the Company during the lifetime of the contract. This will generally only be an issue where the contract commencement and termination dates are far apart.

- Clause 24 (Termination) can be a complex and difficult clause. The first issue is that the Company can always terminate if it wishes to. This is a fact of contracting in the UK Oil and Gas industry and it is very difficult to have this clause removed. Even contracts worth millions of pounds and agreed to run for several years will be subject to this clause which means that, in effect, they are rolling contracts terminable at will on giving notice. It has been known for contracts to be terminated using this clause. However, in general, contacts run their course. One reason for this is that the bidding process for major contracts is lengthy and time consuming and there inevitably will be some interruption to the administration of the business, therefore there is pressure to keep contracts running and not to terminate early. Where the contract is terminated as a result of the Contractor's default, the Contractor has to be given notice and an opportunity to remedy the default. Termination for this reason results in a different obligation on the Company to pay and allows the Company to bring in another party to remedy the work and to offset its payment obligation against the costs it incurs as a result of the default.

If the Contractor becomes insolvent then the effect is similar to a default situation, however there is sufficient flexibility in clause 24.6 to allow the Company to delay paying any monies to the Contractor or its representatives in insolvency until it has finally established the cost of the default or insolvency to the Contract.

- Clause 28 (General Legal Provisions): Clause 28.5 states that English law will apply. This may be thought odd given that many of such contracts take place in waters off Scotland. The explanation is that the oil and gas companies which first established operations on the UKCS were large multinational companies, who had much experience with English law as a system of trade law applied internationally and very little with Scots law.

One issue is the statement that the English courts will have exclusive jurisdiction. This is not now normal; non-exclusive jurisdiction is now generally recommended. If the jurisdiction is entirely with the English courts, there have in the past been problems with enforcing performance of the contact. For example, in a five-year contract the company instructed work from the contractor, but has not paid some outstanding invoices. The company carries out the work, but then withholds delivery of some parts against payment of the outstanding invoices. The company could enforce delivery and if the Scottish courts had jurisdiction (as they may have if the jurisdiction were non-exclusive), the matter would be relatively straightforward; however, with the requirement to go to the courts in England, against the timetable of urgency in running platform, the length of time it would take to enforce the company's rights is such that a negotiated settlement will often be quicker.

- Clause 30 (Resolution of Disputes): This is relatively straightforward and includes a reference to Alternative Dispute Resolution. There is no reference to arbitration, though it would be possible for the parties to agree this.

- Clause 31 (Contracts (Rights of Third Parties) Act): this clause arises out of the English privity of contract rules. Unlike in civil systems and Scots law, there was no English doctrine which allowed third parties rights in contract unless they were parties to the contract. The Act sought to bring in such rights. Generally third parties will not have rights except rights under the indemnity and insurance clauses in favour of 'Company Group' and 'Contractor Group'.

Further reading

3.13

● LOGIC General Conditions of Contract for Services (On- and Off-shore) (Edition 2, October 2003): http://www.logic-oil.com/sites/default/files/documents/Services%20Onshore%20and%20Offshore%20Edition%202.pdf.

B INDUSTRY AGREEMENTS

3.14   This section examines first the contractual arrangement and relationship between the companies that have been issued a licence to undertake oil and gas exploration and exploitation activities in the UK. This contractual arrangement is called the Joint Operating Agreement (JOA). JOAs are usually preceded by an Area of Mutual Interest (AMI) or Bidding Agreement (BA) in anticipation of securing a licence at a licensing round. This section reviews the background and key provisions of AMIs, the nature and functions of the JOA used on the UKCS, its clauses dealing with choice, duties and liabilities of the operator; the joint operating committee; authorisation for expenditure and pass mark; sole risk and non-consent; assignment and withdrawal; and default and forfeiture.

3.15   The unitisation section below considers the situation where oil and gas reserves straddle different licence/boundary areas which necessitate an acceptable arrangement between all the parties involved to regulate the exploitation of the field in an orderly and amicable manner. It is not uncommon to have a reservoir straddling different blocks owned by different licences. Where this is the case, parties are obliged to enter into a unitisation and unit operating agreement to ensure that the fields are exploited in an optimal way and to prevent any disputes as to ownership, waste or duplication. The section considers the legal and contractual arrangement applied in such a situation, its rationale and advantages. It also considers cross border unitisation and joint development agreements between countries.

The upstream preference for joint ventures

3.16   The financial and other resources required by an upstream project are so great that it is unusual for even a large oil company to undertake one on its own. Even the largest oil companies prefer to have a 25% share in four projects than a 100% share of one. Therefore, the norm in the upstream is for a project to be conducted as a joint venture between several companies, with one of those companies designated as the operator and responsible for the actual conduct of operations.

3.17   It is said that an upstream project is usually conducted more efficiently by a joint venture than a single company. However, the interaction between the co-ventures could be time- and resource-consuming. Co-ventures can be an arena for the bitterest disputes. A further observation, which demonstrates that states too believe in the efficiency of a joint venture: it appears that states prefer to let projects to a consortium rather than to a single company, and in some petroleum provinces, such as Norway and Angola, the state actually decides who will be in the consortium.

Unincorporated joint venture

3.18   There are two kind of joint ventures, incorporated and unincorporated. An incorporated joint venture involves the formation of a company to conduct the project, and the co-venturers are the shareholders in the company. The relationship between them is contained in the constitution of the company, ie the memorandum and articles of association, and often a separate shareholder agreement. An unincorporated joint venture does not involve the formation of a new company, and the relationship between the co-venturers is governed by a joint venture agreement of some kind.

3.19   Incorporated joint ventures are common in other industries such as armaments or car-making, but in the upstream there is a very strong preference for unincorporated joint ventures. There are a number of reasons for this preference, but they all derive from the fact that the joint venture company is a legal entity separate from the joint venture shareholders. All the normal rules of company and tax law apply to it, and this significantly restricts the joint ventures' freedom to agree how to manage and conduct the venture.

3.20   Very occasionally an upstream project is conducted through an incorporated joint venture. This is usually because it is the wish, or a legal requirement, of the host state. But for the purpose of this section only the unincorporated joint ventures that are standard in the upstream are considered.

Area of Mutual Interest (AMI) and bidding agreements

3.21   It is usual for a consortium interested in an upstream venture to enter into a preliminary agreement between themselves before they commence negotiations with the resource holder for a project. This preliminary agreement is often called an Area of Mutual Interest Agreement (AMIs), Bidding Agreement, Joint Venture Agreement, or some other such phrase. The purpose of this agreement is to commit the parties to co-operate in single specified project, or may instead refer to a particular bid round, or to a geographical area. It will be limited in time, perhaps to one specified bidding round, or for a stated period. If the project is obtained, the preliminary agreement will be replaced by a full joint operating agreement for the operations phase.

3.22 Preliminary agreements of this type are not usually continuous. The parties have a common interest in pursuing the opportunity that they have identified, which has the effect of aligning their interest. If they cannot negotiate acceptable terms they are free to go off and make other arrangements.

Key provisions

3.23 In essence, a typical AMI will be very simple agreement with four vital provisions:

— opportunity;
— duration;
— no obligation to participate; and
— exclusivity.

Opportunity

3.24 There must be some reason to expect that petroleum rights in some area or project will become available, whether as a concession, a production sharing agreement or some other arrangement. The existence of an opportunity may be public information, for example the announcement of a UKCS licensing round, or it may come as a result of private discussion between one party and a resource holder, in which case that party will usually insist on a confidentiality agreement to protect that information from disclosure to third parties.

3.25 As always, there is a wide spectrum of possibilities on the extent of the proposed joint venture. At one end of this spectrum, a group of companies may agree to pursue jointly a single block in a single forthcoming UKCS licensing round. If they do make a joint bid and the bid succeeds, they will enter into a JOA to cover operations on that block. If no bid is made, or if the bid is unsuccessful, the joint venture agreement terminates and the parties are free to go their own way.

At the other end of the spectrum, two or more companies may agree to work jointly over a wide area, perhaps in an entire country or geographical region.

Duration

3.26 This usually follows the nature of the opportunity identified. The agreement will have to last for long enough to give the joint venture a realistic chance of negotiating the opportunity, but the parties will not generally want to restrict their freedom of action beyond this.

3.27 Therefore, with a joint venture agreement to pursue a single block in a forthcoming licensing round, the agreement will usually last until the later of: (a) a joint decision not to bid; (b) notification of the rejection of the bid; or (c) if the bid is successful, the execution of a full JOA that will replace the initial agreement. However, with a less defined opportunity, the agreement will usually last for a stated period of months or years. It can be very awkward if the parties have underestimated the time required, and the joint venture agreement expires before the opportunity has come to fruition. At this point the agreement falls away, and any party is free to proceed independently and to try to seize the opportunity for itself.

No obligation to participate

3.28   Oil companies jealously and rightly reserve for themselves the actual decisions to participate in a project. They will never accept an agreement which obliges them to participate on terms that are not known, or on terms imposed by another party or parties by means, for example, of a vote. So a preliminary joint venture agreement never obliges the parties to bid or to take up an opportunity if offered. Each party is free to decide that it does not like the opportunity or the terms on which it is offered, in which case it can walk away leaving the opportunity to the other parties. What it cannot do, however, is to take that opportunity for itself, or pursue it independently with third parties.

3.29   Therefore, the effect of a preliminary joint venture agreement is essentially negative. It does not commit the parties to the opportunity, but it does prevent them from pursuing the opportunity independently or with third parties. So it is the exclusivity agreements that are the real heart of the arrangement.

Exclusivity

3.30   A preliminary joint venture agreement is always exclusive, and it binds the parties to work together to pursue the opportunity to the exclusion of all others. Since modern business consist of groups of companies rather than individual companies, the exclusivity provisions routinely apply to the companies' respective groups. The heart of the arrangement is a fairly simple clause similar to 'each party undertakes that for the duration of this agreement it will not, and will procure that its affiliates from time to time do not, pursue any contract other than in accordance with the terms of this agreement'. Notice the reference to party's 'affiliates', 'procure', and 'from time to time'. The restriction does not just apply to companies who are affiliates at the time the agreement is entered into, but to any company that may become an affiliate in the future. It applies to all the members of the group from time to time.

What is a Joint Operating Agreement?

3.31   A Joint Operating Agreement (JOA) is a binding arrangement by which businesses come together as one to search and bore for and get oil and gas on the UKCS under a licence obtained from the government. A JOA has been likened to a sort of marriage between parties, in which parties come together and enter into an agreement for work towards joint ends. It differs from a marriage though in the sense that parties to a JOA lay down rules of conduct which they wish to apply during the course of their relationship. As mentioned above, a JOA is usually preceded by an Area of Mutual Interest or Bidding Agreement in anticipation of securing a licence at a licensing round.

Nature, aim and functions of a joint venture

3.32   The term 'joint venture' is not an English term of art, nor does it benefit from a settled English common law meaning. This confusion occurs as a result of the usage of the term 'joint venture', in quite a number of ways. However the underlying theme, in respect of cases involving joint ventures, is that there exists a common interest in a project or transaction based on a contract. The common interest involves the parties acting in concert and sharing risks towards a joint goal (joint sharing of profits or joint production of a product).

3.33   The common features of a joint venture are:

- there must be community of interests or common goal;
- the venture must have a limited scope and usually relates to a particular project separate from the co-venturers' other businesses;
- the venture must be a defined commercial or business transaction;
- there is common ownership of assets (tenancy in common);
- co-venturers possess the ability to participate in the management of the venture (day-to-day or operational).

As mentioned above, the joint ventures in the oil industry are unincorporated; joint ventures referred to in this section would be the unincorporated joint ventures relating to practice in the oil industry.

3.34   There has been a plethora of information about the differing nature of the joint venture and the partnership and it has been argued that the significance of the difference has legal consequences as well as possible tax effects and tends to affect the concept of the fiduciary relationship between the parties. The oil industry belief and practice is that a joint venture does not create a partnership.

Background of the UKCS JOA

3.35   The JOAs used on the UKCS followed the United States model, developed out of United States oil industry's yearning and subsequent practice of developing and using a standard form agreement.

3.36   During the 1950s in the US the need for a standardised operating agreement became apparent when the oil industry recommended the adoption of an arrangement that would minimise the time spent on contract negotiations. The standardised model form operating agreement that was eventually adopted was that of the Association of Petroleum Landsmen Model Form Operating Agreement Form 610 of 1956 and it was revised many times after.

Note: For details on the AAPL Model Form Operating Agreement please consult the website: http://www.landman.org/docs/forms/1956-joa.pdf.

3.37   In the USA, the AAPL Model Form Operating Agreement is one of the most essential contracts employed by the oil and gas industry. It is expected that every oil and gas professional involved in the drilling of wells in the USA needs to have a basic understanding of the AAPL Model Form Operating Agreement, especially the rights, duties and obligations of the operator as well as those of the non-operators.

3.38   In the UK, the first major step towards the standardisation of JOAs on the UKCS was in 1977 during the 5th licensing round with the JOA developed by the BNOC (British National Oil Corporation). Licences under the pro forma were given to consortia of companies which *had* to include the BNOC as a partner. The BNOC also had to accept the terms of each JOA. As a result the 'BNOC Pro forma Joint Operating Agreement for Fifth Round Licences' emerged. The Fifth round pro forma, which was very similar to the BNOC Sixth round pro forma, has served as a very workable tool in the journey towards standardisation of UKCS JOAs. The 20th round JOAs, produced by the PILOT PPWG in 2002, has been the most accepted standard form currently being used on the UKCS (the most recent standard UKCS JOA was updated in 2013). It should be noted that the standard form JOA is a boilerplate and parties are free to negotiate as to its terms regard being had to overriding licence conditions.

Note: The main difference between the US and the UK JOA is that in the US the operator is in a very strong, dominant position with regard to non-operators, while in the UK, non-operators have more rights than in the US.

Government approval

3.39   The JOA needs the approval of the government (DECC) to become effective. Creating (or novating or amending) a JOA commonly entails the apportionment of at least some of the rights granted by a Petroleum Act licence. As such, it requires the consent of the Secretary of State, who, in the exercise of powers conferred under the Petroleum Act 1998 approves the creation, novation or amendment of any JOA/operating agreement, with respect to the entitlement of the parties to it. Such consent is now given by means of the Open Permission (Operating Agreements) which grants prior approval to most instances of the creation, amendment or novation of operating agreements. The Open Permission is granted under the Petroleum Act 1998, and in particular the Model Clauses of each licence granted under that Act. It permits several companies that together constitute the licensee to novate an operating agreement (including both joint and unit operating agreements) in the course of implementing a licence assignment that has already been approved by the Secretary of State. Open permission only applies to landward agreements. However, in respect of offshore Production Licences, DECC's new e-licence administration system is now live. The Petroleum E-Licensing Assignments and Relinquishments System (PEARS) may be accessed at www.gov.uk/oil-and-gas-petroleum-licensing-guidance.

3.40   In addition, the Open Permission permits the amendment or creation of a JOA/operating agreement in other circumstances, provided additionally that the JOA/operating agreement does not create a new controlling interest in any acreage, nor assign licence rights to anyone outside the licence. In these cases there is also a requirement to notify DECC of certain details of the transaction.

3.41   Companies wishing to create, amend or novate any JOA/operating agreement should examine the text of the Open Permission (Operating Agreements) to decide whether the act has already been granted prior approval. If so, no further permission or approval from the Secretary of State is needed, and in the case of this Open Permission there is no need to notify DECC of intention to use it. Note, however, that companies are still obliged to provide certain information to DECC about the new JOA/operating agreement within two weeks after execution. Such notification may be made by an email to DECC.

3.42   As was stated earlier, the Open Permission is granted under the Petroleum Act 1998, and in particular the Model Clauses of each licence granted under that Act.

Note: Model Clause 41(5) of the Petroleum (Current Model Clauses) Order 1999, SI 1999/160, Sch 9, Pt II, reads as follows:

Restrictions on assignment, etc.

'(5) Where the Licensee is two or more persons, then, without prejudice to the preceding provisions of this clause, none of those persons shall enter into an agreement with respect to the entitlement of any of them to—

(a)   the benefit of any right granted by this licence; or

(b)   any petroleum won and saved from the licensed area; or

(c)   any proceeds of sale of such petroleum,

unless the terms of the agreement have been approved in writing by the Minister, but the preceding provisions of this paragraph do not apply to an agreement for the sale of such petroleum under which the price is payable after the petroleum is won and saved and an agreement in so far as it provides that, after any petroleum has been won and saved from the licensed area, it shall be exchanged for other petroleum.'

Key areas of the JOA

Purpose and scope

3.43   The co-operation takes place within the framework of a jointly-owned authorisation (exclusive licence or contract of work) and is aimed at the production of oil and gas to the mutual commercial benefit of the participants. Mutual co-operation starts with the search for petroleum and ends at the point where the operator delivers to each participant its share of the oil and natural gas production to which the parties are collectively entitled under the rules of the authorisation granted.

3.44   The JOA allows for operations to be undertaken outside the scope of the joint operations under the joint venture through the 'non-consent option'. Through the 'non-consent option', participants could choose to stay out of the operations adopted and approved by the other participants possessing the majority required to take binding decisions, and for a sole risk option, permitting part of the authorised operations to be carried out for the sole risk and account of one or more but less than all the participants.

Participating interests

3.45   The distribution of the participating interests among the participants belongs to the basic conditions of the JOA. In principle, the distribution does not have to be even, but an uneven distribution gives some participants a greater weight than others.

The JOA will set out the participating interest held by each of the parties in the licence expressed as a percentage.

Example:

Company A – 60%

Company B – 15%

Company C – 25%

Operator

3.46   The JOA governs the horizontal relationships between the parties and creates a tenancy in common in respect of the licence. The co-venturers are jointly liable to the government for licence obligations.

3.47   The JOA will allocate the percentage property rights of each party and will state the party's share of the cost which would be commensurate to its percentage share in the venture. The co-venturer's percentage share in the venture is an undivided interest in the joint property which may be assigned, novated or sold by its owner subject to regulatory and pre-emptive restrictions. The JOA provides for an operator who performs the day-to-day activities of the venture, and an operating committee consisting of all co-venturers to supervise and control operations.

Note: In the above example, the operator would be Company A, with the larger participating interest (60%) in the licence.

Note: The Petroleum (Current Model Clauses) Order 1999, SI 1999/160, provides for the appointment of an Operator. Clause 24 of Schedule 10 to the Order reads:

'Appointment of operators

24. (1) The Licensee shall ensure that another person (including, in the case where the Licensee is two or more persons, any of those persons) does not exercise any function of organising or supervising all or any of the operations of searching or boring for or getting petroleum in pursuance of this licence unless that other person is a person approved in writing by the Minister and the function in question is one to which that approval relates.

(2) The Minister shall not refuse to give his approval of a person in pursuance of paragraph (1) of this clause if that person is competent to exercise the function in question, but where an approved person is no longer competent to exercise that function the Minister may, by notice in writing given to the Licensee, revoke his approval.'

3.48 There is generally a provision in the JOA which states that the operator will neither gain nor lose by acting as such. This is primarily to ensure that it does not make a profit as a result of being operator. As a result an operator will be more reluctant than a contractor to assume responsibility for its actions. In these circumstances it would seem fair, and indeed it has become industry practice, to limit the operator's liability towards the non-operators in certain ways. The main provisions in the JOA establishing the liability to the non-operators include: standard of operating, restriction of liability and control by non-operators.

Main duties

3.49 The main duties of the operator consist of preparing and submitting for the review and approval of the management committee:

- annual work programmes and corresponding budgets; special work programmes (evaluation and appraisal of discoveries; abandonment of wells, fields and installations); corresponding budgets and overall plans for the development of a discovery (commercial);
- authority for expenditure (AFE) procedure: some JOA's provide for an authority for expenditure (AFE) procedure which requires the operator before entering into any commitment or incurring any expenditure under an approved work programme and budget, to submit an AFE in respect thereof.

3.50 The operator is also responsible for carrying out of the annual work programme, special work programmes, and overall plans in the form approved by the management committee, subject to the operator's right to incur over-expenditures within certain narrow limits expressed as a percentage of total budget and as a percentage of the individual budget item being overspent.

Powers of the operator

3.51 The extent of powers of the operator is set out in the JOA; the JOA provides for the resignation and removal of the operator. The operator usually acts gratuitously for the JOA and simply takes its profits pro rata from the produced petroleum.

3.52 Apart from the control it has over the day-to-day operations of the joint operations, it simply takes its percentage share. The operator is not usually liable for an honest mistake, misjudgement or negligent act or an omission. It will, however, be liable for wilful misconduct It is not liable for consequential loss, even if were to be held liable for wilful misconduct. The operator is liable to take and maintain all necessary insurances.

Operator standard of operating

3.53   The JOA provides for strict guidance on the manner in which the operator will conduct the operations. These include:

- in a proper and workmanlike manner;
- in accordance with customarily used good and prudent oil and gas field practices;
- with the degree of diligence and prudence reasonably and ordinarily exercised by experienced operators engaged in similar circumstances and conditions;
- in compliance with the requirements of the licence and any applicable law;

The list and the wording of these usually vary between companies and the operator should have careful regard to the wording of these provisions.

Operator's restriction of liability

3.54   The operator's liability has always been restricted but has become even more so in recent years. Usually the operator will only be liable for loss or damage which arises from its wilful misconduct, a term which is defined in various ways. Earlier JOA wording might have caused the operator to be liable for a frolic by a junior employee and, as a result, it has now become acceptable to restrict the liability of the operator to acts or omissions of employees in a managerial/supervisory position. It is hoped that this will restrict the operator's liability to acts of the corporate entity.

Operator's control by non-operators

3.55   The operator should try to give the non-operator a level of control which they feel comfortable with rather than asking them to write a blank cheque and let the operator get on with it. This can be achieved in a number of ways, including: via the voting pass mark, AFE control and ability to non-consent. Although in a legal sense these provisions may not directly affect the ability of the operator to protect itself, they will help in establishing that the various restrictions on liability within the JOA are reasonable.

Removal of operator

3.56   The operator liability provisions have been explained primarily from an operator's point of view, but it can be seen that, given the current industry stance, it is very difficult to establish any sort of liability on the part of the operator. All JOAs contain a 'removal of operator' clause. It is usual to provide for the operator to be removed in the event of wilful misconduct on the part of the operator or in the event that the operator has committed any material breach of, or failed to observe or perform, any material obligation on its part contained in this agreement and such breach or failure has not been remedied to the satisfaction of the joint operating committee within a given period of receipt by the operator of a notice from the non-operator requiring the operator to remedy the same, or within such longer period as may be specified in the said notice.

3.57   Other reasons for operator removal include:

- dissolution, liquidation, winding up, insolvency of the operator;
- the operator ceases to carry on business;
- another participant is willing to take over as operator;
- the Secretary of State withdraws approval of the operator;
- the operator assigns whole of percentage interests to another party who is not an affiliate.

Operating committee

3.58   One of most important subjects with which a JOA deals is the decision-making process. The JOA provides for the establishment of the operating committee for the key decisions relating to the conduct of the joint venture.

> **Note:** A very interesting case on the decision making arrangement within the JOA is the US case *XTO Energy v Smith Productions* (www.supreme. courts.state.tx.us/ebriefs/09/09027002.pdf).
>
> The case concerned the legal construction of the 'subsequent operations' clause of the AAPL Form 610-1982 (Model Form Operating Agreement/ JOA). The key issue was whether under the subsequent operations clause a party can change an erroneously made election to participate in a subsequently drilled well, if that erroneously made election is changed within the 30-day notice period allowed for making the election. In addition, this case discussed the proof necessary to establish a trade usage in the oil and gas industry and whether the trade usage may be used in interpreting AAPL Operating Agreements whose genesis is the custom and usage of the oil and gas industry.

3.59   It is the intention of the JOA that the parties share risks and share investments; the non-operating members participate in the management of such high-risk investment through the operating committee, which supervises and controls the joint operation. Joint ventures can be classified into two distinct management structures: (i) integrated; and (ii) non-integrated.

3.60   The oil industry practice is that of the integrated joint venture where the appointed co-venturer (operator) sees to the day-to-day control; and the operating committee (OPCOM), comprised of representatives of the whole group, supervise and control overall operations, make decisions on policy, approve budgets, contracts and auditing procedures, amongst other ancillary functions.

3.61 The operating committee makes its decision on the basis of a 'pass mark' attained during voting. The 'pass mark' is pre-negotiated and agreed to by the co-venturers in their JOA. The voting in the OPCOM decisions is usually pro rata to the interest of participating members. Pass marks often differ depending on the stage of the work; for instance there would be lower pass marks for exploration (due to obligatory licence requirements) and appraisal than for development.

3.62 Meetings of the operating committee may be held annually in the exploration stage and monthly in the development stage. The exercise of sole risk and non-consent clauses comes into play during voting at meetings of the operating committee, although it is essential that the clauses ought to have been embedded in the joint operating agreement from the onset.

Sole risk and non-consent provisions

3.63 The provision of sole risk and non-consent are one of the ways in which an unincorporated joint venture can be distinguished from a partnership. In a joint venture there exists a right of veto for any member over the drilling of wells. Every new well drilled can be said to be an expansion of the business within the agreed area jointly bid for by the co-venturers, thus the need for all involved to agree on any expansion of their pre-agreed exploration area.

3.64 The purpose of sole risk and non-consent clauses is to allow those who wish to embark on certain work to do so without dissenters. Where there is a disagreement on an important policy decision in the OPCOM, in respect of engaging in such further operations, such disagreement may be resolved by the exercise of sole risk or non-consent clauses, each of which allows non-participation of one or more members.

3.65 The material difference between the two clauses is the amount of support a proposal has obtained at the OPCOM meeting. The two concepts are considered separately, to aid clarity.

Sole risk provisions

3.66 A sole risk clause provides that where a proposal has been made at the OPCOM and has failed to obtain a pass mark, the defeated members may nevertheless go ahead with their proposed project. A joint venture agreement would often include a provision that where a sole risk operation is successful, others may buy themselves back into a share of the production upon the payment of a substantial premium.

3.67   This premium is usually quite substantial (normally a 100% past costs payment and a development carry, usually ten times the amount of earlier payments) and tends to act as a deterrent to the exercise of the sole risk clause and non-participation by non sole risk parties.

3.68   The model sole risk clause envisages four different types of sole risk activities: seismic, drilling, testing and development. The first three may be followed by further activity which is sole risk or joint operations. The operator of the sole risk will often be the operator under the licence. However, if the licence operator is not participating in the sole risk project, in the case of sole risk drilling, it may decline to carry out the drilling and in the case of sole risk development the approval of all the parties to the joint venture is normally required before it is permitted to embark on such development. This is designed to protect the group from danger of the operator being placed in a situation in which an obligation to carry out the sole risk operation prejudices its ability to continue with the joint operations. If the operator does not undertake the sole risk operations, parties are permitted to choose one of their own number to be operator subject to the approval of the Secretary of State for DECC.

3.69   The sole risk area, being distinct from the area of mutual interest, will form a separate area within the joint venture/licence area and thus redefines the scope of the venture. Every new well developed under the sole risk clause is outside the scope of the venture and becomes a sub-venture consisting only of those co-venturers who join in it. The effect of this new structure/group is that all obligations to bear costs and all entitlements to the petroleum derived will be adjusted to rest wholly on the sole risk parties in proportion to their respective interests.

3.70   By and large a sole risk clause aims to give economic reward to proponents of an additional exploration, in an area of mutual interest without the support of the dissenters and excluding any benefit for the non-participants. The rationale behind the sole risk operation is acceptable due to the fact that the joint venture from the onset is an alliance of different companies seeking to gain rewards from exploration. It is, however, noteworthy that in practice the sole risk is used more as a threat to bring parties along in support of a proposal, than it is a means of alternative operations.

Non-consent provisions

3.71   A non-consent clause, in contrast to a sole risk clause, is one which operates where a proposal obtains a pass mark, but the outvoted majority nevertheless elect not to participate in the proposed project. It has been suggested that the reasoning behind the inclusion of the non-consent clause is to provide those co-venturers who opt out with some insulation from risks associated with new drilling. However another school of thought, which one might tend to support, is of the view that non-consent clauses are contrary to the base premise of the joint venture, which is majority rule. Non-consent provisions tend not to apply to licence obligations due to the fact that parties unconditionally accept such obligations by their acceptance of the joint venture licence.

3.72   However, it has been intelligently suggested that a joint venture agreement should allow a right of non-consent, even where no right of non-consent exists in the agreement, in the case of a well which was not included in the annual programme and budget, but added later by means of an amendment to the programme and budget. This argument is persuasive, considering the fact that most companies plan their expenditure on an annual basis and any additional expenditure will pose a problem for a company subject to financial constraints, and possibly subsequent default on its part. It is, however, submitted that any company wishing to engage in joint hydrocarbon exploration ought to be ready to participate in any further exploration confirmed by a majority of its co-venturers in a joint operating committee meeting.

3.73   The position of non-consent parties is quite different from that of a non-sole risk party in relation to the question of whether or not they possess the right to acquire ('buy back') any interest in the project in which the right of non-consent was exercised, and if there is any, how this ought to be achieved. The undesirable nature of the non-consent clause in the oil and gas industry can be evidenced by its non-inclusion in the UKOOA 21st round draft.

3.74   The governing law of UKCS JOAs is usually English law; the JOA would normally contain a clause that disputes shall be subject to the jurisdiction of the High Court of England. The JOA is the main constitution of the parties exploring and producing oil and gas collectively. It does not exist in isolation and might need to be read alongside other agreements entered into by the co-venturers collectively. The JOA would also contain default and forfeiture clauses where a party fails to provide funds when requested under cash calls.

C   UNITISATION

What is unitisation?

3.75   The unitisation of oil and gas fields is the process of merging two or more licence blocks in a field, treating them as one single unit in order to develop the entire field jointly. It is not uncommon for reservoirs of oil and gas to extend beyond the boundaries of an existing licence block into another; in such a situation the most reasonable thing to do is to unitise the blocks, the resultant effect being the enhanced oil recovery, reduction in total costs and maximum economic benefit to all the parties involved.

3.76   The highly migratory/'fugacious' nature of oil and gas in strata means that oil and gas deposits are found in porous rock layers (usually limestone or sandstone) trapped by a layer of impervious rock under very high pressure and which becomes the oil reservoir (a geological formation allowing oil to be collected in pockets). Due to the state in which it is trapped, ie under intense pressure, drilling from any part of the reservoir allows the oil and gas within the reservoir to migrate through the porous rock to the well.

3.77   As discussed above, oil and gas blocks awarded during licensing rounds are an average of about 25 x 10 km; usually these blocks share their boundaries with other allocated blocks. In most licence blocks the boundaries of the oil and gas field are clearly located within the area of the licence block. The field is then developed by the licensees in accordance with the work programme under their licence and the JOA. However in some cases, oil and gas reservoirs straddle different blocks held under different licences, which may require an agreement between the different licence holders to produce and develop the field. In other cases, the reservoir may extend into an unlicensed territory; in this situation the licensee may seek an out of round bid in order to acquire a licence to cover the contiguous block.

3.78   On the face of it, the question may be asked, if oil and gas is fluid in nature and drilling from any part of the reservoir allows oil and gas to migrate through porous blocks to the well head, why do we need to unitise? This was the situation in the early days of exploration in the United States[1], where no provisions for unitisation existed and the 'rule of capture' applied to oil and gas. The atmosphere was very competitive, thus allowing lease owners to drill and produce their own oil as quickly as possible, anticipating production of oil that had migrated from neighbouring areas into their own well. The lease owners went as far as drilling wells along the very edge of their lease lines to achieve this very competitive extraction. Over the course of time this practice was found to be wasteful, as it resulted in unnecessary duplication of expenditure, and imprudent, as less than optimum development was achieved resulting in reduction of total ultimate recovery from the field/reservoir. It was generally accepted that this practice was contrary to good oilfield practice[2].

1   *Kelley v Ohio Oil* (1897) 57 Ohio St 317; 'Oil and Gas Rule of Capture Held not to Limit Recovery for Negligent Recovery of gas from Common Pool', (1948) 62(1) Harvard Law Review, pp 146–148 available at www.jstor.org/discover/10.2307/1336419?uid=3738672&uid =2&uid=4&sid=21101215943427.
2   W English, 'Unitisation Agreements' in MR David, *Upstream Oil and Gas Agreements* (1996), p 98.

Unitisation on the UKCS

3.79   With the benefit of hindsight from the USA experience, the UK licensing regime supports the unitisation of a field where it has been determined that the oil and gas reservoir straddles different licence blocks. This is to ensure the maximum recovery of the resource, which is a paramount goal of both industry and government. The Secretary of State for the Department of Energy and Climate Change, by virtue of the licence powers contained in Model Clauses of the Petroleum Licensing (Production) (Seaward Areas) Regulations 2008[1] is able to approve or compel unitisation. These are set out in the following clauses:

- Model Clause 17—(1) confers power on the Secretary of State to control development and production programmes and provides that:

  'the Licensee shall not—
  (a) erect or carry out any Relevant Works, either in the Licensed Area or elsewhere, for the purpose of getting Petroleum from that area or for the purpose of conveying to a place on land Petroleum got from that area; or
  (b) get Petroleum from that area otherwise than in the course of searching for Petroleum or drilling Wells, except with the consent in writing of the Minister or in accordance with a programme which the Minister has approved or served on the Licensee in pursuance of the following provisions of this clause'.

  The above clause encompasses all forms of oil and gas production which includes by necessary implications production of a unit or field.
- Model Clause 20 specifies the distance of wells from the boundaries of the licensed area to guard against any competitive drilling and rule of capture: 'No well shall except with the consent in writing of the Minister be drilled or made so that any part thereof is less than one hundred and twenty-five metres from any of the boundaries of the Licensed Area'.
- Model Clause 23 deals with the avoidance of harmful methods of working. It requires that the Licensee execute all operations in or in connection with the licensed area in a proper and workmanlike manner in accordance with methods and practice customarily used in good oilfield practice. The licensee is obliged to take all steps practicable in order inter alia to control the flow and to prevent the escape or waste of petroleum discovered in or obtained from the licensed area; to prevent damage to adjoining petroleum-bearing strata; and to prevent the escape of petroleum into any waters in or in the vicinity of the licensed area.

1 Petroleum Licensing (Production) (Seaward Areas) Regulations 2008, SI 2008/225 available online at www.legislation.gov.uk/uksi/2008/225/contents/made.

3.80 The main model clause empowering the Secretary of State to compel unitisation if need be is Model Clause 27[1]:

'(1) If at any time at which this licence is in force the Minister shall be satisfied that the strata in the Licensed Area or any part thereof form part of a single geological Petroleum structure or Petroleum field (hereinafter referred to as 'an Oil Field') other parts whereof are formed by strata in areas in respect of which other licences granted in pursuance of the Act are then in force and the Minister shall consider that it is in the national interest in order to secure the maximum ultimate recovery of Petroleum and in order to avoid unnecessary competitive drilling that the Oil Field should be worked and developed as a unit in co-operation by all persons including the Licensee whose licences extend to or include any part thereof the following provisions of this clause shall apply'.

1   See Petroleum Licensing (Production) (Seaward Areas) Regulations 2008, SI 2008/225 available online http://www.legislation.gov.uk/uksi/2008/225/contents/made, Model clause 27.

3.81   If the above is the case, the Secretary of State is entitled to serve a notice in writing compelling the affected licensees to submit a 'development scheme' for the working and development of the field as a unit[1]. It is important to note that the Secretary of State has not served any such notice to date, but the mere fact that the provision exists is a testament of the government's stance should unitisation be necessary. The Secretary of State is further empowered by Model Clause 27(4) to prepare a development plan:

'if a Development Scheme is not submitted to the Minister within the period so stated or if a Development Scheme so submitted is not approved by the Minister, the Minister may himself prepare a Development Scheme which shall be fair and equitable to the Licensee and all other Licensees, and the Licensee shall perform and observe all the terms and conditions thereof'[2].

1   Model Clause 27(3).
2   Model Clause 27(4).

Unitisation in practice: Unitisation and Unit Operating Agreement (UUOA)

3.82   The unitised area, consisting of tracts from different blocks, is treated as a single unit of oil production. The parties are from different licence groups, however they are treated as one group. In practice this means that licensees will have to negotiate and enter a new type of arrangement commonly known as the 'Unitisation and Unit Operating Agreement' (UUOA). The UUOA acts as the framework arrangement in the conducting of operations on the unitised field. Although licence parties would have entered into a JOA for their different blocks, they have to agree on a UUOA for similar reasons, ie two different licence groups entering into a separate agreement to: (i) provide for the unitisation of the field concerned; and (ii) provide for the development, operation and ultimate decommissioning of the unitised field.

3.83   The negotiation of a UUOA is a time-consuming process and work on the field could be stalled where parties fail to reach a permanent binding agreement. Thus it is the practice for parties/licence groups to enter into preliminary agreements during the early phases of evaluation. These agreements would include, but are not limited to, data exchange, joint well/bottom hole contributions and pre-unitisation agreements.

Government approval

3.84 The parties will have to apply to DECC for approval of the unitisation scheme, which should provide for the maximum recovery of petroleum, and demonstrate that no company has an unfair advantage over the others and that there are appropriate arrangements in place to deal with decommissioning (including the necessary financial and security aspects between the parties).

Key issues in the UUOA

3.85 The UUOA is similar to the JOA in many ways, however there are also some notable elements which are not necessary in a JOA, such as 'unit area, unitised zone, tract, tract participation, determinations and redeterminations' which are probably the most important items in the agreement. Similar to the JOA, the UUOA will contain provisions as to the operator, unit operating committee, voting, sole risk, work programmes, budgets and authorisation for expenditure (AFE), default, procedures for disposal of petroleum and decommissioning. In addition the UUOA would specify the unit area, the 'unitised zone', the tract participation of each licence group and detailed redetermination provisions. Unlike the JOA, which provides for a 'passmark' of the operating committee when making decisions, agreements in relation to unitisation matters are made unanimously.

Tract participation

3.86 It is common that the UUOA will provide for tract participation in the following manner:

'all rights and interests of the parties under the licences are hereby unitised in accordance with the provisions of this agreement insofar as such rights and interests pertain to the unitised zone and each of the parties shall own all unit property and unitised petroleum in undivided shares in proportion to its unit equity'[1].

1 W English, 'Unitisation Agreements' in MR David, *Upstream Oil and Gas Agreements* (1996), p 97.

Determination and redetermination provisions

3.87 The respective interests of the different licence groups in a unit development is a very contentious issue and, as mentioned above, can be a cause of lengthy negotiations. Therefore the practice is that there should be a mechanism for the 'determination' and 're-determination' of the reserves. As more wells are drilled, the technical understanding of the geological formation and the size of the reservoir becomes clearer. The UUOA contains detailed technical rules to be followed in establishing the volume of the reserve and its exact location. These rules are consequently applied during the development phase, with the intention that by the first production date, the first technically based determination can take place. At this stage the percentage interest of the different licence holders would be re-evaluated; some expenditure would have been made and thus a reassessment of liability would be appropriate. Where a group has overpaid, it would be reimbursed and similarly if more interest has been allocated to a group it follows that it would have to pay up its extra recalculated contribution.

3.88   According to English, there are a variety of methods for calculating the quantity of petroleum in a unitised zone. The most common include: hydrocarbon pore volume (HCPV), hydrocarbons initially in place (HCIP), moveable hydrocarbons initially in place (MCHIIP), initial recoverable reserves (IRRES), and economically recoverable reserves (ERRES). The stock tank oil originally in place (STOOIP) method has been the most favoured approach in UK unitisation. STOOIP relates to the total volume of oil originally in the reservoir. This has been considered to be the easiest and most equitable method in determination, although it is agreed that not all the oil in the reservoir can be accessed. It can be determined with finality as soon as development drilling has been concluded. The number and timing of redeterminations during production of a unit field are also specified in the UUOA. Redeterminations are very costly and very time-consuming, often resulting in disputes and litigation. It has been argued that with advanced technology, the number of redeterminations should drop[1].

1   W English, 'Unitisation Agreements' in MR David, *Upstream Oil and Gas Agreements* (1996), p 318

Role of the expert

3.89   The UUOA will also provide for procedure to be followed for re-determination and referral to an expert in the very likely event that parties are not able to agree on a determination and re-determinations. The usual issues that occur during negotiation of the expert procedure provisions in the UUOA are: the matters that can be referred to an expert; who can make such referral; expert selection, technical rules to be followed by an expert, methods employed in expert resolution[1] and remuneration of an expert. The expert, although referred to as 'him', is usually an independent company with the necessary skill and expertise to carry out this function. The expert's role falls in between the traditional expert who provides an opinion by which parties will agree to abide and an arbitrator who will decide based on the respective merits of competing claims. A number of recent cases have examined the role of the expert and the manner in which the procedures were dealt with[2].

1 The most common methods used by experts include the 'pendulum procedure' method where the expert is required to adopt the position of one or the other of the parties in dispute and does not settle for any middle ground; and the 'guided owner' approach (see *Amoco (UK) Exploration Co v Amerada Hess Ltd*), where the expert is privy to all discussions and will be aware of the circumstances and positions of parties and thus base his decision on same.

2 *Amoco (UK) Exploration Co v Amerada Hess Ltd* [1994] 1 Lloyd's Rep 330; *Shell UK Ltd v Enterprise Oil plc* [1999] 2 Lloyd's Rep 456; *Neste Production Ltd v Shell UK Ltd* [1994] 1 Lloyd's Rep 447.

Trans-boundary unitisation

3.90   Sometimes the oil is present in reservoirs straddling the international boundaries/lines of international maritime delimitation of two different states. In such a situation the joint development of the field by the two governments through their national oil companies or licence groups from the two countries will occur. A number of joint development agreements have been signed between different countries. In this case domestic law on joint development of fields will be inapplicable since the jurisdiction of each state ends at its boundary, thus agreements have to be reached by the two states involved to act as a foundation for the UUOA among the two separate entities (NOCs or licensees) from the different sides of the boundary.

3.91   In the UK, the Secretary of State is again empowered by Model Clauses to give directions via a notice in writing as to how licence rights in cross boundary fields are exercised. Model Clause 28[1] states that:

'(1) where the Minister is satisfied that any strata in the Licensed Area or any part thereof form part of an Oil Field, other parts whereof are in an area to which the Minister's powers to grant licences pursuant to the Act do not apply and the Minister is satisfied that it is expedient that the Oil Field should be worked and developed as a unit in co-operation by the Licensee and all other persons having an interest in any part of the Oil Field, the Minister may from time to time by notice in writing give to the Licensee such directions as the Minister may think fit, as to the manner in which the rights conferred by this licence shall be exercised'.

1 Set out in the Petroleum Licensing (Production) (Seaward Areas) Regulations 2008, Schedule.

3.92   These powers are very wide and the Secretary of State is conferred with great discretion in this matter. The reasons for this are sensible: the government has greater interest in unitisation of a field across the median line compared to that wholly within the UKCS, as it has to assert its control over this national resource and ensure the maximum revenue in terms of tax (similar to the licence group's position in trying to get the larger tract participation).

3.93   The UK entered into bilateral agreements with neighbouring countries, such as Norway and the Netherlands, in the North Sea involving a number of trans-boundary oil and gas fields on the UKCS including the following: Frigg, Statfjord, Murchison (unitisation with Norwegian companies) and the Markham field (unitisation with a Dutch company).

UK and Netherlands

3.94   The bilateral maritime delimitation agreement between the UK and the Netherlands was signed on 6 October 1965 to establish the boundaries between the UK and the Dutch Continental Shelf[1]. The first unitised field to be developed between the two countries was the so called 'Markham' field. The Markham Field reservoirs were discovered in 1985 by Ultramar Exploration (Netherlands) BV and on 26 May 1992 the two countries signed the Markham Agreement to provide for the joint exploitation of the reservoir.

1   The Agreement between the Government of the Kingdom of the Netherlands and the Government of the United Kingdom of Great Britain and Northern Ireland relating to the delimitation of the continental shelf under the North Sea between the two countries, 6 October 1965 (entered into force: 23 December 1966). See UN website at www.un.org/Depts/los/LEGISLATIONANDTREATIES/STATEFILES/GBR.htm.

UK and Norway

3.95   The two countries have had a number of years of very close co-operation on the development of trans-boundary oil and gas resources. On 10 March 1965 the bilateral delimitation agreement was signed to provide for guidance in the event of a cross-border oil and gas discovery, including how the field should be developed and how the proceeds from such development should be apportioned[1]. The agreement paved the way for the three cross-border unitisation agreements for the Frigg, Stafjord and Mutchison Fields;

- the Frigg Field was discovered in 1969 and in 1972 it was found to straddle the boundary between the two countries. The Frigg Field Agreement was signed on 10 May 1976 by the countries and provided for consultation between the two governments with a view to determine the limits of the estimated total reserves and its apportionment. The agreement provided for a single operator that would develop the field as a single unit; and the countries would share in the proceeds from the field in accordance with proportion of the deposit within their respective jurisdiction. The agreement established a commission to oversee the operation and administration of the field;
- the Statfjord Agreement was signed on 16 October 1979 and followed the same format as the Frigg Field agreement. It required the field to be exploited as a single unit. However, apart from matters including approval of the unit operator, determination of the limits of the reservoir,

taxation, etc the individual licensee had more autonomy on the way in which the field was to be exploited.

1   Agreement between the Government of the United Kingdom of Great Britain and Northern Ireland and the Government of the Kingdom of Norway relating to the delimitation of the continental shelf between the two countries, 10 March 1965 (entry into force: 29 June 1965; see copy of agreement at www.un.org/Depts/los/LEGISLATIONANDTREATIES/STATEFILES/GBR.htm.

3.96   In 2005 the UK Energy Minister and his Norwegian counterpart signed the UK/Norway Framework Treaty[1]:

'The treaty removes the need for negotiating separate treaties for specific projects in the North Sea and paves the way for unprecedented co-operation on North Sea oil and gas projects between the two states'[2].

The Treaty, in Chapter 3, contains detailed provisions in respect of trans-median unitisation between the two states. Since the Treaty was signed, two field development plans have been approved: Enoch and Blane.

Note: Enoch and Blane trans-boundary developments: The UK and Norway approved on 1 July 2005 the development of Enoch and Blane fields. Both fields have remained undeveloped for years, partly because they are trans-boundary. Enhanced co-operation between UK and Norway in general, and in particular the signing of the Framework Agreement Concerning Cross-Boundary Petroleum Co-Operation, encouraged new trans-boundary projects. The approvals of the developments of Enoch and Blane fields mark important milestones in the bilateral co-operation between UK and Norway.

The Framework Agreement for Trans-boundary Projects signed in April 2005 paved the way for new projects. In the past trans-boundary fields like Enoch and Blane have been subject to individual treaties between UK and Norway. With the new Framework Agreement in place, this is history. The agreed principles for cross-border co-operation facilitate a transparent approval process. The agreement unlocked new trans-boundary projects in the North Sea including the mature areas, and optimal use of existing infrastructure. It is generally accepted that the cross-border projects like Langeled, Playfair, Boa, Statfjord Late Life, Tampen Link, Enoch and Blane, illustrate that the UK-Norwegian co-operation is working.

Blane: The Blane field lies partly on the UK Continental Shelf (UKCS) and partly on the Norwegian Continental Shelf (NCS). Blane is a sub-sea development tied back to Ula, which is a Norwegian field located north-east of Blane. At Ula the well stream is processed for further transport in existing export infrastructure. The sub-sea installations related to Blane are placed on the seabed on the UKCS. Blane came on stream in 2006. The total crude oil production was 186,778 tonnes in 2007 and 536,565 in 2008 respectively. The field's reserve is estimated to be 5.1 million standard cubic

---

meters of oil equivalents. The first operator for Blane was Paladin Expro Limited. The UK partners in the BLANE field, along with their percentage interests, are: Talisman Energy (UK) Ltd (30.49); Nippon Oil Exploration And Production UK Ltd (17.07); Eni UK Ltd (16.95); Dana Petroleum (BVUK) Ltd (15.24); Roc Oil (GB) Ltd (15.24); Eni ULX Ltd (5.01).

Enoch: The Enoch field lies partly on the UKCS and partly on the NCS and is located south-west of the Norwegian Glitne field. Enoch was also planned as a sub-sea development tied back to the Brae field located on the UKCS. At Brea the well-stream was processed for further transport into existing export infrastructure. The sub-sea installations related to Enoch were placed on the seabed on the UKCS. Hence, all the installations associated with Enoch are located on the UKCS. Enoch came on stream by the end of 2006 and in 2007 produced 237,240 tonnes of crude oil and in 2008 produced 271,879 tonnes. The field's reserve is estimated to be about 2.4 million standard cubic meters of oil equivalents. The first operator for Enoch was Paladin Expro Ltd. The UK partners in the Enoch field, along with their percentage interests, are Talisman North Sea Ltd (30); Dyas UK Ltd (17.50); Dana Petroleum (BVUK) Ltd (15); Roc Oil (GB) Ltd (15); Dana Petroleum (E&P) Ltd (11); Endeavour Energy UK Ltd (10); Talisman LNS Ltd (1.5). On the Norwegian side the following companies are involved Statoil, Total E&P Norge AS, Det Norske Oljeselskap AS and DONG Norge AS.

1 The treaty can be downloaded from www.official-documents.gov.uk/document/cm67/6792/6792.pdf.
2 See DECC, 'UK/Norway Oil and Gas Cooperation Treaty', available at http://webarchive.nationalarchives.gov.uk/+/http://www.berr.gov.uk/energy/international/uk-norway/page28322.html.

Activities

3.97

1 Why do parties operating in the oil and gas industry enter into joint operating agreements? What are the benefits of such an agreement?
2 Who makes the decisions for the joint operations?
3 What could non-operators do if they are unhappy with the operator?
4 What other joint obligations exist under the licence and how are these obligations met?
5 Access a copy of the trans-boundary agreement between the UK and Norway and make sure that you understand the key aspects. (a) Highlight the strengths and weaknesses of this arrangement. (b) Do you think this type of arrangement could be used as a template by developing countries?
6 What are the main similarities and differences between an unitisation agreement and a joint operating agreement?

7   In the UK, the role of the expert and the procedural methods of dispute resolution in unitisation arrangements were examined in a number of court cases between major companies operating on the UKCS. In view of these cases what advice would you give to the companies concerning the role of the expert and the areas of dispute resolution in the unitisation arrangement?

Note: You should look at the following cases: *Amoco (UK) Exploration Co v Amerada Hess Ltd* [1994] 1 Lloyd's Rep 330; *Shell UK Ltd v Enterprise Oil plc* [1999] 2 Lloyd's Rep 456; *Neste Production Ltd v Shell UK Ltd* [1994] 1 Lloyd's Rep 447.

Further reading

3.98

- GMD Bean, *Fiduciary Relationships, Fiduciary Duties and Joint Ventures: the Joint Operating Agreement* (1989, University of Cambridge), Ch 1.
- T Daintith & G Hewitt, *United Kingdom Oil and Gas Law* (2012, Sweet & Maxwell), Chs 6 and 7.
- S Sayer, 'Negotiating and Structuring International Joint Venture Agreements' (1999) 5(1) The centre for Energy, Petroleum and Mineral Law and Policy, p 1.
- S Shaw, 'Joint Operating Agreements' in MR David, *Upstream Oil and Gas Agreements* (1996, Sweet & Maxwell).
- S Styles 'Joint Operating Agreements' in G Gordon, J Paterson and E Usenmez, *Oil and Gas Law: Current Practice and Emerging Trends* (2nd edn, 2011, Dundee University Press), Ch 12.
- MPG Taylor, TP Winsor & SM Tyne, *Joint Operating Agreements* (1992, Longman), Ch 6.
- John R Reeves, The Development of The Model Form Operating Agreement: an Interpretative Accounting (1995 University of Oklahoma College of Law); AB, Dartmouth College, 1992, Summer, 2001, 54 Okla L Rev 211
- W English, 'Unitisation Agreements' in MR David, *Upstream Oil and Gas* (1996, Sweet & Maxwell)
- N Macleod, 'Unitisation' in G Gordon, J Paterson and E Usenmez, *Oil and Gas Law: Current Practice and Emerging Trends* (2nd edn, 2011, Dundee University Press), Ch 13.
- DECC, Oil and gas: fields and field development: www.gov.uk/oil-and-gas-fields-and-field-development.
- DM Ong, Joint Development of Common Offshore Oil and Gas Deposits:'Mere' State Practice or Customary International Law? (1999) 93 The American Journal of International Law, 771.

- *Amoco (UK) Exploration Co v Amerada Hess Ltd* [1994] 1 Lloyd's Rep 330.
- *Kelley v Ohio Oil* (1897) 57 Ohio St. 317; *Neste Production Ltd v Shell UK Ltd* [1994] 1 Lloyd's Rep 447.
- *Shell UK Ltd v Enterprise Oil plc* [1999] 2 Lloyd's Rep 456.
- R King 'The Accountability of Experts in Unitisation Determinations: *Amoco (UK) Exploration Co v Amerada Hess Ltd*' (1985) 12 Oil & Gas Law and Taxation Review 185.

D   CONTRACTUAL ASPECTS OF ACQUISITION

3.99   In this section the contractual aspects of acquisition of oil and gas assets are analysed. As a result of commercial relationships that exist in the oil and gas offshore industry, certain specific provisions have to be made to accommodate supplementary relationships. These relationships might occur before, during or after the grant of a licence to explore and produce oil and gas. These include arrangements between the existing parties or increasingly, because of the nature of the services required, they may be between the licence holders through the operator or main contractor with outside companies and contractors.

3.100   The acquisition and disposal of oil and gas assets in the form of assignments of UKCS oil and gas upstream licence interests have increased dramatically over the last couple of years. Assignments, in the context of the UKCS, refers to acquisitions and disposals of interests in the relevant petroleum production licences which will generally include the relevant working interests under the governing joint operating agreements (JOA), joint bidding agreements (JBA) and unitisation agreements (UOA), and any relevant agreements relating to transportation, data, purchase and sales, employees, tax and other field agreements depending on the particular deal in question[1].

1   See G Picton-Turbeville, 'Oil and Gas Acquisition Agreements' in MR David, *Upstream Oil and Gas Agreements* (1996), p 188.

3.101   The reasons behind decisions to invest in or dispose of existing licence are not far fetched. Over the last few years the UKCS has developed into a mature basin and it has become common for major IOCs to restructure their portfolios and divest of oil and gas assets outside certain core areas where investment is focused. The assets on the UKCS may have also become too costly to operate due to the company's sheer size, number of staff, overhead costs which may not be commensurate to its investment and anticipated returns. On the other hand the buyer, usually a Small and Medium-sized Enterprise (SME), may consider the assets more valuable, and may be planning to enter the UKCS for the first time by acquiring existing licence interests.

3.102   This is not to say that a larger company may not be interested in acquiring existing licence interests. It is not uncommon for an established player to acquire existing licence interests to increase its percentage interest to gain a dominant vote in an existing JOA. It may also be looking to acquire production to finance exploration commitments, or may have interests in adjoining blocks or fields. It might also understand the overall geology of the area, thus having better information as to the prospective value of the assets, or it might be buying to secure transportation rights. These possibilities and reasons are not a closed list but reflect the majority of cases.

Types of acquisition deals

3.103   There are two major methods of acquiring interests in existing oil and gas assets: the asset deal and the share deal.

Asset deal

3.104   The **asset deal** is an arrangement where the buyer directly acquires the licence interests and associated assets from the company which owns them. This is a complete transfer of ownership from one company or group of companies to the buyer. The main advantage of this kind of arrangement is that the buyer achieves a clean cut off from the moment the assets are transferred and only acquires liabilities it is aware of at the point of transfer (which would have been taken into consideration in the purchase price). It does not take on unknown liabilities and thus simpler due diligence is necessary. The disadvantages of having this sort of arrangement is that the deal is subject to pre-emption rights[1] of the seller's co-venturers; there are far more consents to be obtained; operatorship is subject to the approval of the co-venturers and the Secretary of State, and corporation tax losses cannot be claimed as the acquiring company is a new corporate entity[2].

Note: The number of consents from government has been reduced by the introduction of the Master Deed[3] regime in the case of transfer of percentage interests between existing licences, (provided no licence assignment is required) the Open Permission (Operating Agreements) granted by the Secretary of State (26 April 2012), see https://www.gov.uk/government/uploads/system/uploads/attachment_data/file/49092/5152-OpenPermJOA.pdf.

By virtue of Model Clause 40, the Secretary of State has to give its approval in writing to any transaction involving the assignment or transfer of any benefit under the licence which in practice is now obtained by electronically sending a standard application form to the Secretary of State who looks at the financial and technical capability of the applicant in considering whether

---

to approve the transfer. Also Model Clause 24 makes the appointment of a new operator subject to the Secretary of State's approval.

1   An obligation on a party to offer a deal which has been negotiated with a third party to its co-venturers. See 'New Pre-emption Arrangements' available at www.logic-oil.com/master-deed.
2   See See G Picton-Turbeville, 'Oil and Gas Acquisition Agreements' in MR David, *Upstream Oil and Gas Agreements* (1996), pp 189–196.
3   See: The Master Deed at www.logic-oil.com/master-deed.

3.105   Apart from the straight asset deal, there exist a number of variations including the following:

- farm-in: Where consideration for the asset is performance of a field obligation or reimbursement of seller's costs of the operator performing the duty;
- earn-in: A variation of the farm-in relating to a situation where the farm-in relates to a work obligation and where the Secretary of State is reluctant to allow transfer of interests until completion of the relevant work obligation;
- swap: This is where an exchange is the consideration paid for the asset.

Share deal

3.106   The other method of acquiring interest is by way of share deal, which involves acquisition by the buyer of some or all the shares in the company and companies which hold the relevant licence interests. A share deal either takes the form of a public takeover or privately negotiated acquisition. The advantages of the share deal are the lack of pre-emption rights, simpler implementation, the requirement for fewer consents and the easy assumption of operatorship and assumption of corporation tax losses.

Note: Although strictly speaking there is no need for government consent in a share deal, the approval of the Secretary of State needs to be obtained if the target company is the operator, as the share deal would be caught by the 'control clause'. Model Clause 41(3) gives the Secretary of State the power to revoke a licence where there is a change in control. A share deal is caught by this provision, so where the share deal involves the buyer replacing the seller as operator it is necessary to obtain approval from the Secretary of State prior to completing the agreement. In practice a standard letter is obtained from the Secretary of State stating that he would not exercise this power. This is not legally binding and it should be noted that the Secretary of State may also revoke the licence by virtue of Model Clause 24(2) if he is of the view that the operator lacks competence. See the Petroleum Licensing (Production) (Seaward Areas) Regulations 2008, SI 2008/225 available at www.legislation.gov.uk/uksi/2008/225/contents/made.

3.107   It is the internal structure of the company or companies having its shares acquired that are modified, as opposed to a substitution of the company by the new company in the case of an asset deal; in the share deal scenario the corporate entity remain the same. The disadvantages of the share deal are that the buyer acquires all the assets, which includes unwanted assets and liabilities of the target company.

Acquisition process

3.108   Where one of the above methods of acquisition has been chosen (in this case an asset sale) and after due diligence by both parties, the parties enter into a sale and purchase agreement.

> **Note:** The seller: needs to check all the legal, financial and commercial issues to include confidentiality and assignment provisions of its JOA and assembles all relevant material in a 'data room' (a virtual room accessible online, usually for a definite time period, where interested parties can view these documents).
>
> The buyer: needs to investigate the title; check for encumbrances and charges on the asset; review all agreements including the JOA, the bidding agreement, unitisation agreements and any other relevant document which confer rights, obligations and interests on the seller; pre-emption rights; restrictions on assignment/change of control in order to find out if there are no restrictions on novation; abandonment/decommissioning provisions; and contingent liabilities.

3.109   The following steps are then necessary to complete the asset acquisition[1]:

- the seller applies for consent from the Secretary of State for licence assignment;
- the Secretary of State approves, conditional on the confirmation of Master Deed[2] or traditional deed of assignment;
- the buyer, seller and remaining participants create and execute their own deed of assignment or execution deed in Master Deed form;
- the buyer and seller inform the Secretary of State of execution and completion;
- the Secretary of State updates his records

Like any other transaction, the seller will give certain warranties to the buyer in respect of the assets in order to provide the buyer with a remedy should they be untrue, which may have occasioned the buyer to have overpaid for the assets. Examples of warranties might relate to the absence of any litigation on the asset, absence of default in the JOA, accuracy of information and agreements, disclosure of the assignment/change of control provisions etc.

These warranties protect the buyer by making the seller give precise disclosures at an early stage in respect of issues that may potentially be of concern, thus the buyer has a full picture of the assets and liabilities he is taking on. From the seller's point of view it will want to exclude certain warranties in respect of reserves or reservoir performance[3]. The scope of the warranties will depend largely on the nature of the target assets, and on the negotiating strengths of each party.

The buyer acquires its legal title to the assets when all parties execute the deed above prior to informing the Secretary of State. It should be noted that there are many other agreements (JOAs, unit agreements, petroleum sales agreements, transportation agreements, processing agreements etc) that are required to be novated at the same time.

1   N Wisely, 'Acquisition and Disposals' in G Gordon, J Paterson and E Usenmez, *Oil and Gas Law: Current Practice and Emerging Trends* (2nd edn, 2011, Dundee University Press), Ch 16.
2   Available at www.logic-oil.com/master-deed.
3   See N Wisely, 'Acquisition and Disposals' in G Gordon, J Paterson and E Usenmez, *Oil and Gas Law: Current Practice and Emerging Trends* (2nd edn, 2011, Dundee University Press), Ch 16.

E   TRANSPORTATION AGREEMENTS

3.110   This section examines the contractual arrangements put in place for getting oil and gas from the wellhead to the market place. In doing so, the contractual considerations relating to the following are covered:

● offtaking and transporting oil and gas (pipeline or ship);
● typical terms of a gas pipeline transportation and processing agreement (TPA);
● transportation (or transhipment) of crude oil and Liquefied Natural Gas (LNG) or Gas to Liquids (GTL).

Transporting oil and gas: getting it to market

3.111   Simply having title or rights to large reserves of petroleum is of little use to a producer unless it can physically get the petroleum to its customers. It is a feature of the oil and gas industry that petroleum is rarely situated close to the population and market, which actually needs and can afford to pay for it. The UK North Sea is probably the most obvious exception to this general rule, with substantial reserves of petroleum conveniently situated just off our shores.

3.112   However, it is very rare to have such a happy coincidence and sometimes it seems that most of the petroleum in the world is actually located in the most unstable and unfriendly (environmentally or politically) regions of the world. Areas such as Africa, the Middle East and Russia spring readily to mind.

So how can petroleum be commercialised? In other words, how can it be transported from the site of production to the point where it can be sold?

Oil and gas (pipeline or ship)

3.113   Large-scale production of petroleum requires bulk transportation, which can only be provided by shipping or pipelines. The mode of transportation is largely dependent on whether you wish to transport oil or gas, as there are fundamental differences between the physical characteristics of oil and natural gas.

Oil

3.114   Oil is an inert liquid, which can be pumped through a pipeline, stored and transported by tanker (whether seagoing, road or rail) or even carried away barrel by barrel if necessary. This means that, unlike gas, a pipeline is not essential to the development and commercialisation of an oil field, though a pipeline will allow greater volumes to be transported more quickly, thereby increasing revenues.

Natural gas

3.115   In contrast, the volume of gas means that it cannot be economically transported by tanker (leaving aside Liquefied Natural Gas (LNG) or Gas To Liquids (GTL) which are considered below). Therefore, the only economic 'primary' method of transporting gas from its place of production is by pipeline, and so gas pipeline infrastructure is essential in commercialising gas reserves.

Due to the volume and physical characteristics of gas, gas pipelines tend to be more expensive to build, with higher capital and operating costs. This is because the gas needs to be compressed under high pressure and also gas pipelines typically have to be more structurally sound than oil pipelines, once again increasing costs.

Contractual matrix for the transportation of petroleum

Inter-linking nature of chain of contracts

3.116   Every piece of equipment and infrastructure involved in the search for, development, production and sale of petroleum requires a contractual framework, setting out the rights and obligations of each party involved.

All of these contracts compose a complex 'suite of agreements' and each element should be compatible (or 'back-to-back') with each other. In particular they must attempt to anticipate the elements in the chain of contracts where commercial and/or operational risk will result from a failure to ensure 'back-to-back' terms.

For example, a producer may be obliged under a Gas Sales Agreement (GSA) to deliver specific quantities of gas to its buyer on a particular day. This promised delivery, however, can only be performed if the transporter fulfils their obligations under the transportation arrangements. Thus a failure by the transporter to fulfil their obligation to deliver the gas for and on behalf of the producer may result in liquidated damages being claimed by the buyer of the gas against the seller. It will therefore be essential for the seller to have 'back-to-back' rights under the transportation agreement to make a claim against the transporter for such losses.

3.117   The transportation and processing arrangements are of huge physical, commercial and legal significance in the relationship between the producer of the petroleum and its buyer. That is, the TPSA is a central agreement in the chain of commercial agreements running from the point of production to the point of sale (covering JOAs/UUOAs, inter field arrangements such as allocation and attribution, terminal services and the GSA).

3.118   An added issue is that petroleum, and natural gas in particular, may contain other elements (such as traces of oil in gas and vice versa) and require processing to separate out such unwanted hydrocarbons as well as produced water and hazardous impurities such as hydrogen sulphide or carbon dioxide. The extent of processing required will of course depend upon its original composition and its proposed end use.

3.119   The producer is required to obtain the rights to flow petroleum through each part of the transportation system and have it processed either as part of the transportation agreement or separately (it is not unusual to combine both the transportation and processing elements into the same agreement and these are commonly referred to the 'transportation and processing agreement' or TPA).

3.120   Depending on circumstances it may be necessary to put two or more TPAs 'back to back' as follows. If the intended delivery is into an international gas system there may need to be additional provision made for secondary processing at, for example, a border delivery point where the shipped gas will be brought to final sales specification. This processing could include the removal of unwanted substances, solid or liquid, which may have been picked up during the longer residence time in the trunk pipeline. This final process will trim the gas to ensure that it is within the agreed specification as regards calorific value, dew point etc.

Pipelines and transportation agreements

3.121   When producers plan the development of a petroleum field they generally have two options for the export by pipeline of the petroleum:

- to build and own a dedicated pipeline running from their field to deliver the petroleum from the field (or fields) to its intended place of delivery; or
- to contract to have the petroleum transported through an existing, adjacent pipeline.

3.122   If the producers choose the first option they will become pipeline owners. In practice, the producers from several adjacent fields may club together to build the pipeline, but the key characteristic of this approach is that each party will retain an equity ownership in the pipeline, which it then uses. The relationship between the owners will be documented by contract, for example in a pipeline operating agreement.

3.123   The alternative option to ownership therefore is for the producers to make arrangements with the owners of an existing, adjacent pipeline for the transportation of their petroleum. In this case, the producers will enter into a transportation agreement (see below) with those owners for the use of a portion of the pipeline's capacity and will pay a fee, or tariff, for the provision of the transportation service. Both options are considered below.

Producer as pipeline owner

3.124   As previously mentioned, where the producers elect to construct and own their own pipeline, the producers will typically enter into a pipeline operating agreement ('POA') amongst themselves. Broadly, the POA will look much like a JOA. It will, for example, set out the ownership interest of each of the producers, provide for an operating committee composed of the representatives of each of the producers, set out how much of the pipeline capacity may be used by each of the producers (which will generally be in proportion to their ownership interest percentages), and allocate costs and liabilities associated with the pipeline (again generally in proportion to ownership interest percentages). The agreement will sometimes also have provisions governing the terms upon which spare capacity in the pipeline might be offered to third parties.

3.125   Where the producers elect to own the pipeline jointly through the medium of a joint venture company in which they are the shareholders, the POA would then additionally contain many of the elements of a shareholders' agreement.

3.126   Somebody will need to take responsibility for the day-to-day physical operation of the pipeline, and so the owners will appoint an entity, the operator, to operate the pipeline on their behalf in a way similar to that under a JOA. Alternatively, the operator could be an entirely separate entity, appointed and acting under a separate operating services agreement, for a fee, and assuming a greater level of liability. Ideally, in the interest of operational efficiency, a pipeline will have one operator for its entire length, although this might not always turn out to be the case.

3.127   Assuming that the producers have elected to build and own their own pipeline, the next decision to be made is whether that pipeline will be used only to transport petroleum for the producers' intended purposes (in other words using the pipeline purely as a dedicated, contract-specific vessel), or whether the pipeline might be treated as a commercial, income-generating multi-user pipeline, through exploiting the options for the carriage of third party petroleum for a tariff.

3.128   If the producers decide to build and operate the pipeline as a multi-user pipeline then the cost consequence of doing so is that the pipeline will be sized in excess of the producers' particular commercial needs, with the excess annular capacity being available for third party petroleum transportation, and this will increase the cost of construction (although the intention is that tariff receipts from third parties will recoup these costs). The decision as to whether to oversize the pipeline and to use it as a commercial asset is largely a commercial and economic issue for the producers.

TPA required: where producer does not own pipeline

3.129   As mentioned above, the alternative option to ownership is for the producers to make arrangements with the owners of an existing, adjacent pipeline for the transportation of their petroleum. In this case, the producers will enter into a transportation agreement (see below) with those owners for the use of a portion of the pipeline's capacity.

Common terms of a TPA

3.130   A TPA will typically provide for the following matters. Much of what follows will be the subject of keen negotiation between the owners of the pipeline ('the transporter/processor') and the producers (who at this stage are also called 'the users').

Commencement

3.131 The commencement date for the TPA must be specified or ascertainable. There may be conditions precedent to commencement: these are things that must be done or obtained in order for the actual project to take place and for the signed TPA to become fully legally binding on the parties. Examples of conditions precedent are receipt of all necessary governmental approvals and completion of the construction of the pipeline or related facilities.

It is in the interests of the users to ensure that the transporter/processor is legally bound to begin transporting the newly produced gas at the commencement date and must pay for any losses incurred by the user as a result of the transportation system not being ready.

Duration

3.132 Some TPAs are expressed to be for a set duration, for example until 2020. However, as is touched on above, having reserves of petroleum is of little use without having an export route or means of transporting the petroleum to customers. Therefore, the user will wish to be able to transport their petroleum for the entire life of the field, which may well be beyond this date. On the other hand, the transporter/processor will probably want to be able to terminate the TPA if and when delivering the gas becomes uneconomic for them under the agreed tariff. A common compromise is the sharing of the operational and repair costs of the transportation system between the transporter/processor and the users. Alternatively the TPA may provide for the re-setting of the tariff in certain circumstances.

3.133 In addition, the TPA may provide for early termination, for example on default in payment of the tariff by the user, or if a force majeure event persists for an extended period, or if there is failure (by the transporter/processor or the users) to transport a minimum quantity of petroleum in a contract year.

Capacity reservation

3.134 Firm capacity rights are the firm rights to transport a certain quantity of petroleum through a transportation system in a contract year[1]. Therefore, a user must ensure that such reserved capacity is sufficient to handle the expected production of petroleum for the life of their field, and any anticipated variances in production rates[2].

1 A contract year in a TPA is typically from 1 October to 31 September to follow what is known as the Gas Year.
2 The system will need to be operated on either a volume basis or an energy content basis. It is often convenient to book capacity on a volume basis, but for all allocation and attribution calculations to be based on energy content.

3.135   This may be a constant capacity for the life of the service period or there may be a procedure for varying the reserved capacity periodically, for example:

- a capacity schedule set out in a schedule to the TPA to reduce the transportation capacity as the production of petroleum from the field declines; or
- a maximum capacity is booked, but the user may reduce capacity as required provided a minimum capacity is booked.

3.136   The nature of the GSA and the options the seller has to fulfil this agreement will determine the flexibility required. For a simple supply agreement of a constant volume over a fixed period of years then the capacity required will be the Maximum Daily Contract Quantity (swing times ACQ/ days in contract year): see above on GSAs. If the GSA is a 'depletion' type sale then procedures will be required to allow reduction of booked capacity as the field delivery declines.

3.137   This clause always represents a commercial compromise between the user, who generally wants as much flexibility as possible, and the transporter/ processor, who wants fixed capacity throughput obligations. Generally, the user will be required to book capacity for each year, month and day and this cannot exceed reserved levels without the consent of the transporter/processor. This allows the transporter/processor to allocate spare capacity to other shippers.

3.138   There may be additional problems relating to PSC or JOA terms. Long term GSAs will almost certainly require reasonably predictable and constant volume flows, which are compatible with these capacity reservation terms. However, in a stand-alone PSC or JOA arrangement a user's volumes may go up or down.

3.139   One way to allow the shipper flexibility is to permit them to reassign their booked capacity. This is becoming increasingly common in some countries. If this facility is allowed then this reduces the need for including flexibility during the contract life. In this case provision would need to be made to ensure that the assignee can notify the transporter/processor of their nominations and the combined nominations fulfil the original reservation requirements.

Nominations

3.140   Capacity rights tend to be maximum limits on how much petroleum can be transported by that user in a year. However, the actual quantities to flow on a day-by-day basis will have to be nominated by the user to the transporter/ processor.

3.141   These are usually done in various steps, perhaps starting 24 months prior to the relevant time with a best estimate. The TPA will contain detailed operational procedures for notifying the actual quantities of petroleum to be carried in the pipeline on a day, and rules establishing the extent to which the users can vary the rate of delivery of petroleum into, or the offtake of petroleum from the pipeline during the day. A common approach is that estimates of likely requirements for capacity are given and such estimates provide a non-binding forecast of how much gas the user wishes to be transported and processed far in advance on an annual, monthly and weekly basis. These estimates will then progressively become more and more binding (in other words the most recent estimate must be within a certain range of plus or minus a certain percentage of the previous estimate) on the user until the actual nominations, which are a binding notification given for the following week or perhaps day of transportation/processing. These procedures must be consistent with the user's petroleum supply agreement requirements.

Variations

3.142   Variations are the fine-tuning of the nominations, and the exact process of arriving at a nomination of throughput will depend on the commercial environment and interfaces, particularly downstream of the processing plant. It is vital that the nomination provisions in the TPA and onward sales agreements are wholly compatible. If they are not compatible then serious commercial risk could be introduced to the supply chain. If, for example, the gas is being delivered to a power station operating in other than base load operation it may be necessary to make provision for increasing nominations on a 'within day' basis, in other words increasing or decreasing volumes on as little as only an hour's advance notice.

Common stream and quality specification

3.143   Petroleum from different sources or fields being transported through a single pipeline is said to be 'commingled' in a 'common stream'. Essentially the effect of this is that if one field inputs petroleum with impurities then this could damage the pipeline itself, and/or effectively damage other users' petroleum which is in the same common stream ('poisoning the stream').

3.144   This has the effect that a buyer of such petroleum may be entitled to reject this 'off-specification' petroleum. However, gas tendered for delivery which fails to meet the precise specification contained in the agreement may not harm the pipeline and processing system, and therefore, in addition to the transporter/processor's right to refuse to accept the gas tendered, it is common to provide that the transporter/processor should use its reasonable endeavours to accept off-specification gas tendered, subject to agreement on any liabilities incurred. If the gas is accepted, provision may then also be made for a further charge for processing to deal with the off-specification gas. If the off-specification gas is not accepted there are a number of implications for the user: that day's nomination (or some of it) has been wasted and potentially the user will be in breach of any GSA to which it may be party.

3.145 Therefore, the TPA will have to deal with who is liable where such an event has occurred so that an innocent user is recompensed for any losses they incur as a result of the off-specification petroleum delivered into the system by another user.

Allocation, attribution and measurement

3.146 Allocation and measurement procedures are required to ensure that each shipper is credited with what they deliver and what they offtake. That is, where more than one party is delivering gas into the pipeline and processing system, provision must be made to ensure that they are each credited with what they deliver and attributed the correct offtake. Where gas is delivered in a commingled stream, allocation rules determine how much is attributable to each shipper and to how much lean gas and NGLs a shipper is entitled.

3.147 Allocation normally takes place on an energy content basis and is often calculated over a period of a calendar month. The transportation system operator will provide a full accounting of all gas and NGLs attributed to each user by a given date each month. The volumes lifted by a user are compared to the volumes to which it is entitled and reconciliation may be required in the event of over or under lifting of petroleum.

Priorities

3.148 In a system where there are other users (including the transporter/processors themselves who have perhaps reserved transportation and processing capacity for their own production) and the capacity has been reduced or restricted, then a user will want to ensure that there is a pro rata apportionment of capacity among all shippers (in the proportions that their original reservation of capacity has to the available capacity on the day in question). This is based on pro-rating by way of pre-booked capacity. This is probably the best and most fair system in that it minimises the element of 'gaming' between the various shippers. An alternative is to pro-rate against the shipper's throughput nominations currently in force, or against longer term shipping estimates.

3.149 This 'pre-booked' approach sets out the most common system for allocation among system users in the event of a shortfall in capacity such that no one shipper is hit by the full impact of any restriction in capacity; the impact is shared by all of the shippers in proportion to how much capacity they had originally reserved.

Transportation tariffs and send or pay or minimum bill/ quantity

3.150   This is the fee payable for the transportation and processing services under the TPA. Some systems use a two-part tariff based on capacity reserved and the volume of commodity shipped (a capacity/commodity tariff). In this approach it would be normal to include in the commodity element all operating and other costs that vary with the volume of gas transported and a fixed monthly charge per unit of capacity reserved.

3.151   Some systems have alternative tariff structures: it may be a fixed monthly rate, or there may be different charges for volumes greater than the reserved monthly capacity. The tariff charge will usually rise in accordance with an index or formula.

Send or pay

3.152   Send or pay clauses[1] allow the transporter/processor to impose a minimum charge in exchange for the user being allocated a minimum amount of guaranteed capacity. The charge will be made whether or not the whole capacity is used. This has the advantage of providing the transporter/processor with a guaranteed minimum income. It works on the basis that the user will deliver a minimum quantity of gas both over the term of the TPA and in each individual year or pay a charge based on the shortfall. This is similar in principle to the take or pay clause in a gas sales agreement.

1   Also sometimes called minimum bill or minimum quantity clauses.

3.153   Almost universally, there will be an allowance in the send or pay provision for force majeure or other events occurring which affect the user and transporter/processor, reducing their minimum capacity obligations. Where these deductions are not agreed to, the send or pay provision is often called a 'hell-or-high water', or 'all events', clause.

Force majeure

3.154   Force majeure is a concept that excuses parties to a contract from performing their obligations if the performance of such obligations is being prevented by an unforeseeable event outwith the control of that party. An example would be a hurricane or perhaps a new law or regulation preventing performance under the contract. Force majeure has its origins in the French and continental legal systems but is not a 'term of art' in English law. Nevertheless, force majeure provisions are now ubiquitous in all types of commercial contracts, with the concept of force majeure being expressly provided for and defined in 'common law' style contracts.

3.155 Because such a clause potentially means that a party may be excused non-performance under the contract (for example a failure to re-deliver gas), force majeure clauses are often contentious and take a long time to negotiate. Also there are different styles of force majeure clause (ie general or specific listing/exclusion of events) and a party may insist on its own particular events of concern even though in cases the differences are often more apparent than real.

3.156 Some commonly contentious points are acts of government, particularly in Production Sharing Agreements (PSCs) areas or where there is other government participation. That is, petroleum companies are reluctant to allow government entities to shelter behind acts of government and will often seek direct government assurances, and extension of relief to events affecting third parties (for example pipeline operator). Financiers will also always be concerned as to the impact of force majeure and if the project is being financed the bankers should be consulted at an early stage in the development of the contract.

3.157 It is important for the force majeure clauses in all the related contracts in the upstream/midstream/downstream chain to be as consistent as possible, especially between the TPA and the GSA.

Warranties

3.158 The user will usually give assurances or warranties as to good and unencumbered title to the petroleum delivered into the system and the transporter/processor will give warranties as to the petroleum redelivered by it and warranties that all necessary internal authorisations have been obtained and complied with.

Payment and default

3.159 Generally the users will be required to pay the transportation tariff monthly, although the send or pay payment is more typically made quarterly, semi-annually or annually. If the users do not make payment when due then the transporters/processors will have the right to suspend transportation/ processing of the users' petroleum, and if the default in payment continues beyond a particular grace period the owners will generally have the right to terminate the TPA by notice.

Title and risk

3.160   The title to, and risk of loss of, petroleum in the pipeline will normally be retained by the users, whilst its custody passes to the transporters/processors for the duration of the transportation/processing service. Where the pipeline serves a number of fields, the petroleum will be in a commingled stream consisting of a mixture of the petroleum from all the fields contributing petroleum to the pipeline, and each of the various users will own an undivided interest in the commingled stream. Title and risk in the petroleum will normally pass from the user to its buyer at the redelivery point.

Liabilities and indemnities

3.161   The liabilities clause in a TPA is often lengthy, complex and heavily negotiated. Having set out their respective obligations, the parties here spell out the consequences of a breach, such as an unexcused failure by the owners to provide the transportation/processing service or a delivery of off-specification petroleum into the pipeline by the users.

3.162   There is a potentially complex web of causes of action between the users, the owners, and other users of the pipeline. A single breach may give rise to two separate causes of action between the users and the owners, one in contract and one in tort. For example, if the users deliver off-specification petroleum into the pipeline they may be liable in contract to the transporters/processors for failure to comply with the quality provisions in the TPA, and may also be liable in tort to the transporters/processors if the off-specification petroleum damages the pipeline. A properly drafted liabilities clause will address both causes of action so that, for example, the transporters/processors could not avoid a limitation on their right to recover against the users in a contractual cause of action by then suing the users in tort.

3.163   Additional complexity arises with the presence of other users who are not necessarily in a contractual relationship with the existing users, but who may be injured by acts or omissions of the existing users, or, conversely, may injure the existing users by their own acts or omissions. The relationship may simply be ignored in the TPA, and the users will be left to sue one another in tort with respect to any damage resulting from their use or misuse of the pipeline. Alternatively, the transporters/processors may attempt to create a contractual pattern of liability, which will apply to all users of the pipeline, by providing in the agreement for liability among the users and by having all users enter into a single agreement (often called 'club rules' or 'User Agreements') setting out the allocation of liability amongst them all.

3.164   It is common for the parties to exclude liability for consequential losses. The parties may also put a monetary cap on their overall liability, either on a per incident basis or over the life of the TPA.

Liability for failure to provide transportation service

3.165   It is common for the transporters/processors to seek to be liable only for a failure to provide the transportation/processing service if they have been guilty of wilful misconduct[1]. As the loss that the users are most likely to incur is a liability for damages to their petroleum buyer, or at least a loss of revenue from that buyer, and given the usual exclusion of liability of the transporters/processors for consequential losses, it is questionable whether the transporters/processors have any real remedy against the owners for a failure to provide the transportation service unless such damages (or even a proportion thereof) are expressed as being recoverable.

1   This is the same concept as used in JOAs.

Transhipment: transportation by ship

General issues

3.166   Where a pipeline is either uneconomic or not feasible for other reasons, shipping or other types of bulk transportation may be possible. Crude oil/GTL tankers and LNG shipping are both considered below.

Crude oil tankers: specific points

3.167   These are probably the most well-known alternative to pipelines and are sometimes referred to as 'moving pipelines'. Oil tankers are typically relatively 'low tech', although safety and environmental standards (such as the phasing in of double hulls) mean that new tankers at least are more sophisticated today. These are huge vessels designed to carry as many hydrocarbons in liquid form as possible, including GTL (gas to liquids – liquefaction of gas via the changing of the chemical properties of the gas to create a fluid which can be transported just like oil).

LNG tankers: specific points

3.168   LNG stands for liquefied natural gas. LNG is natural gas which has been cooled to the point that it condenses into a liquid, at a temperature of around -161°C (-256°F), using liquid nitrogen. This reduces its volume by six hundred fold, meaning that it can be transported in specially designed vessels in large enough volumes to make a trip economic. This offers an economic alternative to transportation by pipeline.

3.169   The gas must be cooled (liquefied) at a 'liquefaction plant' and then pumped onto a specially designed LNG tanker, which essentially is a gigantic floating freezer. Despite their cargo, LNG ships have a very good safety and reliability record, which has been gained through high standards of construction and much higher standards of maintenance than in conventional ships. Typically, especially under long-term LNG sales contracts, a seller will charter a number of vessels to allow continuous pick up and deliveries to meet its obligations under its sales contract. The engineering side is particularly critical as LNG ships are powered by steam turbines. They are virtually the only steamships still operating and therefore the number of ship's engineers with steam experience is very limited.

3.170   This means that LNG ships and crew are more expensive than the charter party for a conventional oil tanker and since they are so hard to come by these tend to be on long-term charters. It is normal for the initial charter period to match the length of the initial sales contracts for the project to ensure that shipping capacity is available for the project life. Traditionally this has been 20–25 years. Shorter charters may also be used to obtain ships for trading activities to carry spare capacity etc. These are often for 1–5 year periods.

3.171   An LNG charter party may allow for an initial charter period, which can be extended for the length of an extension period and further extended for the length of an additional charter period at charterer's option. It is good practice to provide for a right to extend. Most LNG projects last longer than the initial contract period and it would be unfortunate to lose the shipping at the end of the initial 25 years. This is a risk when the market is tight, and in these circumstances the ships can be difficult to replace. LNG ships are capable of lasting 40 years provided they are maintained to a high standard. Normally they will undergo a major mid-life refit. However, extending the charter in tranches as proposed here allows the charterer to monitor the condition of the ship as it ages. The charterer usually has exclusive use of the ship throughout the charter period.

3.172   Accordingly, LNG shipping has been characterised in the trade to date by a number of key features, which makes it very different from other forms of bulk transportation such as crude oil. These include:

- dedicated fleets working on each deal;
- high cost of ships;
- shipping integrated into the buyer or the seller's project and commuted on a long-term basis;
- scheduling must adjust to address needs of the supplier, the buyer, the suppliers' other buyers and inherent shipping risks;
- LNG ships are technically sophisticated;
- safety and reliability of utmost importance.

3.173   Shipping is the vital link in the integrated LNG chain between upstream plant and downstream customer. LNG projects were traditionally financed to service one customer (or group of associated customers) and as a result it was a relatively straightforward, though time-consuming, task to set up transportation as part of the long-term relationship between the buyer and the seller. That is:

- ex-ship (or DES) basis: means that the seller delivers the LNG to the buyer's home port;
- FOB (or Free on Board): means that the buyer sends his/her own ship to pick up the LNG cargo from the seller's home port;
- CIF: means that the seller provides shipping and insures the cargo but title is transferred to the buyer on the high seas.

Thus shipping relationships developed initially to encompass predominantly ex-ship delivered contracts, with the seller being responsible for safety and reliability of the ship, but the buyer accepting all shipping costs.

Ex-ship or FOB

3.174   Advantages and disadvantages from the supplier's perspective of ex-ship sales:

Advantages:

- the seller retains control of scheduling/supply chain;
- the seller retains possible extra price margin;
- the seller is in control of safety standards;
- the seller retains flexibility to deliver to alternative customers in the case of buyer's default;
- easier for the seller to manage boil-off on a maximum operational and economic basis.

Disadvantages:

- higher capital outlay;
- shipping risk/under utilisation of shipping capacity;
- ship/shore liabilities at unloading point.

F   PETROLEUM SALES ARRANGEMENTS

3.175   This section considers the sales arrangements for petroleum products, namely:

- crude oil;
- natural gas; and
- Liquefied Natural Gas (LNG).

Main areas of law which may be applicable to petroleum sale and purchase agreements (SPAs)

3.176   Legal issues in connection with SPAs arise under public and private law and, in international SPAs, under public international law. The public law aspect arises from state ownership and licensing of oil and gas reserves and may also arise from regulation of the gas industry. The private law aspects arise out of the contractual arrangements.

3.177   The main areas are as follows:

- **The law dealing with the granting of rights to produce oil and gas:** The petroleum regime of the jurisdiction in which the gas reserves are located forms the basis for the seller's title in respect of the gas to be sold. The regime may take a number of forms, for example concession agreement, production sharing arrangements, or a licensing regime.

  In the case of LNG, the buyer and seller will almost certainly be in different jurisdictions and the seller is often a state (or part state) owned company. The buyer must establish the identity of production licence/concession holders and ensure that the seller has title to the gas.

- **The law relating to sale of goods:** This will include issues of time at which ownership and risk in the goods (namely the petroleum) pass to the buyer.

- **Contract law generally:** The law of misrepresentation could apply to statements about the quality and composition of the gas to be sold. The law of frustration will apply where a contract becomes impossible to perform.

- **Regulatory legislation relating to the buyer:** Where the buyer is a public utility, it will have been granted a licence to carry on an activity as a gas distributor. Both buyer and seller must consider the terms of that licence in light of the SPA.

- **Tax law relating to production and sale of hydrocarbons:** Production taxes are important for evaluating the profitability of a project. Sales taxes may give rise to disputes as to whether they should be borne by seller or buyer.

- **Competition law:** As production licences are often held by more than one party, this area of law may apply to sellers. The competition law relating to monopolies and abuse of a dominant position may be applicable to the buyer.

- **Arbitration law:** An agreement to refer disputes for resolution by an independent arbitral tribunal is commonly found in international contracts.

- **Governing law of the contract:** It is necessary to specify the applicable law where the parties are incorporated in different states. The choice of law determines the rules which will apply to the interpretation of the contract. As the parties to GSAs are usually located in different jurisdictions, conflicts of law may be an issue but can be avoided by choosing a third party law, such as New York or England.

In contrast to some continental legal systems, under New York or English law it is not permitted, when interpreting the contract, to refer to any document other than the contract itself. Also, the intentions of a party are established by a strict interpretation of the language used in the contract.

Crude oil sales

3.178   Crude oil is the world's most actively traded commodity. The largest markets are in London, New York and Singapore but crude oil and refined products—such as gasoline (petrol) and heating oil—are bought and sold all over the world in localised markets.

3.179   Crude oil is typically sold by a producer or its agents through a variety of contractual arrangements including spot transactions (that is, one-off deliveries of relatively small amounts). Although 'spot markets' for gas and LNG do exist and are developing, one of the main differences between them and crude oil is that the actual physical contracting for crude oil is essentially done on one of a number of standard form contracts, usually for a duration of no longer than one year.

3.180   Oil is also traded on a 'non-physical' basis via futures and derivatives markets, in other words not generally to supply physical volumes of oil, more as a mechanism to allow speculation in pricing differences and/or to distribute risk.

3.181   Another main difference between gas/LNG sales and those of crude oil is that there are generally accepted benchmark prices easily available for crude oil. On any business day the average price for crude oil for the day so far can be found in the mainstream media. If no other information is given, an oil price appearing in the UK or European media reports will probably refer to the price of a barrel of Brent blend crude oil from the British North Sea sold at London's International Petroleum Exchange (IPE). This is not the case for gas /LNG, where pricing is much less transparent and highly localised.

3.182   Accordingly, it is not the aim of this book to concentrate on the contracts for crude oil, as these are fairly short term or spot market standard forms. Instead, the much more complex and longer duration contracts for the sale of natural gas and LNG are concentrated on.

Gas sales agreements and LNG SPAs generally

3.183   Gas and LNG are very different from crude oil both from a practical and a pricing perspective, as mentioned above. Gas in its natural state is certainly not as portable as oil, and is therefore less tradable. Also gas contracts have typically looked to secure longer term customers and revenue streams for its producers. Therefore there is no one benchmark price for gas, and the pricing of it will vary from contract to contract and region to region.

3.184   There is a 'spot market' in the UK where gas prices are published and there are short-term standard contracts to allow trading of gas as a commodity in a style similar to gas, such as 'Beach 2000' which sets out basic terms for physical delivery 'at the beach' in the UK. There are also various standard contracts for the 'non-physical' trading of gas on the various commodity or energy exchanges or markets throughout Europe, for instance the 'NBP' terms. Such 'non-physical' contracts may simply sell rights to gas already within the relevant national gas transmission system and no physical delivery of gas to a buyer ever actually takes place.

3.185   However, the following paragraphs focus on long-term GSAs and LNG SPAs for physical delivery, which can last 25 years or more, although shorter terms are becoming more and more common.

3.186   GSAs and LNG SPAs sometimes need to be longer-term agreements to provide certainty to producers and their financial backers. It costs a lot of money to search for and develop oil and gas reserves and the seller will look to a GSA to be signed to provide certainty that it has a buyer to provide a guaranteed revenue stream in order to pay for the cost of the development of such reserves.

3.187   Companies looking to develop a gas field may also be required to raise the necessary funds by bringing in 'venture capitalists' as investors, who will provide funds for the development in exchange for shares in the project and/or company (equity) or borrow money from a bank (debt). In either case having a good financially strong buyer and guaranteed revenue stream will provide some security to financial backers and help make the project 'bankable'.

3.188   The commercial risks for the buyer arise mainly from concerns for security of supply on the one hand and price and market uncertainty on the other. Also, market uncertainty is in some markets connected with regulatory uncertainty. A good example of this is eastern Europe, where countries such as Romania have to balance attracting inward investment to produce their own oil and gas reserves with protecting their domestic industries and consumers from the real international market prices for oil and gas. This can lead to a position where a company looking to develop a gas field is faced with a gas price that is kept artificially low by the government, or even worse fundamental uncertainty as to what price they can charge altogether. A contract which aims to run for upwards of 15–25 years must attempt to manage such unforeseeable events, and each deal will need to be individually tailored to the local circumstances. That said, there are essentially two different main types of longer-term contract, although some contracts may be a hybrid version comprising elements of both.

Depletion contracts

3.189   Under a depletion contract the seller sells all, or a fixed percentage, of the estimated economically recoverable reserves of a given field (the ERR). The contract quantities will be fixed based on the seller's analysis of the reservoir and the facilities to be installed. The GSA will normally be structured to last for as long as the given field's ERR last. Subject to specified substitution rights, the seller dedicates the field, or an agreed proportion of the field, to the buyer.

Supply contracts

3.190   Supply contracts are normally contracts for fixed quantities for a fixed term (or duration) in which the seller agrees to provide up to the agreed amount of gas per day during the contract period. The seller can source the gas from wherever it chooses so long as it meets the delivery specification.

3.191   With the exception of early Norwegian supplies to Europe, depletion contracts have tended to be used in markets where the producing fields are close to the market and where the buyer enjoyed a monopoly in his franchise area. In this case there was little or no prospect of the producer being allowed to sell his gas to other buyers. This gives the producer the assurance of an outlet for his gas while the buyer gains the assurance of a dedicated field.

3.192   Depletion contracts are, however, less popular in a competitive market and, although they still exist, the modern GSA in more developed gas markets is more likely to be a supply contract. Contracts which involve major transportation distances such as those feeding the European markets from Russia or Algeria have traditionally been supply agreements, based upon major, world class, reserves of non-associated gas but with the source not specified. Smaller supplies of associated gas would then be accommodated into the main supply.

Comparison and distinctions between supply and depletion contracts

3.193   The major difference between the two types of contract is that a depletion contract requires the acceptance of some degree of reservoir risk (in other words volume risk) by the buyer, the ongoing determination and warranty of economically recoverable reserves and the establishment of depletion quantity reductions over the contract term.

3.194 Sometimes a sort of hybrid contract is created, which is usually a supply contract, but with the source of the gas specified. This will also involve the buyer in an element of reservoir risk because it is unlikely that a seller will commit to finding gas from other sources if the named reservoir does not produce as expected.

3.195 **LNG specific points:** LNG SPAs tend to be supply type agreements. It is also worth noting that an LNG project needs to combine its SPA with a GSA to ensure a 'feed stock' of gas to be liquefied. Because this will probably be a GSA with a separate supplier of gas an LNG SPA would normally have a clause providing for evidence that the seller has access to sufficient reserves of gas, and warrants that both buyer and seller will have the facilities to produce and receive the LNG and that the buyer (or seller) will provide adequate transport. In these circumstances the buyer may require a certificate to be given by a recognised international oil and gas surveyor certifying the quantities of the relevant reserves.

Contents of a typical GSA or LNG SPA

3.196 A typical GSA or LNG SPA will include the following types of provisions. Please note that although most of the following points will apply equally to both GSAs and LNG SPAs, any major differences in respect of LNG SPAs are highlighted where relevant.

Duration

3.197 Whereas oil sales contracts are typically of short duration, up to one year, GSAs required in connection with a major project development are typically long term, 15–25 years. The reason for the difference of duration stems from the broad worldwide market for oil and the relative ease of transportation of oil as compared to natural gas. Because of the capital costs involved in developing major gas fields, a gas producer traditionally ensures that, before developing a new field, it has entered into long-term GSAs for the sale of a large part of the field production.

The buyer, particularly if it is a public utility, has traditionally been most concerned to ensure security of supply over a long time, and will also seek a long-term contract. In markets such as the USA and the UK, where competition has been introduced in the gas and electricity markets, this reliance on long-term contracts is changing.

Where a gas sales contract has an impact on the EU or US gas markets, EU or US Anti Trust legislation must be taken into account in setting the terms of gas sales contracts, including duration, as certain provisions commonly included in such contracts may be found to be anti-competitive (although the

EU Commission has recently indicated, informally as part of the investigation into the European gas market, that it understands that long-term GSAs may be necessary in some circumstances).

3.198   LNG specific points: Traditionally the duration of an LNG SPA is 20–25 years from the date of first supply. Long terms are useful for sellers looking to assure offtake and maximise their perceived return, but are not essential. Shorter-term contracts of 5–10 years have often been used for incremental quantities from existing plants.

There is some indication that buyers are now looking for rather shorter terms. Financing has generally to be repaid over about 10 years of operation and this sets a practical minimum duration of about 15 years where financing is involved (longer than the finance period to provide a margin of security).

Delivery point, property and risk

3.199   The delivery point is the point at which the gas is delivered from seller to buyer (usually at a point in the pipeline). Title and risk need not necessarily pass at the same point, appropriate treatment of these issues will depend on the circumstances, the type of buyer and GSA.

3.200   LNG specific points: LNG contracts are normally on an FOB or delivered sale (DES or ex-ship) basis where in the first case the buyer provides transport and the cargo is transferred to the buyer at the seller's loading point, whereas with a delivered sale the seller provides shipping and the cargo transfers to the buyer at the receiving point. In a CIF sale the seller provides shipping and insures the cargo but title is transferred to the buyer on the high seas.

Conditions precedent

3.201   Since long-term GSAs are typically and ideally signed well in advance of the completion of the development, this will usually also mean that a number of tasks and consents will still need to be completed and obtained in order to bring the project to completion and into production.

3.202   Accordingly the conditions precedent (CP) clause expressly states that the GSA does not become fully effective until all of these requirements have either been satisfied or waived. Otherwise the seller could have assumed obligations to deliver gas, but it either physically and/or legally cannot because certain tasks or consents have not been satisfied and/or obtained.

3.203   The CP clause imposes an obligation on both parties to get the necessary government, financing, planning etc permissions and approvals to perform the contract. Also, if there are major matters that either party must conclude before it is agreed that the contract can become effective, these matters are set out as 'conditions precedent' (sometimes called 'suspensive conditions') and a timetable set for their fulfilment, which needs to be tailored for each agreement.

3.204   Some of the matters to be considered are:

- achievement of financial close/entry into financing agreements;
- all necessary authorisations on both sides, specifying each important item individually;
- any legal opinions if foreign jurisdictions necessary;
- any other documents which are contingent on the parties entering the GSA such as the award of major construction contracts.

3.205   The clause is structured so that the applicable dates for the satisfaction of each individual CP should be included against such CP, for example,

'Execution by the Buyer of the Financial Documents by 31 December [ ]'.

3.206   A contract with a large number of CP is correspondingly uncertain. It is therefore good practice to minimise the number of these. If all the major contracts related to the project are signed simultaneously, CP can be reduced or eliminated, but if financing for construction of facilities is required, usually the contract will be signed ahead of finalising financing.

It is always preferable to limit (either in terms of their number or the time taken in their fulfilment) the number of CP whose fulfilment depends mainly on commercial actions to be taken by one of the contracting parties. The existence of such CP inevitably increases the uncertainty mentioned above, and to some extent tends to create a commercial option should market conditions change after the contract is signed.

It is impossible for the parties themselves to guarantee that all required government permissions will always be in place. It is therefore quite common to seek direct assurances from the relevant governments.

Start date

3.207   The start date is the date on which the seller's obligations to deliver gas to the buyer pursuant to the GSA first begins.

As with the issue of CP, signing the GSA well in advance of actual construction and the obtaining of clearances means that at the time of signing the exact start date is probably still unclear. This important date is therefore ascertained via a 'funnelling' mechanism whereby a range of potential dates 'windows' are funnelled down to a final fixed date.

In practice either the seller or the buyer will initiate the 'funnelling' process depending upon which one has to install facilities or take significant action to enable the supply to start.

Delivery of gas may be needed to 'commission' the new facilities and this 'commissioning gas' will have to be paid for. However, there is likely to be a discussion about a price discount for commissioning gas because in accordance with the agreement the volumes are less certain than those delivered after the start date and will not, in theory, attract the same value in the market place. The argument is likely to be particularly forceful if the seller requires the commissioning period and the buyer does not.

Transportation and third party access

3.208   It is important for the seller to be certain that the buyer has adequate facilities or rights to use facilities to receive the natural gas to be supplied and to transport it from there. It is usual and prudent to include in the GSA a warranty by the buyer to this effect.

3.209   **LNG specific points:** This is much more complex in LNG sales. Much discussion of the shipping arrangements will take place, often referred to as the annual programme. There is no doubt that having control of ships allows far more flexibility of trade, which is becoming more valuable as wider trading opportunities open up. Buyers are also aware of this and there is often considerable negotiation over the issue of control of shipping and therefore whether the sale is to be FOB at the liquefaction plant or delivered at the re-gasification facilities.

The most important issue in practice is to assure a reliable shipping operation and this in turn depends on a high standard of construction and maintenance of ships. If the seller does not control the ships it must nevertheless take steps to satisfy itself that the ships are of sufficient quality to perform reliably.

Gas quantities and nominations

3.210   The quantities in the GSA may be defined in volumetric terms or as units of heat.

Quantities is a very important area, as it defines the extent of each party's obligations to each other.

Delivery obligations of the seller and obligations of the buyer

3.211   The seller agrees to deliver a certain quantity of gas to the buyer and the buyer agrees to pay for such quantity of gas. The seller's obligation under the GSA is to deliver the nominated amount (up to the maximum amount provided for under the GSA) on any given day. These are usually expressed as follows:

- *Daily Contract Quantity (DCQ):* This is an agreed daily quantity by reference to which the buyer makes its nominations for the deliveries of gas on each day;
- *Annual Contract Quantity (ACQ):* This is the quantity of gas which the buyer expects to take in a contract year. It is equal to the product of multiplying the DCQ applicable for the relevant contract year by the number of days in that contract year;
- *Maximum Daily Contract Quantity (MDCQ):* The GSA will specify the maximum amount of gas that the buyer is entitled to require delivery of; for example this could be expressed as 120% of the DCQ for example.

Normally the seller is not obliged to provide gas in excess of this maximum quantity but may agree to use reasonable endeavours to do so, at an agreed premium.

3.212   LNG specific points: LNG is sold in fixed quantity cargoes so the quantities shall really consist of scheduling enough ships and trips to meet the demand and flexibility required under the SPA. Therefore, it is an even more complex issue than when a pipeline is involved under a GSA.

Underdelivery of gas by seller

3.213   An underdelivery occurs when the seller delivers a quantity of gas which is less than that which it is contractually required to deliver during a day. The underdelivery may have been caused by the default of the seller in performing its contractual obligations or by force majeure (see below).

3.214   The sanction for breach (other than for force majeure) was traditionally shortfall pricing, in other words liquidated or agreed damages paid by reducing the price of a corresponding quantity of gas subsequently delivered by the seller, although this remedy may not be appropriate in competitive markets. This saves the seller and buyer negotiating what the buyer's actual losses were each time a claim is made, ie the damages are agreed and fixed in advance.

3.215   The primary purpose of this provision is to set a limit on liability for breaches of contract mainly applicable to the seller, as the buyer's liability has already been fixed due to the minimum quantity obligation.

3.216   The buyer's liability for failure to take is limited to the payment of take-or-pay. Sellers are not always content to accept that this should be the sole remedy for buyer failure and retain the additional right to sue for damages. Very occasionally a monetary cap may be set on liability.

3.217 Limitations on liability can be quite difficult to negotiate. Typically (but not always) the GSA will exclude liability for indirect and consequential losses except in the case of a party's wilful misconduct.

Knock on effect on the buyer of an underdelivery

3.218 The buyer under a long-term GSA could be:

(a) a wholesale buyer of gas (or liquefaction plant which sells LNG) who then sells the gas onto its own industrial and domestic customers further down the line; or

(b) a large industrial user itself who uses the gas for its own processes, for example manufacturing; or

(c) a power generator who needs gas to fuel its gas turbines from which it produces electricity, once again for industrial and domestic users.

3.219 However, one thing that all buyers of gas have in common is that if they do not get the gas that they need then there may be consequences for them, especially for the wholesale buyer who looks to meet demand for gas from its customers.

3.220 What this means is that the buyer of gas has to make sure that it has security of supply so that it can meet its downstream obligations. If it does not do so, it may incur losses under its 'downstream' contracts with its customers as a result.

Need for flexibility

3.221 Many buyers' demand for gas varies throughout the year, and in the course of each day; reasons can range from seasonal effects, daily patterns of electricity usage, etc.

3.222 Since energy demand is higher in the winter months in the northern hemisphere as a result of a greater need for gas for heating and generation of electricity it is not unusual to set a higher DCQ in the winter than in the summer months. Conversely, in the southern hemisphere and hotter regions energy demand and the DCQ tends to be higher in the summer months due to the demands of air conditioning. This is known as seasonal swing.

3.223 Downward flexibility or swing is the difference between what the seller expects or is obliged to supply on a normal day (the DCQ), and the low point of demand that it is obliged to supply on any day under the GSA on request from the buyer (the MDCQ, which is a fixed percentage, for example 80%, of the DCQ).

3.224   Upward flexibility or swing is the difference between what the seller expects or is obliged to supply on a normal day (the DCQ), and the peak demand that they are obliged to supply on any day under the GSA on request from the buyer (the MDCQ, which is a fixed percentage, for example 120%, of the DCQ).

3.225   Buyers want to have as much flexibility (both downward and upward) or swing as possible to help them balance their demand peaks and troughs, but this comes at a cost, since capacity in wells, pipelines and other facilities has to be increased. A combination of the buyer's need for upward flexibility, willingness to pay, capacity in existing facilities, market competition and gas availability will dictate the price to be paid for such flexibility.

3.226   As with many of the other provisions there is likely to be much more flexibility in contracts where the supply source and buyer are in close proximity. Contracts between indigenous producers and local markets may contain upward flexibility of up to 130% or even more (early contracts in the UK contained 167% daily swing).

3.227   International contracts tend to have lower swing factors, more likely 110%, or in some cases 120%. In more recent contracts into the UK market daily swing has been negligible, but there has been an element of seasonal swing obtained by having a higher DCQ in winter and a lower one in the summer.

Nominations

3.228   Nominations allow the fine-tuning of matching demand by the buyer and its customers and supply. The GSA should stipulate:

(i)   the quantities that can be nominated on a daily basis;
(ii)   how, and within what time limits, nominations (in other words nominations for the amount of gas required on a day) must be made;
(iii)   how daily nominations, generally required to be taken at equal hourly offtake rates, may be varied; and
(iv)   what happens if nominations are not made?

3.229   There is no one all-purpose nomination regime. The agreed regime will depend on the operational constraints on the seller, the requirements of the buyer and the negotiating position of each party.

3.230   Typically, the GSA provides that the buyer nominates the daily quantity it wants delivered, and provided it does so within the time and quantity limits as specified in the GSA, this will be 'properly nominated'. It is the properly nominated quantity that the seller is obliged to deliver. However, there are GSAs, which are essentially 'seller nominated', whereby the seller nominates what it thinks it can deliver and the buyer just has to accept what is given (within a certain range).

3.231 The GSA sets when nominations (and any variations to nominations) are to be made. It is important to ensure that the nomination regime in the GSA is compatible with the nominations regime in international or downstream transportation pipelines and/or any applicable network code.

Excess gas

3.232 If, on any day, the buyer requests more than the maximum daily amount provided for in the contract ('excess gas'), the GSA provides that the seller is not under a firm obligation to deliver excess gas but is under an obligation to use its reasonable endeavours to do so.

Excess gas will be paid for at the excess gas price, which may well be higher than the contract price, especially if the excess counts towards take or pay (see below), or may be lower if the seller is seen to benefit from faster depletion of the reservoir (this could particularly be the case under a depletion contract).

3.233 LNG specific points: In LNG SPAs because of the physical restrictions on nominations and flexibility (ie it depends on how many ships you have) providing flexibility, for example seasonal flexibility, can be very expensive for the seller. Most LNG contracts require deliveries to be scheduled reasonably evenly throughout the year. Some buyers have very seasonal offtake (usually a winter peak) and would like more LNG in winter than summer to reduce their storage needs. It may be possible for the seller to balance two markets with different requirements but any request for seasonal supply needs to be studied very carefully.

Take or pay obligations of the buyer

3.234 Minimum bill quantity (MBQ) or take or pay (TOP) clauses require the buyer to pay for a minimum quantity of gas over a specified period of time (usually one year) even if it fails to take delivery of that quantity. Therefore a TOP clause assures the seller of a regular cash flow.

3.235 These are legally enforceable obligations, provided that the obligation to pay is linked to the overall consideration and that the obligation in itself is not seen as overly oppressive or as a penalty.

3.236 The TOP level acceptable to the seller will need to be sufficient to cover costs incurred by the seller, including any finance costs, consisting of the costs of production and transportation of the gas, as this is the only income it can be sure of.

3.237 In return, the buyer is granted, and must annually elect between exercising either, the right to:

- *Carry Forward*: to enable the buyer to establish a credit against future TOP liabilities in years when they have taken a quantity in excess of the MBQ. That is, adjustment should also be made for any outstanding balance of carry forward quantities (that is, any gas taken by the buyer in excess of the TOP quantity in the previous contract year, which can be carried forward to reduce any deficiency and thus to reduce the TOP liability for the next year); or

- *Make Up:* to enable the buyer to recover quantities of gas for which they have made TOP payments in years when they take a quantity in excess of the MBQ. That is, the GSA may contain provisions for any gas which the buyer has not taken in a given year but which has been paid for by way of its TOP obligation to be classed as make-up gas. In the next contract year, once the buyer has taken and paid for the TOP quantity, any quantities taken over that amount are taken free of charge (as they have already been paid for) up to the make-up quantity.

3.238 Almost universally, there will be a reduction in the TOP quantity for the occurrence of force majeure events which affect the buyer's ability to take delivery of gas. There will be a reduction for events affecting the seller's ability to deliver for any reason. That is, in calculating the TOP payments, adjustment should be made to take into account any gas the buyer fails to take for reasons of force majeure and for any amounts the seller has failed to make available for delivery.

Maintenance of facilities

3.239 Facilities require periodic maintenance, and this will result in such facilities being unable to operate either totally or in part. Generally, the GSA will provide for co-ordination of maintenance to minimise the down time of all parties. In markets where there is less demand for gas in certain months, maintenance will typically be scheduled in such periods, thereby minimising disruption. From the buyer's perspective, this should be back-to-back with its downstream gas sales obligations.

3.240 From the seller's perspective, the maintenance period has to accommodate all buyers to the greatest extent possible, and information as to all of the buyers' maintenance periods must therefore be gathered before fixing the seller's facility's maintenance period.

3.241 For clarity of responsibility, it will be necessary as usual to identify the responsibilities of buyer and seller as regards construction, operation and maintenance of facilities. Where, however, a regulated transmission network is used for transportation, the standards applicable to that system will usually be the contractual benchmark for compatibility and performance issues.

3.242   Although the issue is usually one of co-ordination of maintenance downtime, whether or not maintenance reduction days reduce TOP obligation will be discussed.

3.243   It may be that that the buyer's facilities will require maintenance and not the seller. As with the start up procedures, this is all a question of who controls the facilities that need maintaining. It is usual for a proportion, if not all, of the seller's maintenance to be taken off the TOP quantities. It is less likely that a buyer's requirement for maintenance will cause such a reduction.

Specification of the gas

3.244   This clause provides for the agreed gas delivery specification and the parties' rights if gas delivered by the seller does not meet the delivery specification.

3.245   Gas delivered by the seller must comply with the specification. The gas specification will be agreed based on the characteristics of the gas supply source and on the operational requirements of the facilities into which the gas will be delivered and/or consumed downstream of the point of sale.

3.246   The GSA will typically contain provisions which detail the parties' rights and liabilities if 'off spec' gas is delivered. If the off spec gas is not accepted there are a number of implications for the buyer: that day's nomination (or some of it) has been wasted and the buyer will be unable to operate their facilities and/or meet their own output obligations.

3.247   The buyer will generally have the right to reject off spec gas at the point of delivery. However, the buyer can do this only if it is notified in advance. Thus the GSA differentiates between off spec gas accepted knowingly and off spec gas accepted unknowingly.

3.248   If off spec gas is accepted knowingly, the GSA provides for a discount off the price of all off spec gas accepted; this gives buyers an incentive to take off spec gas and not reject it. If off spec gas is accepted unknowingly, the buyer will want an indemnity against all costs and liabilities incurred as a result of accepting the off spec gas, including consequential losses.

Typically sellers will try to limit this liability to the costs of cleaning and clearing the buyer's facilities and/or treating the gas to make it marketable/useable. It is not uncommon for the seller to cap their potential liability for such damages.

Force majeure

3.249   Force majeure is a concept that allows a party to a contract to be excused from its obligations in the event of an unforeseeable event, which is outwith the control of that party, 'hindering or preventing' performance of such obligations.

3.250   This concept, derived from Civil Code systems, is alien to English law but is now ubiquitous in 'common law' style and international commercial agreements. It is expressly provided in such contracts to avoid a termination via frustration of the contract as a matter of law. Frustration is a difficult and imprecise concept in contract law and requires a court decision to operate.

3.251   Force majeure clauses often take a long time to negotiate as there are different styles of force majeure clause (namely general versus specific listing/exclusion of events) and a party may insist on its own particular events of concern. The differences are often more apparent than real. Some commonly contentious points are acts of government; buyers are reluctant to allow government entities to shelter behind acts of government and will often seek direct government assurances, and extension of relief to events affecting third parties (for example pipeline operator).

3.252   Financiers will always be concerned as to the impact of force majeure and if the project is being financed the bankers should be consulted at an early stage in the development of the contract. It is important for the force majeure clauses to be as consistent as possible in all the related contracts in the upstream/midstream/downstream chain.

Termination

3.253   Like other commercial contracts, GSAs tend to expressly set out the duration and expiry of the contract and under which circumstances the contract can be terminated. Such 'termination events' typically include:

- default by the seller:
  - total or partial failure to meet delivery quantity obligations;
  - failure to meet the quality/pressure specifications;
- default by the buyer:
  - of take or pay obligations;
- other termination events:
  - on expiry of the specified term of the contract;
  - exhaustion of ERR;
  - insolvency of either party;
  - long-term force majeure.

Dispute settlement

3.254 There are usually two levels to dispute resolution, the first of which is resolution of disputes of a technical nature by experts. The second is resolution of disputes of a legal nature (national courts or arbitration). The parties must agree on governing law for the contract. In international contracts, the parties generally will agree on a neutral law known for having a well-developed body of commercial/contract law (English law is a common choice).

3.255 Dispute resolution in international GSAs is usually via international arbitration, for example International Chamber of Commerce, UNCITRAL, London Court of International Arbitration, etc, with arbitration to be held in a neutral venue.

3.256 The dispute settlement clause can be very difficult to negotiate because of national sensitivities. However, in practice it is almost impossible to get international finance unless:

(i) a well-established commercial legal system is used (generally English); or

(ii) international arbitration is accepted.

Even when these provisions exist there can still be problems if there is any concern that a judgment would be difficult to enforce.

3.257 Arbitration is a lengthy and expensive process and for minor disputes experts should be used where possible.

If possible the same legal system should apply to all the related contracts in a contract chain to minimise the risk of differences in interpretation.

Contract pricing of gas

3.258 In contrast to crude oil, the price and pricing of gas is not uniform throughout the world. In addition, gas prices, as those of oil, are exposed to market variations during the life of a GSA. Gas pricing is market-dependent and markets change over time. Price in gas agreements is generally determined from a base price to which an escalation formula is applied. Escalation formulae will generally be of a multiplicative or an additive type.

3.259 Traditionally, prices in long-term contracts have been set so as to make the gas competitive with alternative fuels, and are therefore linked to oil product prices. This concept of inter-fuel competition to set the price of gas (from its 'market' value) is used in most continental European cross border contracts. The various potential competing fuels are kerosene, gas oil, low sulphur fuel oil, high sulphur fuel oil, coal etc. Each country/area will have a different relevant mix of competing fuels.

Bulk supply agreements may have an additional factor in their price escalation mechanisms— the special price review, which differs from the review described above in that its frequency is restricted, and that it is only undertaken if one or both parties request it, in line with the procedure set out in the contract.

Under this procedure, the general rule is that the parties have a right to call for a special review of the prevailing gas price under the contract despite the operation of the agreed price formula. Either party may call for the review at intervals of no less than (say) three years (and there may be one opportunity during the contract life for either party to call for an additional review). The aim of this procedure is to ensure that the gas price has not strayed out of line with prevailing market conditions. Although one of the reasons to call for a review may be the seller's contention that prices under other bulk import contracts are generally higher, an overriding consideration is usually that the buyer must be able to sell profitably the contracted gas into the market against competing fuels. In a liberalising market, there is concern that the price review procedures (both special and routine) may become unstable as gas prices become increasingly set by reference to other gas prices. However, it is quite likely that the periodic price review will continue to have a place in long-term agreements.

Because energy markets are extremely volatile, and subject to drastic political, governmental and regulatory intervention, accommodating such aspirations over a 15–25 year period is quite a challenge.

3.260   LNG specific point: Pricing of LNG globally is essentially similar to that of gas. In other words it is sometimes linked to the price of alternative fuels, and is highly localised and has no real benchmark. Before negotiating a price, therefore, it is very important to assess the current state of the relevant market and to learn the latest developments in pricing.

Activities

3.261
- You are advising a client who wants to acquire some North Sea Assets. How does he go about doing this, and what due diligence should he conduct?
- A gas producer has a field in which it is very difficult to know exactly how much gas is there and how much can be produced on a day-by-day basis. Given these difficulties what type of gas sales agreement (GSA) would be advisable and what other features might mitigate the seller's liability under the GSA?
- Your client, a small new entrant to the UKCS, is looking to enter into a gas transportation agreement with the owners of an existing pipeline,

to export gas from their nearby new development. There are no real technical problems in 'tie-ing in' or connecting physically to the pipeline and the tariff arrangements are acceptable to your clients. The field to be developed is expected to produce gas and is expected to have a life of 10–12 years, although this will probably be extended by prudent management of the reservoir. A draft transportation agreement has been sent for your client's review and in particular includes:

— a ten year fixed term;
— a minimum bill (or send or pay) obligation of 80% of the nominated firm capacity;
— a provision that problems with production will not constitute a force majeure event;
— a provision that if there is a problem in the transportation system then the producer's capacity may be reduced.

Explain to your client the main effect and implications of the above and any recommendations you may have.

Further reading

3.262   It is highly recommended that you consult as many of the following as background for better understanding:

- U Vass, 'Access to Infrastructure' in G Gordon, J Paterson and E Usenmez, *Oil and Gas Law: Current Practice and Emerging Trends* (2nd edn, 2011, Dundee University Press), Ch 7.
- N Wisely, 'Acquisition and Disposals of Upstream Oil and Gas' in G Gordon, J Paterson and E Usenmez, *Oil and Gas Law: Current Practice and Emerging Trends* (2nd edn, 2011, Dundee University Press), Ch 16.
- MR David, *Upstream Oil and Gas Agreements* (1996, Sweet & Maxwell).
- S Gyaltsen & A Turton 'The Master Deed and Changes in the North Sea' (2003) 9 International Energy Law & Taxation Review, pp 258–260.
- R Major, 'A practical look at pre-emption provisions in upstream oil and gas contracts' (2005) 5 International Energy Law & Taxation Review, pp 117–123.
- P Roberts, *Gas Sales and Gas Transportation Agreements Principles and Practice* (3rd edn, 2011, Sweet & Maxwell).
- M Hammerson, *Upstream Oil and Gas: Cases, Materials and Commentary* (2011, Globe Law and Business).

See also:

- Code of Practice on Access to Upstream Oil and Gas Infrastructure on the UK Continental Shelf: www.oilandgasuk.co.uk/knowledgecentre/InfrastructureCodeofPractice.cfm.
- LOGIC, The Master Deed: www.logic-oil.com/master-deed.

- Oil and Gas UK, Sale and Purchase Agreement: cdal.com/cmsfiles/ modules/publications/pdfs/REF09B.pdf.

G CONTRACTUAL ARRANGEMENTS FOR THE DECOMMISSIONING OF OFFSHORE INSTALLATIONS

3.263 As a result of commercial relationships that exist in the oil and gas offshore industry, certain specific provisions have also to be made to accommodate supplementary relationships. These relationships might occur before, during or after the grant of a licence to explore and produce oil and gas. These include arrangements between the existing parties or increasingly, because of the nature of the services required, it may be between the licence holders through the operator or main contractor with outside companies and contractors.

3.264 The following section covers the contractual aspects relating to the decommissioning of offshore installations in the UKCS, in particular examining the relationship between the various licensees (operator and co-licensees) to execute their obligation towards the government to remove all the equipment used during the exploration and production stages.

3.265 The following areas are addressed:

- overview of decommissioning agreements;
- international requirements;
- UK: national requirements and obligations;
- relevant provisions of the Petroleum Act 1998;
- the industry contractual arrangement.

Overview of decommissioning agreements

3.266 Decommissioning of oil and gas installations and pipelines on the UKCS has become a much debated and highly topical issue in the industry in recent years, in contrast to being merely a footnote some 30 or so years ago. As the fields on the UKCS matured and field production declined, the crucial question of who is to bear the cost of dismantling and bringing ashore, or in the alternative, the liabilities of leaving *in situ* disused offshore installations, became a relevant one. The cost of decommissioning UKCS offshore infrastructure over the next 20–30 years has been estimated to be between £19 and £23 billion and indications from projects so far suggest this figure could increase unless savings can be gained as experience grows[1].

Note: The costs associated with individual decommissioning programmes can vary from £5 million for a small sub-sea development with equipment only on the seabed, to £500 million for a full-scale decommissioning project involving large steel or concrete platforms and other facilities such as pipelines, loading systems, seabed templates and manifolds. The estimated costs for current decommissioning projects are £160 million for the North West Hutton field and £260 million for the Frigg field, as against £14 million for decommissioning the Durward and Dauntless subsea facilities approved for decommissioning in 2000[2].

---

1   See Oil and Gas UK (OGUK) 2009 Economic Report at www.oilandgasuk.co.uk.
2   Department of Trade and Industry (now DECC), *Decommissioning Offshore Energy Installations: A Consultation Document,* June 2007. Available online at http://webarchive. nationalarchives.gov.uk/+/http://www.berr.gov.uk/consultations/page39781.html

3.267   In response to the fairly new or apparent condition to make provision for decommissioning, at present the government through the Secretary of State for the Department of Energy and Climate Change (DECC) regulates the oil and gas industry in respect of decommissioning issues, by powers vested in him by virtue of the Petroleum Act 1998 and the Energy Act 2008.

3.268   The government stipulates that a decommissioning programme (referred to in the PA 1998 as an 'abandonment programme') has to be prepared in respect of all producing fields prior to end or cessation of production[1]. This is to act as a safeguard and ensure that the cost of decommissioning disused installations should not be borne by taxpayers. In response to the necessity of providing security, it is usual practice that joint venture partners enter into a decommissioning security agreement to ensure that there is adequate security for decommissioning costs. The agreement also serves as a proper and timely balance to the securitisation of decommissioning funds on the one hand; and the transfer of interests and release of interest holders on the other, albeit the latter is subject to the approval of the Secretary of State.

Note: There are four distinct stages involved in a decommissioning project:

- the available options for decommissioning are developed, assessed and selected, balancing environmental factors, cost, technical feasibility, health and safety, and public acceptability factors;
- the operator applies to the government to finish production, having proved the reservoir is no longer viable. The government will then grant a 'cessation of production' (COP) permit. At this stage the wells will be securely plugged deep below the surface;
- the operator gains government approval to proceed with its recommended decommissioning option and offshore operations begin to remove all or parts of the structure to shore;

> - sections are removed to shore and then re-used, recycled or disposed of.

1 See Petroleum Act 1998, Pt IV at www.legislation.gov.uk/ukpga/1998/17/contents.

International requirements

3.269   The decommissioning of offshore oil and gas installations and pipelines on the UKCS is regulated through the Petroleum Act 1998 (PA 1998). The UK's international obligations on decommissioning are governed principally by the 1992 Convention for the Protection of the Marine Environment of the North East Atlantic (OSPAR Convention). Agreement on the decommissioning regime to be applied to offshore installations in the OSPAR maritime area was reached at a meeting of the OSPAR Commission in July 1998. The responsibility for ensuring that the requirements of the PA 1998 are complied with rests with DECC:

- the UK's **international obligations** on the decommissioning of offshore installations are to be found in United Nations Convention on the Law of the Sea (UNCLOS) of 1982, which entered into force in on 16 November 1994 and was acceded to by the UK on 25 July 1997. Article 60(3) is the main provision on decommissioning;
- the **regional obligations are mainly found in the** Convention on the Protection of the Marine Environment of the North East Atlantic (OSPAR Convention). OSPAR is the main regional instrument covering decommissioning and was agreed to in 1992, which applies to the North East Atlantic, including the North Sea and parts of the Arctic Ocean. The OSPAR Convention is applicable to the UK and came into force in 1998.

Note: The OSPAR Convention[1]:

- requires the application of:(i) the precautionary principle; (ii) the polluter pays principle; (iii) best available techniques (BAT); and (iv) best environmental practice (BEP), including clean technology;
- provides for the Commission established by the OSPAR Convention to adopt binding decisions;
- provides for the participation of observers, including non-governmental organisations, in the work of the Commission;
- establishes rights of access to information about the maritime area of the Convention.

---

1 Background to the Convention available on the OSPAR website at http://www.ospar.org/documents/dbase/publications/p00461_background%20doc%20cemp_assessmt%20criteria_haz_subs.pdf

3.270   OSPAR Decision 98/3: In July 1998 at the First Ministerial meeting of the OSPAR Commission, a new regime for the decommissioning of disused offshore installations was established under the new Convention. Ministers unanimously adopted a binding Decision (OSPAR Decision 98/3 on the Disposal of Offshore Installations) to ban the disposal of offshore installations at sea.

Note: The OSPAR Decision does not apply to pipelines.

3.271   Under the terms of Decision 98/3, which entered into force on 9 February 1999, there is a general prohibition on the dumping and leaving wholly or partly in place of offshore installations. The Decision requires that topsides of all installations must be returned to shore. The Decision further stipulates that all installations with a jacket weight less than 10,000 tonnes must be completely removed for reuse, recycling or final disposal on land. This can be seen to be a result of the Brent Spar incident where environmental factors played a paramount role.

3.272   Decision 98/3 provides three instances where derogation from the main rule is permitted[1], these are:

- footings of large steel jackets weighing more than 10,000 tonnes;
- disused offshore installation, which can be shown to have deteriorated or damaged; and
- concrete installations.

This is due to the difficulty that may be encountered during their removal.

1   See OSPAR Commission, Inventory of Oil and Gas Offshore Installations in the OSPAR Maritime Area (OSPAR Publication No 334) (2007).

3.273   Decision 98/3 makes it clear that the derogation provision for the footings of large steel installations applies only to those installed before 9 February 1999, and as a result all steel installations placed in the maritime area after that date must be totally removed. The 'Sintra' Statement, a ministerial document which accompanied Decision 98/3 made it clear that there were no plans to create new concrete installations in any new oil field developments in the maritime area and thus concrete installations were only permitted when strictly necessary for safety or technical reasons. The competent authority for the contracting party may permit such derogation where an assessment in accordance with Annex 2 to the Decision shows that there are significant reasons why an alternative disposal option, ie a derogation, is preferable as opposed to re-use or recycling or final disposal on land. It has been agreed that these cases should be considered individually to see whether it may be appropriate to leave the footings of large steel installations or concrete structures in place. The decision to permit derogation is subject to the relevant contracting party consulting all contracting parties of OSPAR in accordance with Annex 3 to the Decision. The permit shall conform to conditions listed in Annex 4 to the Decision. Decision 98/3 provides for review by the OSPAR Commission at regular intervals, to consider in the light of experience in decommissioning and in the light of research and exchange of information whether the derogations from the general ban on dumping continue to be appropriate. The first such review was conducted in 2003 and concluded that insufficient decommissioning experience existed to justify changing the derogation criteria.

UK: national requirements and obligations

3.274   The legislation governing the offshore installations and pipelines regime in the UKCS are the Petroleum Act 1998 (PA 1998) and the Energy Act 2008. Owners of an offshore installation or pipeline cannot proceed with its decommissioning unless they have obtained prior approval of a decommissioning programme under the PA 1998. The PA 1998 refers to an 'abandonment programme' although the preferred and generally accepted term is a 'decommissioning programme'.

3.275   The treatment of offshore installations and pipelines is contained in the PA 1998, Pt IV. It is obvious from the wordings of the PA 1998, s 29, that the Act envisages a situation where the installation or pipeline is not totally removed. This partial removal has to conform to the OSPAR allowed derogations. The PA 1998 stipulates that a decommissioning programme should contain an estimate of the cost of the measures proposed; specify the times at or within which those measures are to be taken or make provision for determining those times; and, where an installation or pipeline is to remain in position or be only partly removed, include provision for maintenance where necessary.

Note: DECC's Guidance Notes for Industry on Decommissioning of Offshore Installations and Pipelines explains the operational aspects of the decommissioning regime of Pt IV of the PA 1998. The Guidance Notes are not prescriptive in nature and provide a framework for the decommissioning regime as envisaged by the wordings the Act. The government through these Guidance Notes intends to make the process of submission and approval of decommissioning programmes as flexible as possible within the statutory and policy constraints.

Relevant provisions of the Petroleum Act 1998

3.276   The main provisions of the PA 1998, Pt IV, which is statutory backing to the overriding need to secure and safeguard decommissioning of installations and pipelines at no expense to the government or the taxpayer, are listed below:

- s 29 enables the Secretary of State, by written notice, to require the submission of a costed and definite decommissioning programme for each offshore installation and submarine pipeline. Where some part of the installation or pipeline is to be left in situ, provisions as to its maintenance should be also be included. Those persons given notices are jointly and severally liable to submit a programme. Under s 34 the Secretary of State is empowered to re-issue a notice in certain instances, ie where he has rejected an earlier submitted programme or where he has withdrawn approval previously given, although the latter instance is conditional on the application of parties. Section 31(5) allows the Secretary of State to give a further notice before the programme is submitted, either to supplement or to add to any conditions contained in the first notice;

- s 30 lists the parties upon whom a notice may be served in respect of an offshore installation. They are:
  - (a) the operator;
  - (b) the licensee;
  - (c) a person outside paragraphs (a) and (b) who is a party to a joint operating agreement or similar agreement relating to rights by virtue of which a person is within paragraph (b);
  - (d) a person outside paragraphs (a) to (c) who owns any interest in the installation otherwise than as security for a loan;
  - (e) a company (to be substituted for body corporate) which is outside paragraphs (a) to (d) but which is associated with a company (body corporate) within any of those paragraphs.
- s 30(2) lists the parties upon whom a notice may be served in respect of submarine pipelines;
- the Secretary of State, by virtue of s 30(3), may by written notice require a person appearing to him to be within any of the paragraphs of s 30(1) or (2) to give him, within such time as may be specified in the notice, the name and address of every other person whom the recipient of the notice believes to be within any of those paragraphs in relation to the installation or pipeline concerned. This is to identify all possible future recipients of s 29 notices should a situation arise that the liable parties are not able to decommission. This is a safeguard against the government or the taxpayers having to pay for any expenses occurring from default. The next subsection goes on to stipulate that a person who without reasonable excuse fails to comply with a notice under sub-s (3) shall be guilty of an offence. Approval or rejection by the Secretary of State of submitted programmes is dealt with in s 32. Where there is a failure to comply with a notice or there is rejection of a submitted programme, the Secretary of State is empowered to prepare a programme and recoup expenses from the liable party;
- s 34, entitled 'revision of (approved) programmes', deals with alterations of programmes either at the request of those who submitted it or *suo motu* by the Secretary. This section, when read with s 35, covers the transfer of assets; it is under these provision/s that liability can be transferred legally. These sections guard against claims of lack of knowledge by all

parties as there are detailed provisions dealing with notices and written representations for all concerned;

- s 34(3) reinstates the government stance on identifying the liable parties and safeguarding the taxpayers, stating:

> 'Secretary of State shall not propose that a person who is or **has been** within paragraph (d) or (e) (but no other paragraph) of section 30(1) or paragraph (b) or (c) (but not paragraph (a)) of section 30(2) shall have a duty to secure that a programme is carried out unless it appears to the Secretary of State that a person already under that duty has failed or may fail to discharge it.'

The purport of the above is the widening as far as possible, of the class of people who may be identified to carry out decommissioning in the event of default by the primarily liable parties. Thus, where a party has sold its interests in a licence and has transferred its liability for decommissioning, by the application of withdrawal and subsequent substitution with a new programme, it is by no means free from future obligations to decommission; the words 'has been' are strong enough to make it liable. This is untenable and it is proposed that the government delete these words in the light of the decommissioning security agreements which are in now in place (DCPD) and which safeguard funds earmarked from early stages for the sole purpose of decommissioning.

Part IV of the PA 1998 stipulates that once a decommissioning programme is approved by the Secretary of State, the duty of the persons who submitted it, to ensure that it is carried out, is joint and several.

- s 36 deals with the duty to carry out an approved programme and s 37 deals with default in carrying out an approved programme. Section 38 provides the Secretary of State with means to satisfy himself that any person who has a duty to secure that an approved decommissioning programme is carried out will be capable of discharging that duty both financially and technically and, where he is not so satisfied, require that person, by notice, to take such action as may be specified. Where there is a failure by those given notice to submit a programme or secure that it is carried out, s 37(3) enables the Secretary of State to do the work and recover the cost from those given notice. Section 36, like s 30(3), is a safeguard against possible taxpayer liability in the event that recipients are unable to offset their duty to decommission;
- s 39 empowers the Secretary of State to make regulations relating to decommissioning of offshore installations and pipelines. In this respect, the regulators stance of making regulations less rigid, less prescriptive and more flexible is seen by its guidance notes noted above;
- ss 40 and 41 are omnibus penalty provisions for offences committed under Pt IV of the Act. Section 40 provides for maximum sentences for: (a) summary conviction, to a fine not exceeding the statutory maximum; (b) on conviction on indictment, to imprisonment for a term not exceeding two years, or to a fine, or to both;

- s 42 confirms the Secretary of State's authority to act in accordance with Pt IV of the Act. It also provides certain instances where redress can be sought by aggrieved recipients (although within 42 days of their alleged grievance). In all other situations not covered by the exceptions in s 42(2), the validity of any of the acts of the Secretary of State shall not be questioned in any sort of legal proceedings;
- miscellaneous provisions in respect of notices, definition of terms and interpretation are contained in ss 43, 44 and 45 respectively.

The above provisions form the main legislative framework of the UKCS decommissioning regime and are premised on ensuring that the proper parties (including former s 29 notice holders) responsible for the decommissioning process follow it through, without any negative impact on the taxpayer, whilst conforming to international and regional obligations.

Industry: decommissioning contractual arrangement

3.277   In 2007 the industry developed the Decommissioning Cost Provision Deed (DCPD) as its standard arrangement for decommissioning security[1]. The DCPD was a result of a long period of consultation on developing a standard decommissioning securities arrangement, based on industry practice to satisfy obligatory and contractual ends. The arrangement is both a safeguard to decommissioning funds and a commercial agreement between the co-venturers aimed at curbing double securitisation and onerous financial obligations. The DCPD is to accompany the JOA in governing interests, liabilities and obligations of joint venture partners with respect to decommissioning.

1   Guidance Notes Decommissioning of Offshore Oil and Gas Installations and Pipelines under the Petroleum Act 1998 (revised in January 2009). Available online at www.oilandgasuk.co.uk/templates/asset-relay.cfm?frmAssetFileID=236.

3.278   As discussed above, the JOA is the commercial arrangement entered into by the joint venturers in a licence towards the attainment of their common goal. The main elements of decommissioning obligations under the JOA are in respect of the decommissioning budget, decommissioning plan and decommissioning programme. The operator (responsible for the day-to-day running of the venture) nominated by the co-venturers, is responsible for preparing the budget, plan and programme. The industry practice is that the operator is also responsible for satisfying these decommissioning obligations, once it calculates that 50% of the recoverable reserves of the field have been produced, or earlier if so specified by the joint operating committee (the body comprised of co-venturers which is responsible for the general management of the venture)[1].

1   P Dymond and Stronachs, 'Decommissioning', in J Wills and EC Nelson (eds) *The Technical Guide to the UK Oil and Gas Industry* (2007), p 516.

3.279 The DCPD is designed to replace or supplement existing provisions in a JOA, relating to decommissioning security. The DCPD and the JOA are interwoven and there are common areas such as default, forfeiture, confidentiality and withdrawal clauses. Where there is a conflict between both agreements in relation to decommissioning security, the provisions of DCPD are intended to supersede those of the JOA. The DCPD is an important step towards the management of joint obligations in respect of decommissioning and at the same time is consistent with the goal of maximising recovery of oil and gas on the UKCS[1].

1   See L Moller, 'The cost of Decommissioning: Government and the Industry Attempts at Addressing Decommissioning Liabilities' (2007) 5(4) Oil, Gas and Energy Law Intelligence.

3.280 Execution of the DCPD could coincide with that of the JOA, but this might yield an absurd result in a situation where there has been setting up of trusts and payment of trusts fees from the onset without any resultant development or commercial discovery at the end. It is therefore commercially wise to attach a pro forma DCPD, leaving a few terms to be negotiated, and agree to negotiate and execute before the Field Development Plan. This may delay the FDP, but is a safeguard that development of the field cannot commence without a DCPD in force[1].

1   See J Aldersey-Williams, 'Decommissioning Security' (2007) 5(4) Oil, Gas and Energy Law Intelligence.

3.281 The DCPD contains clauses on the objects, the determination of a decommissioning plan, security documents to be held under the trust structure, computation of the licensees' shares of decommissioning costs, alternative security, default, payment of decommissioning costs, assignment and withdrawal, expert resolution, confidentiality, notices, third parties and miscellaneous provisions. The DCPD employs a trust structure to hold the decommissioning fund, which could either be cash or the acceptable alternative forms of security. The fund is controlled and administered by a trustee. Each licensee executes two trust deeds, one for cash and one for alternative provision so as to properly distinguish 'cash security' from 'alternative provision security'. The trust mechanism is the safeguard to decommissioning funds and the securitisation method employed for decommissioning obligations. The licensees pay cash into the trust every year, or alternative security computed for that relevant year towards decommissioning obligations. The trustee is authorised to invest these funds in certain specified securities and should seek to obtain a yield equal to the discount rate applied under the DCPD. The essence of this is that if the licensees paid their security in full each year, at the date of decommissioning the fund held by the trustee should have matured and equate with the cost of decommissioning.

3.282 The government, understanding that the trust fund set aside for decommissioning could in an event of insolvency fall into the hands of the insolvency office-holder, has stated that it would make statutory provision for the safeguarding of such funds. This is to be achieved by excluding such funds from the application of the Insolvency Act 1986, thus safeguarding decommissioning funds from falling to the insolvency office-holder. There is a precedent of this sort to be found in s 29 of the Coal Industry Act 1994 which protects security which has been provided for subsidence.

> **Note:** DSAs are traditionally used in a number of commercial transactions: (a) between parties to a JOA to secure their decommissioning obligations; (b) in connection with a sale and purchase agreement (SPA) to protect the assignor from the assignee's default; (c) between assignee and co-venturers, to guard against the co-venturers being unduly liable to the extent of the assignee's insolvency, since liability is joint; (d) given by the assignee to the Secretary of State where the Secretary is concerned about its financial status.

3.283   The DCPD, in order to protect all parties, makes specific provisions which dispense with the need to enter into individual DSAs in the above instances and invariably save a lot of money for a new entrant. In order to protect the former licensees who may be liable under the PA 1998, Pt IV there are options to remain as parties to the DCPD with no obligation to provide security but with the ability to enforce its terms through the 'second tier participants' mechanism. In this way the former licensee can ensure that the decommissioning plan is carried out and if it in any event is made liable for decommissioning, it can recoup its expenses from the trust set up. Thus, a former licensee who is satisfied that the DCPD is robust enough to guard its interest, may permit the security to be given under the SPA to be offset by the security provided by DCPD. This dispenses with double security. The second tier participants possess various rights under the DCPD including approval of any further amendments to the agreement[1].

1   J Aldersey-Williams, 'Decommissioning Security' (2007) 5(4) Oil, Gas and Energy Law Intelligence.

3.284   However, the inclusion of retaining former licensees as second tier participants is subject to negotiation and agreement by all parties. Some partners may not want former licensees to be parties to the DCPD; also former licensees may not wish to cease to be parties to the agreement. In these cases the former licensees are protected under the DCPD by the 'third tier participant' mechanism for those who may be given a benefit under the agreement through the Contracts (Rights of Third Parties) Act 1999, even though they might not be parties to the DCPD. This situation covers possible liable parties and gives them a right to recoup expenses from the security held by the trust.

3.285   In the case of the Secretary of State seeking a DSA from an assignee, the robust trust mechanism and various provisions contained in the DCPD safeguard the government and taxpayer from risk of decommissioning liability on default. The trust envisages a situation where provisions are made every year into the trust to secure obligations arising from decommissioning. The government also gets comfort from the fact that all co-venturers are jointly liable. In the event that the Secretary of State has to carry out decommissioning in most cases where the operator is insolvent the Secretary of State is entitled by the DCPD to recoup his expenses from the trustee.

3.286 Where an interest is to be assigned, the DCPD provides that the assigning party should ensure that the assignee enters into a novation in such form agreed by the parties (in line with the JOA). The assignee also pays the appropriate provision amount or alternative provision, computed in respect of the interest it acquires. Once the security has been provided the assignor may apply to be released in whole or in part from its own security. The amount of security reimbursed would depend on the SPA. Where the assignor and the assignee agree for the assignee to simply carry on with the obligations, the amount of security to be reimbursed would be for the relevant year in which the sale occurs. Where security is not included in the sale, then the assignee would be liable to pay for previous years up to the relevant year. Irrespective of the commercial arrangement between the vendor and buyer, the trustee is only allowed to reimburse the assignor on the receipt of the Type V notice which the vendor is entitled to serve only after the assignee has made payment of either the provision amount or alternative security. Thus, the co-venturers are safe in respect of security; they need not ask the assignee for extra security since the assignment can only take place after proper consideration by the all of them collectively and the trustee in any event would not release the outgoing party's contribution until replaced by the assignee's. In reaching an agreement whether or not to allow the sale, they (joint venturer) ought to have considered the financial standing of the incoming party, as the assignee would have the benefit of the same rights and be subject to the same obligations under the DCPD previously held by the assignor to the extent of the assigned interest.

Finally, the DCPD is regarded as a robust commercial arrangement which provides for all parties who were, are, or are likely to be liable for decommissioning obligations on the UKCS.

Activities

3.287
- You are advising a client who wants to acquire some North Sea assets. How does he go about doing this and what due diligence does he have to conduct in view of the decommissioning obligations in the licence?
- Do you think decommissioning should be a contractual or legal requirement?
- What decommissioning advice would you give your client when he wants to farm into a producing field in the UK North Sea?

- Are the UK's decommissioning obligations a deterrent to investment?

Further reading

3.288 It is highly recommended that you consult as many of the following as background for better understanding:
- J Aldersey-Williams, 'Decommissioning Security' (2007) 5(4) Oil, Gas and Energy Law Intelligence available online at www.gasandoil.com.
- P Dymond and Stronachs, 'Decommissioning' in J Wils & EC Neilson, *The Technical and Legal Guide to the UK Oil and Gas Industry* (2007, Aberlour), Ch 15.7–15.14.
- L Moller, 'The cost of Decommissioning: Government and the Industry Attempts at Addressing Decommissioning Liabilities' (2007) 5(4) Oil, Gas and Energy Law Intelligence.
- J Paterson, 'Decommissioning Offshore Installations' in G Gordon, J Paterson and E Usenmez, *Oil and Gas Law: Current Practice and Emerging Trends* (2nd edn, 2011, Dundee University Press), Ch 7.
- J Aldersey-Williams, *The Decommissioning Cost Provision Deed* (2008) International Energy Law Review.

See also:

- Code of Practice on Access to Upstream Oil and Gas Infrastructure on the UK Continental Shelf.
- PILOT Brownfields Workgroup on Decommissioning, Decommissioning Cost Provisions Deed, August 2007.
- PILOT Brownfields Workgroup on Decommissioning, Guidance Notes for Decommissioning Cost Provision Deed, August 2007.
- DECC Oil and gas: decommissioning of offshore installations and pipelines (Decommissioning programmes, including dates, locations, installations decommissioned, method of decommissioning and close-out reports where available.) Available at: www.gov.uk/oil-and-gas-decommissioning-of-offshore-installations-and-pipelines.

H RISK MANAGEMENT IN THE OIL AND GAS INDUSTRY

Contractual risk management

3.289 This section considers the manner in which companies usually address the contractual risk relating to the industry with a special focus on the indemnification provisions and the mutual hold harmless practice adopted by the UKCS oil and gas industry. The following concepts are discussed in detail:

— indemnification;
— Mutual Hold Harmless.

3.290   Because there are frequently a large number of contractors rendering services on an oil platform at any given time, and given the non-existence of privity of contract between them, it is important to have properly drafted clauses, covering insurance of risk, or mutual indemnity clauses between the company and the contractors. Where the framework for the management of risks is not properly in place, problems of allocation of liability will arise where a contractor has caused harm to other contractors working on the platform. Thus, it is important to have a coherent and robust risk management structure. Towards this end the mechanisms used in the offshore oil and gas industry for control and management of risk are examined. Clauses that cover insurance, defects liability and limitation of liability in the standard contracts are analysed and the usual subjects of cover are highlighted. The LOGIC Industry Mutual Hold Harmless (the standard contractor risk management agreement) is also considered in detail.

Background

3.291   The management of risk in international oil and gas project contracts, particularly the up and midstream oil and gas projects, is of great importance to the parties involved in the project contracts and their legal advisors at the negotiating, drafting and interpretation stages. The inherent risk associated with oil and gas operations is anchored on the enormous potential liabilities envisaged, which includes but are not limited to, the huge capital invested, properties, the environment, the lives at stake and of course the commodity itself. The oil and gas industry ('the industry'), in its quest to manage risk in a manner that suits the developing trends of shifting contractual risk, have, contrary to common law's perception of how such risk should be allocated, modified a number of contractual provisions to achieve their precise intention—commercial expectation[1]. These modified contractual provisions are commonly grouped into three categories: (a) indemnification provisions, which include the hold harmless provisions; (b) exemption clauses, which purport to exclude or restrict the liability that would otherwise attach to a breach of contract[2]; and (c) limitation of liability provisions[3].

1   The intention of parties to the oil and gas project contracts is to re-allocate, between the parties to the contract, the risk of the occurrence of certain types of loss and thereby saying that neither of them should bear sole responsibility for the stated species of loss, which is indeed contrary to the general indemnity provision, which imposes the obligation to bear the risk of a particular type of loss on one party. By re-allocating the risk, parties are permitted to assess and accept risks more easily. Thus, delay in claim settlement is avoided, and certainly reduces fighting of lawsuits. See D Peng, 'Mutual Indemnities in North Sea Contracts—Liability and Insurance Clauses', in D Peng (ed), *Insurance and Legal Issues in the Oil Industry* (1993) at p 157. This explanation for re-allocating risk by the industry has been criticised to be overstated because it is limited to personal injury and that the explanation would not be sufficient as regards damage to property. See also G Gordon 'Risk Allocation in the Oil and Gas Contracts' in G Gordon, J Paterson and E Usenmez, *Oil and Gas Law: Current Practice and Emerging Trends* (2nd edn, 2011, Dundee University Press), Ch 14.

2 Examples of such clauses include, but are not limited to, disclaimer clauses, exculpation clauses and many more.

3 Limitation of liability clauses do not completely relieve a party from liability but, instead, cap the amount of liability. In other words, the clause guarantees that a party will not be held liable for damages above a stated amount; for example see Texas Act § 127.005(c) which provides that parties to a unilateral indemnity contract are allowed to create otherwise prohibited indemnity obligations so far in writing the indemnitor states that its obligation is supported by insurance not required to exceed $500,000. See Allen H Gwyn, 'Legislative and Judicial Responses to Limitation of Liability Provisions', (1996) 16 Construction Lawyer 62 at 61.

The contractual indemnification provision

3.292   The industry developed this risk management model—the contractual indemnification provision—to shift the risk of liability from the negligent party (the indemnitee), to an innocent party (the indemnitor).

> **Note:**
> * an *Indemnitee* is a person or a certain entity who receives reimbursement from another for resulting losses and liabilities;
> * an *Indemnitor* is a person or a certain entity who reimburses another for a loss suffered because of a third party's or its own act or default.

3.293   The contractual indemnification provision as employed by the industry has been criticised as being inequitable and an exertion of unfair bargaining power on small contractors by the big oil companies and oil well operators in some common law jurisdictions[1], while some other common law jurisdictions have embraced the provision. Thus, in the UK where this provision has been embraced, steps are being taken to proffer solutions to the inherent problems which exist in the drafting of the indemnity clause, vis-à-vis the complex and hazardous nature of the industry's project operations[2].

1 See Hunter H White, 'Winding Your Way Through the Texas Oilfield Anti-indemnity Statute, The Fair Notice Requirements and Other Indemnity Related Issues' (1996) 37 S Tex L Rev 161, p 163. See also *Getty Oil Co v Insurance Co of North America* 845 SW 2d 794, 803 (Tex 1992).

2 The Industry Mutual Hold Harmless Scheme (IMHH) went live in 2002 with the primary objective to address the contractual gaps which traditionally exist between oil industry contractors working on the UKCS who are not in contract with each other (available at www. logic-oil.com/imhh).

3.294   Generally, risk allocation under the law of contract and tort in a common law jurisdiction is subject to considerations such as breach of care (whether statutory or otherwise), remoteness of damages; steps taken by the non-breaching party to mitigate its loss and compensatory damages; and the party in breach of contract or duty is under the obligation to make good the losses suffered by the non-breaching party[1].

> **Note:** The non-breaching party is the Indemnitor, while the breaching party is the Indemnitee.

1 See G Gordon, 'Risk Allocation in the Oil and Gas Contracts' in G Gordon, J Paterson and E Usenmez, *Oil and Gas Law: Current Practice and Emerging Trends* (2nd edn, 2011, Dundee University Press), Ch 14.

3.295   This fault-based risk allocation position is usually taken in instances where there has been no contributory or participatory fault on the part of the, so called, non-breaching party[1]. Under the principle of the tort of negligence, where a person owes a duty of care and breaches it with losses arising therefrom, the person at fault is therefore under the obligation to make a payment of compensatory damages to make good that arising loss[2]. Thus, liability should follow a breach of duty or be based on fault[3].

1 See Genevieve Macattram, 'How Can the Indemnity Clause Expand or Limit the Responsibility for Liability of the Parties in International Oil and Gas Contracts?' pg 13, available at www.dundee.ac.uk/cepmlp/car/html/CAR10_ARTICLE2.PDF.
2 See *Clerk and Lindsell on Torts* (19th edn, 2005), paras 9.01–9.04.
3 See G Gordon, 'Risk Allocation in the Oil and Gas Contracts' in G Gordon, J Paterson and E Usenmez, *Oil and Gas Law: Current Practice and Emerging Trends* (2nd edn, 2011, Dundee University Press), Ch 14. See also G Treitel, *The Law of Contract* (11th edn, 2003), p 926.

3.296   In contrast, the contractual indemnification provision employed in allocating risk in most standard service contracts is founded on the view that liability should be accepted by the party in the best position to insure against or otherwise absorb the particular loss in question, and should not follow a breach or fault[1]. Therefore, the industry has used the contractual indemnification provision to circumvent, so far as possible under contract law, the general principle of the law of tort of negligence.

1 See G Gordon, 'Risk Allocation in the Oil and Gas Contracts' in G Gordon, J Paterson and E Usenmez, *Oil and Gas Law: Current Practice and Emerging Trends* (2nd edn, 2011, Dundee University Press), Ch 14.

3.297   The contractual indemnification provision is a clause in an agreement between two or more parties, whereby one party undertakes or agrees to become financially responsible or covering liability, for loss or damage arising from a claim or demand made by a third party, which the other party should ordinarily have been liable for[1]. Therefore, the contractual indemnification provision will not only exclude a party from its liability in negligence to the other party but would further require the non-breaching party to indemnify the breaching party against the consequences arising from his own negligence. Thus, the contractual indemnification provision would hold the indemnitee harmless for damages, by shifting liability as between the contracting parties to the indemnitor.

1 *Black's Law Dictionary* defines an indemnity clause as a contractual provision in which one party agrees to answer for any specified or unspecified liability or harm that the other party might incur. It is also termed 'hold harmless clause' or 'save-harmless clause': *Blacks' Law Dictionary* (8th edn, 2004).

3.298   The court, in interpreting the contractual indemnification clause, intends to deduce the intention of the contracting parties as at negotiation stage. This is because the subjective intention of the parties would not be reliable to determine such intention, as it depends on whether a party is the indemnitor or indemnitee[1]. The court would ordinarily assume that the parties intended for liability to follow a breach of duty or fault, as the court is of the view that it is inherently improbable for one party to the contract to intend to absolve the other party entirely from the consequences of its own negligence[2]. Therefore, contrary to the intention of the parties, effect would not be given to the contractual indemnification clause unless the wording of the clause is clear and unambiguous to address the important public policy considerations surrounding indemnification of an indemnitee against liability for death, or injury to personnel or damage to property caused by its own negligence.

> **Note:** The indemnification clause is usually interpreted in the light of the contract as a whole and not in isolation[3].

1   See Genevieve Macattram, 'How Can the Indemnity Clause Expand or Limit the Responsibility for Liability of the Parties in International Oil and Gas Contracts?', pg 10 available at www. dundee.ac.uk/cepmlp/car/html/CAR10_ARTICLE2.PDF.
2   See *Chitty on Contract* (29th edn, 2004), vol 1, para 14-010; Treitel *The Law of Contract* (11th edn, 2003), p 222 and also *Sonat Offshore SA v Amerada Hess Development Ltd* [1988] 1 Lloyd's Rep 145 at 157.
3   See *RE Jordrell* (1890) 44 Ch D 590; *Glen's Trs v Lancashire and Yorkshire Accident Insurance Co Ltd* (1906) 8 F 915.

3.299   Unlike the common law presumption of liability following a fault or a breach of duty, the judiciary through case law take the stand that parties could, through the terms of their contract, re-allocate risk. Most importantly, the wording of such indemnification clause must be clear and unambiguous. Therefore, since the courts, as regards contractual indemnification, are of the general view that it is 'inherently improbable that one party to a contract should intend to absolve the other party from the consequence of his own negligence'[1], parties must therefore use clear and unambiguous words to re-allocate risk when they intend to. The judiciary's approach to the express negligence test vis-à-vis indemnification clauses was impressively expressed by Devlin LJ in his comments in *Walters v Whessoe Ltd and Shell Refining Co Ltd*[2]:

> 'It is well established that if a person obtains an indemnity against the consequences of certain acts, the indemnity is not to be construed so as to include the consequences of his own negligence unless those consequences are covered either expressly or by necessary implication. They are covered by necessary implication if there is no other subject matter upon which the indemnity could operate. Like most rules of construction, this one depends upon the presumed intention of the parties. It is thought to be unlikely that one man would agree to indemnify another man for the consequences of that other's own negligence that he is presumed not to intend to do so unless it is done by express words or by necessary implication'.

1   *Gillespie Bros Ltd v Roy Boulles Transport Ltd* [1973] QB 400 at 419. See also Treitel *The Law of Contract* (11th edn, 2003), p 222.
2   [1960] 6 Build LR 23, CA (Civ).

3.300   Furthermore, in the classic case, *R v Canada Steamship Lines Ltd*[1], the court in its quest to deliver a fair and equitable judgment summarised three propositions included in the judgment of the board of the Privy Council, Lord Morton of Henryton:

- where the indemnification clause expressly states that a party is exempted from the consequences of its own negligence or his servants, or refers to some synonym for it, effect must be given to such a clause[2];
- where the clause does not expressly refer to the word negligence, the court must consider if the words used can in their ordinary meaning be wide enough to cover the negligence of the party or his servants[3]; and
- where it has been identified that the words used are wide enough, the court must further consider whether there is another head of damage (such head must not be too remote from what the *proferen* could have expected to gain protection from) other than negligence upon which to base the claim.

1   [1952] AC 192, [1952] 1 Lloyd's Rep 1 at 8. This case will hereinafter be referred to as 'Canada Steamship Lines case'.
2   To satisfy this test, there must be a clear and unmistakable reference to 'negligence' or to some similar word for it. See *Smith v South Wales Switchgear Co Ltd* [1978] 1 WLR 165, at 169 and 173.
3   As regards this test, an example of a clause which excluded liability for any damage or breach of duty is; '…which may arise from or be in any way connected with any act or omission of any person …employed by [the defendant]'. It has been held to be wide enough to cover negligence on the part of the defendant's servant. Thus, phrases such as 'however arising' or 'any cause whatsoever' have been held to cover losses by negligence. See *Lamport & Holt Lines Ltd v Coubro & Scrutton (M & I) Ltd* [1982] 2 Lloyd's Rep 42; *Rutter v Palmer* [1922] 2 KB 87 at 94; *Scottish & Southern Energy plc v Lerwick Engineering & Fabrication Ltd* [2008] SCLR 317 at 318, and also *Chitty on Contract* (29th edn, 2004), vol 1, para 14-011.

3.301   However, in *EE Caledonia Ltd v Orbit Valve Co*[1], the court relied on the above three propositions in arriving at a decision regarding the enforcement of indemnification agreements under the English law. One of the operators in the Piper Alpha disaster accepted the liability that the negligent act of one of its employees had contributed to the death of another's employee. After the operator had compensated the family of the deceased, it sued to recover under the indemnity clause where it had been indemnified against the death of the contractor's employee even when negligence has been established. The contractor argued that the clause in question did not expressly or clearly refer to negligence as expected by common law. In applying the propositions laid down in *Canada Steamship Lines* case, the Court of Appeal refused to give effect to the clause on the grounds that the second test was not satisfied. It has been observed, however, that although the wording was not necessarily directed to the indemnified party's negligence, still the court could have inferred and decided that the said wording had intended to exclude other heads of claim, particularly breaches of statutory duty[2].

1 [1995] 1 All ER 174, [1994] 1 WLR 1515, CA, referred to henceforth as the '*Orbit Valve* case'.
2 See the words of Steyn LJ in the *Orbit Valve* case.

Industry Mutual Hold Harmless Scheme (IMHH)

3.302   It is pertinent to mention therefore, that as far as oil and gas operation contracts are concerned, there are two common types of contractual indemnification provisions, namely the simple and the mutual indemnification provision[1].

Note:

- the *Simple Indemnification* provision is a clause in an agreement whereby the indemnitor agrees to be financially responsible for payment to the indemnitee in the event that the latter suffers loss in a specified circumstance;

- the *Mutual Indemnification* provision, also called 'mutual hold harmless indemnities' or 'knock for knock indemnities' or 'cross-indemnities', is a contract in an agreement where each party agree to be financially responsible for, and indemnify the other(s) against resulting injury or death to its own personnel or damage to its own property, regardless of fault.

---

1 See G Gordon, 'Risk Allocation in the Oil and Gas Contracts' in G Gordon, J Paterson and E Usenmez, *Oil and Gas Law: Current Practice and Emerging Trends* (2nd edn, 2011, Dundee University Press), Ch 14; see also Toby Hewitt, 'Who is to Blame? Allocating Liability in Upstream Project Contracts', (2008) 26(2) Jnl of Energy & Natural Resources Law, p 182.

3.303   However, the industry, in its operation contracts, exploits the mutual indemnification provision more. Thus, attention will be focused on the 'mutual hold harmless' or the 'knock-for-knock' indemnities regime. The industry is of the view that the question is really not whether the loss or the damage suffered by the indemnitee was wholly or partly arising from the consequences of its own negligence but rather, whether the terms of a properly construed indemnity clause will cover the loss suffered by the indemnitee. Therefore, whether or not the word 'negligence' is used in the indemnity clause, effect should still be given to any clause which by implication has the same effect as a clause where such word has been used[1].

1 This of course was the situation in the judgment delivered by the Court of Appeal in the *Orbit Valve* case, where the plaintiff claimed an indemnity in respect of payment made to an employee of the defendant who had died in a fire on board the plaintiff's offshore platform. The contract contained a straightforward mutual indemnity clause in respect of each party's employees. The clause did not, however, contain any provision that the indemnity would apply even if the loss in question were caused by negligence, thus the word 'negligence' was not used. The claim failed on the ground that the death had been caused by the indemnitee's own negligence and it was therefore stated that it was 'prima facie implausible that the parties

would wish to release one another from the consequences of the other's negligence and agree to indemnify the other in respect of such consequences'. However, see the decision in the *London Bridge* case.

The position of the industry before 2002

3.304 In addition, by the very nature of an oil and gas production platform, where the expertise of countless contractors and sub-contractors is engaged, there arose the need to bridge the gap between the operator and these participating contractors and sub-contractors[1]. The vigilance of the industry was therefore aroused by a combination of privity of contract law, and the fact that not all the different contractors and sub-contractors would have entered into a contract with each other but only with the operator of the platform[2]. The industry, with the view to bridge the gap that existed between one contractor group and another contractor group invented the back-to-back indemnity principle[3]. It could be observed, however, that this link although effective, would mean that the operator would spend a lot of time administering the indemnity agreement and there is also the tendency for the operator to become responsible for a greater degree of liability beyond that which it had anticipated.

1   The doctrine of privity of contract is a principle of law which states that only parties to a contract are bound by the terms of that contract. See The Standard Bulletin, 2nd Edition, (October, 2007), p 5.
2   Under this principle, the operator will bear the risk and provide indemnity for the contractor in respect of any claims in relation to not only its own personnel and property but also that of other contractors with which this contractor is not in any contractual relationship with and the contractor will then in turn provide indemnity in respect of the personnel and property of the sub and sub-subcontractors in his group and not only in favour of the operator but for other lead contractors. See generally G Gordon, 'Risk Allocation in the Oil and Gas Contracts' in G Gordon, J Paterson and E Usenmez, *Oil and Gas Law: Current Practice and Emerging Trends* (2nd edn, 2011, Dundee University Press), Ch 14.
3   See Contracts (Rights of Third Parties) Act 1999, s 1. Available at: www.legislation.gov.uk/ukpga/1999/31/contents. See also The Standard Bulletin, 2nd Edition, (October, 2007), p 5.

3.305 It should be noted, however, that before the enactment of the Contracts (Rights of Third Parties) Act[1] 1999 (the C(RTP)A 1999) under English law, contractors which were not in contractual relationships with contractors in other groups (which are usually referred to as third parties to the existing contract) would not be beneficiaries of the existing indemnity agreement[2]. The C(RTP)A 1999 therefore now allows persons who are not parties to an agreement to enforce rights or benefits under the agreement. Thus, although these third party contractors or sub-contractors can now claim as beneficiaries, they can not enforce the terms of an indemnity agreement to which they are not parties. In other words, even with the enactment of the C(RTP)A 1999 and the back-to-back indemnity approach, gaps would still exist between the different contractors and sub-contractor groups[3].

1   See Contracts (Rights of Third Parties) Act 1999, s 1. Available at: www.legislation.gov.uk/ukpga/1999/31/contents. See also The Standard Bulletin, 2nd Edition, (October, 2007), p 5.

2 Under the United States Laws, efforts are also being made to change the law governing the right of persons who are not parties to a contract and who intend to claim benefits from it. See Francis Dawson, 'New Zealand Privity of Contract Bill', (Winter 1982) 2 (3) *Oxford Journal of Legal Studies* pp 448–454.

3 See The Standard Bulletin, 2nd Edition, (October, 2007), p 5.

The position of the industry since 2002

3.306   The industry, therefore, for a wide range of reasons (to address the contractual gaps which customarily existed between the different contractor and sub-contractor groups working on the production platform, to prevent contractors from taking out extensive insurance cover against unforeseen emergency which may cause injury or death to other's personnel or damage to property, and to reduce or extricate the operator's administrative work in relation to back-to-back indemnity), produced the Industry Mutual Hold Harmless ('IMHH') Scheme through the IMHH deed[1]. Under the patronage of LOGIC the IMHH deed was structured to facilitate the allocation of risk for personnel, property and consequential loss as envisaged by them[2]. In the opinion of the industry, this approach was designed to create a clearer and predictable allocation of liabilities mechanism and also prevent an overlap of insurance covers for identical risks[3].

Note: The existing (2012) IMHH deed is the most up to date and **is valid** to the end of 2021. Available at www.logic-oil.com/imhh.

---

1 For the aims and objective of the IMHH Scheme, and the IMHH deed visit www.imhh.com.

2 See G Gordon, 'Risk Allocation in the Oil and Gas Contracts' in G Gordon, J Paterson and E Usenmez, *Oil and Gas Law: Current Practice and Emerging Trends* (2nd edn, 2011, Dundee University Press), Ch 14.

3 See Nick Brown, 'Talk on IMHH at Legal Innovation Day', 18 November 2003.

3.307   Therefore, as far as the scheme is concerned, participants—the various contractors on the production platform—are required to enter into the scheme at once, for a long term by signing up for same. It should be noted, however, that participants to the scheme must still include an indemnity clause in their contractual agreements even though they have signed up for the deed[1]. Thus, the deed does not take precedence over the actual agreement or contract[2].

1 See generally G Gordon, 'Risk Allocation in the Oil and Gas Contracts' in G Gordon, J Paterson and E Usenmez, *Oil and Gas Law: Current Practice and Emerging Trends* (2nd edn, 2011, Dundee University Press), Ch 14.

2 Ibid and also Clause 11 of the IMHH Deed, available at www.logic-oil.com/imhh.

3.308   In conclusion, although some problems have been observed in relation to the IMHH deed[1], it is undoubtedly a step in the right direction to give effect to the industry's intention so far as risk allocation in the oil and gas industry is concerned, and of course also to resolve the above stated difficulties which existed before 2002.

1 It has been observed, amongst other potential dangers of the IMHH, that the deed stands
   the risk of latent drafting error and/or a change in practice law of the contractors who are
   not exactly oil and gas industry specialists. See generally G Gordon, 'Risk Allocation in the
   Oil and Gas Contracts' in G Gordon, J Paterson and E Usenmez, *Oil and Gas Law: Current
   Practice and Emerging Trends* (2nd edn, 2011, Dundee University Press), Ch 14.

The rationale behind the contractual indemnification clause

3.309 It has, however been said, that the main reason for inventing and
then embracing the application of this indemnity clause is to aid the quick
determination of liability and reduce the lengthy process of awarding costs to
the injured party or the family of the deceased, where a death has occurred[1].
This assessment is based on the countless number of contractors and sub-
contractors on a typical production platform and the gaps which may exist
within the contractual chains between these contractors[2]. However, this reason
has been criticised to relate only to claims resulting from personal injury or
death and would therefore not be a sufficient explanation for the application
of the contractual indemnification clause as regards damage to property
or economic losses[3]. Although it is true the industry frowns at unnecessary
publicity and would therefore encourage a swift and a predictable resolution
of litigation or resulting disputes, it would seem exaggerated for anyone to
conclude that it is the major reason why the contractual indemnification clause
was initiated[4].

1 See D Sharp, *Offshore Oil and Gas Insurance* (1994), p 108.
2 See also the dicta of Lord Bingham in *London Bridge* case, para 7 [2002] 1 All ER (Comm)
   321; see also D Peng, 'Mutual Indemnities in North Sea Contracts—Liability and Insurance
   Clauses', in D Peng (ed), *Insurance and Legal Issues in the Oil Industry* (1993) at p 157 who
   argues that the main reason for this provision is to avoid delay in the settlement of claims and
   reduce litigation.
3 See G Gordon, 'Risk Allocation in the Oil and Gas Contracts' in G Gordon, J Paterson and E
   Usenmez, *Oil and Gas Law: Current Practice and Emerging Trends* (2nd edn, 2011, Dundee
   University Press), Ch 14.
4 Ibid.

3.310 More writers, commentators and even judges have however observed
that the primary reason for initiating the contractual indemnification clause was
to avoid the duplication or multiplicity of insurance coverage[1]. The possibility
of duplicating insurance coverage is very high, on the basis that the owner of
a piece of equipment will want to insure same against the risk of demolishing
the whole platform and the risk of it injuring or killing other people. However,
other contractors on the same production platform would also feel the need to
insure themselves against such possible exposures[2]. Thus, as regards this one
piece of equipment, several insurance covers would have been carried out, by
the owner and many other contractors who have anticipated their exposure
to the equipment. Supporting this reasoning, Lord President Roger in the
London Bridge case[3] stated that the contractual indemnification clause was
'fundamental to the economics of the North Sea operations'. His Lordship

based his reasoning on the high risk involved in the operations of a typical production platform. Thus, the more insurance covers taken out, of course at a high premium due to the hazardous nature of the oil and gas industry, the more expensive the contract price becomes. The very high premium would therefore prohibit or discourage the involvement of smaller contractors and would create a scenario where the increased cost of insurance is finally borne by the operator.

1   See D Peng, 'Mutual Indemnities in North Sea Contracts—Liability and Insurance Clauses', in D Peng (ed), *Insurance and Legal Issues in the Oil Industry* (1993) at p 157. See also Toby Hewitt, 'Who is to Blame? Allocating Liability in Upstream Project Contracts', (2008) 26(2) Jnl of Energy & Natural Resources Law, p 183. See the words of Lord President Roger in the *London Bridge case* at 2000 SLT 1123 at 1150I.
2   Ibid
3   Ibid. See also the words of Lord Bingham where he, with apparent approval, described contractual indemnification clauses as a market practice which had developed to take into account the unique characteristic of the offshore platform operations (at p 557). See also T Daintith & G Hewitt, *United Kingdom Oil and Gas Law*. (2012, Sweet & Maxwell).

3.311   At first glance however, the reasons put forward as the driving force behind initiating the contractual indemnification clause seem contrary to the intended applicability status of the clause, but after being given a proper and in-depth analysis, it seems like a sound economic and operational reason to initiate the clause[1].

1   See G Gordon, 'Risk Allocation in the Oil and Gas Contracts' in G Gordon, J Paterson and E Usenmez, *Oil and Gas Law: Current Practice and Emerging Trends* (2nd edn, 2011, Dundee University Press), Ch 14.

The practicality of the Mutual Hold Harmless Regime

3.312   As mentioned above, the IMHH regime, as initiated by LOGIC, had been accessed initially by the IMHH deed, but now the deeds of adherence are being engaged[1]. In theory, the underlying objective of the IMHH regime is to provide an efficient and convenient procedure through which various sets of mutual indemnities in a typical oil and gas production platform can be neatly co-ordinated between parties[2]. Thus, the intention of the regime is to provide a full and primary mutual indemnity on the basis of the group, whether small or large. It should be noted that in practice, although the risk allocation regime is not free of drawbacks, it will still be viewed as a forward-looking success and a step in the right direction.

1   See Sch 2 to the IMHH Deed for a pro-forma deed of adherence.
2   See G Gordon, 'Risk Allocation in the Oil and Gas Contracts' in G Gordon, J Paterson and E Usenmez, *Oil and Gas Law: Current Practice and Emerging Trends* (2nd edn, 2011, Dundee University Press), Ch 14.

3.313   One of the application problems that has tainted the success of the regime is based on lack or inadequate knowledge or awareness as regards the application of the regime[1]. For example, the majority of the contractors, whether from a big or small oil and gas company, were of the view that the IMHH deed covered third party visitors to the production platform, or believed that once a contractor signs up that is all that is required of it and thus, it could now claim indemnity against losses resulting from the consequence of even its own negligence[2]. Such misconceptions expose the contractual chain to the danger of gaps as far as insurance covers are concerned. Thus, to make the regime go from theory to practice, it can not be overemphasised that the continued education and training of the personnel of the industry is vital[3].

1   See G Gordon, 'Risk Allocation in the Oil and Gas Contracts' in G Gordon, J Paterson and E Usenmez, *Oil and Gas Law: Current Practice and Emerging Trends* (2nd edn, 2011, Dundee University Press), Ch 14.
2   IMHH deed cl 11, states that the deed shall not take precedence over, amend, modify or apply to the terms of any agreement between signatories entered prior to, on or after this deed becoming effective in relation to such signatories.
3   See G Gordon, 'Risk Allocation in the Oil and Gas Contracts' in G Gordon, J Paterson and E Usenmez, *Oil and Gas Law: Current Practice and Emerging Trends* (2nd edn, 2011, Dundee University Press), Ch 14.

3.314   Furthermore, industry players also have the tendency to become unduly relaxed by believing all the contractors on the production platform are signatories to the IMHH deed. This is a very unsafe assumption because, for example, drilling contractors might be reluctant to sign up to the IMHH deed, because they are unable to provide an estimated value of the scheme and the latter's advantages to them. Their reluctance is based on their costly equipment and the large number of personnel engaged on a typical production platform. It is thus inadvisable for industry players to make assumptions about the prevalence of the IMHH deed, because it makes the underlying objective of the regime impracticable, as the aims tend to be defeated.

3.315   For a new contractor planning to engage itself with the activities on a production platform, it will be difficult for it to determine or ascertain whose property or personnel will be on the platform at the time of entry and whether or not they are signatories to the IMHH deed. Indeed, they will not know whether the contractor has first and foremost incorporated the contractual indemnity clause in its agreement and intends to be bound by the deed because it is a signatory.

3.316   Having mentioned some of the identified drawbacks of the regime, they are not enough to condemn the success of the regime; it could only affect its practicality to some extent. However, with adequate awareness, the relevant personnel would become more enlightened.

> **Note:** a good understanding of the 'indemnification' provisions and the 'knock for knock'/'mutual hold harmless' provisions, in contracts used in the offshore oil and gas industry will be very beneficial to your industry experience.

Activities

3.317
- What is the difference between a simple and mutual indemnification clause?

Further reading

3.318
- Case: *Westerngeco Ltd v ATP Oil & Gas (UK) Ltd* [2006] EWHC 1164, [2006] 2 All ER (Comm) 637.
- G Gordon, 'Risk Allocation' in G Gordon, J Paterson and E Usenmez, *Oil and Gas Law: Current Practice and Emerging Trends* (2nd edn, 2011, Dundee University Press), Ch 14.
- LOGIC, *Indemnity Mutual Hold Harmless Deed:* www.imhh.com/deed/ IMHH_Deed.pdf.
- Clerk, Dugdale & Lindsell, *Clerk & Lindsell on Torts* (2005, Sweet & Maxwell).
- T Hewitt 'Who is to Blame? Allocating Liability in Upstream Project Contracts' (2008) Journal of Energy & Natural Resources Law: the Journal of the Section on Energy and Natural Resources Law of the International Bar Association 26, 177.
- DD Peng, *Insurance and Legal Issues in the Oil Industry* (1993) International energy and resources law and policy series. London, Graham & Trotman.
- Sharp, DW, *Offshore Oil and Gas Insurance* (1994, Witherby & Co).
- Treitel, *The Law of Contract* (2003, Sweet & Maxwell).
- Industry Mutual Hold Harmless at http://www.imhh.com/about.cfm
- LOGIC, General Conditions of Contract for Services (On- and Off-shore) (Edition 2, October 2003): www.logic-oil.com/sites/default/files/documents/Services%20Onshore%20and%20Offshore%20 Edition%202.pdf

I ADMINISTERING AND MANAGING THE CONTRACT

3.319 This section deals with some key aspects of the administration and management of the contract, including some practical issues of an oil and gas contract from the point of view of a contractor. Reference is made to the LOGIC model contract and it will be assumed that the contractor has a contract for continuing work during the whole period of a contract.

> **Note:** Readers should refer to the LOGIC General Conditions of Contract for Services (On- and Off-shore) (Edition 2, October 2003) on the LOGIC website at: www.logic-oil.com/sites/default/files/documents/Services%20 Onshore%20and%20Offshore%20Edition%202.pdf.

Administering the contract

What is contract administration?

3.320   There are various meanings of 'contract administration' in use throughout the business world. Generally, contract administration is concerned with the operational aspects of the routine administrative and clerical functions associated with the organisation. Specifically it involves monitoring the day-to-day activities carried out by the staff of the organisation/company after a contract has been awarded, to determine how well the company and the contractor performed to meet the key requirements of the contract.

3.321   It encompasses all dealings between the parties (ie the company and the contractor) from the time the contract is awarded until the work has been completed and accepted or the contract is terminated, payment has been made, and disputes have been resolved. Thus, contract administration constitutes that primary part of the procurement process that assures the company gets what it paid for and the contractor gets reimbursed for services rendered.

3.322   Usually, in contract administration, the focus is on obtaining supplies and services, of requisite quality, on time, and within the budget. While the legal requirements of the contract determine the proper course of action of company staff in administering a contract, the exercise of skill and judgment is often required in order to effectively protect the company's interest.

3.323   The importance of contract administration to the success of the contract, and to the relationship between the parties (ie company and contractor), should not be underestimated. Clear administrative procedures ensure that all parties to the contract understand who does what, when, and how.

3.324   Contract administration requires appropriate resourcing. In the case of the company input, this will primarily be the responsibility of the contracts manager. The procedures that typically combine to make up contract administration are as follows:

- keeping proper records;
- asset management;
- ordering procedures;
- payment procedures;

- financial control;
- dispute management.

> **Note:** Contract administration is fundamental to the smooth running of any contract (ie construction or oil and gas contracts).

What are the key objectives of contract administration?

3.325

- **To establish and implement fair contract terms:** The success of a contract depends on whether the product is of the required quality, within budget, delivered/completed by the required date with the party (ie company or contractor) making a reasonable profit. If these simple criteria are not achieved, one of the parties is likely to be dissatisfied, resulting in time-wasting and costly disputes for both parties. It is very important, therefore, that when contracts are set up they acknowledge the need to achieve these basic objectives.

  Sufficient time should be allocated for the performance of the contract. Success is unlikely if an unrealistically short time is allowed for execution or if an unreasonably low tender is accepted. The contract administrator must actively encourage the use of sensible guidelines/parameters concerning the duration and budget of the contract and must remain mindful of them during the progress of the contract. In the case where the contract administrator works for one of the parties (eg company) he would assist in the management of the contract to ensure it is carried out within the client's budget and timescales, but must recognise that the other party (eg contractor) must be allowed to perform his works as efficiently as possible;

- **To ensure knowledge and pursuit of obligations:** Contracts place obligations upon both of the contracted parties. Good contract administration will ensure that the parties are aware of what and where their obligations lie and that every endeavour is made to fulfil them. However this cannot be done passively and an effective administrator would usually encourage the parties to tackle problems immediately and resolve them in the manner required by the contract rather than allowing them to escalate;

- **To communicate and disseminate information:** Good communication is essential both within and between the two parties to ensure that information is issued in adequate time for work to proceed as programmed and that potential problems, changes, claim items, etc, are advised as early as possible enabling the most desirable method of overcoming any problem to be established and put in hand. Late notification or direction is likely to result in the contract taking longer than anticipated and incurring additional costs. If these are not addressed immediately, they may lead to unnecessary claims and disputes;

- **To confront and resolve problems:** A reluctance to confront bad news often leads to poor contract management. In some cases, a contractor may be averse to notifying his senior management of problems he is experiencing or anticipating until it is too late and unavoidable. However, early advice from the administrator often enables alternative methods to be used to execute work, or agreement with the client's agents to achieve the desired result by a different route. A client's agent may try to ignore/reject legitimate claims for additional time and/or expense because he does not want to upset the client. However, disputes will have to be resolved eventually, much better that they are tackled actively and positively at an early stage so that the problem can at least be minimised, which in itself aids resolution.

The role of the contract administrator

3.326   A good contract administrator is essential to ensure the execution of a successful contract. The role of the contract administrator is fundamental to the smooth running of any contract (ie construction or oil and gas contracts; etc) yet this is often given inadequate attention until a serious problem arises. In order to be effective, it is therefore important that the role and responsibility of the administrator is clarified and prioritised from the outset of the contract.

3.327   Contract administrators work for companies, contractors, engineers and architects, etc. They monitor and actively seek to ensure compliance with the contractual provisions relating to the duties and rights, information flow, notices, valuations, deadlines, payments assessments, claims for money, variations and extensions of time.

Think: Who is the contract administrator in your company/organisation?

- logistics manager;
- contracts manager;
- commercial director;
- secretary;
- clerk.

What makes a good contract administrator?

3.328   In order to achieve the above objectives a contract administrator must be competent, resolute and objective. He must be competent in order to gain the respect of those he deals with and discourage abuse of authority and contractual situations, both of which are likely to lead to unnecessary disputes. He must be resolute to ensure that matters are dealt with as required by the contract and objective to ensure that, within the contract parameters, the interests of both parties (ie the company and contractor) are properly balanced. Importantly, in most cases the administrator is a member of a team (usually consisting of technical, financial and business colleagues) and he must therefore be a team player because he depends on the wider team to carry out his functions. He cannot achieve his task of successfully completing the contract on his own.

> **Note:** Contract form is no substitute for good contract administration.

3.329 The form of the contract is usually the first thing to be criticised when problems arise during the execution phase. For example 'the form of contract was not wholly appropriate' and 'had a different form been used the difficulty being experienced would have been avoided'. These are mainly misconceptions.

3.330 The construction industry (and also the oil and gas industry) is notorious for projects resulting in significant claims and disputes. This often results in the adoption of new and bespoke contract terms and conditions to avoid litigation. Examples include bespoke partnering agreements and alliance agreements, which often sit over the contract terms and conditions and which are intended and are often successful in reducing confrontation in construction contracts. However, as most cases show, new contract forms and new approaches to contracting do not in themselves resolve contractual problems.

> **Note:** You should know by now that the UKCS oil and gas industry adopted the standardised contracts under LOGIC for their operations in the North Sea.

3.331 Importantly, whatever contract form is used it is essential that it is administered properly. This is no less important with partnering and alliance agreements. Poor contract administration is likely to result in claims and disputes, whatever the form of contract. Equally, good contract administration will minimise or avoid claims and disputes. Partnering agreements often seek to enforce measures that a good contract administrator would practise whatever the contract form.

3.332 Contract administration should therefore be given consideration from the outset of a contract. It should serve to ensure that both contracted parties understand and uphold the contract, that information is communicated effectively and that potential problems are dealt with efficiently and expeditiously. If a contract administrator is effective, his presence will be felt by the team as a supportive force driving the contract towards its goal. If the role of contract administrator is ignored or carried out poorly, the contract is unlikely to be completed successfully.

Managing the contract

3.333   What follows is an overview of the process of managing the contract once it has been agreed and signed by the parties. For the purpose of this discussion, please again examine the Services (On- and Off-shore) Contract, on the LOGIC website at: www.logic-oil.com/sites/default/files/documents/Services%20Onshore%20and%20Offshore%20Edition%202.pdf.

3.334   Clause 4 of the General Terms and Conditions provides for the contractor's general obligations.

- Clause 4.1 requires the contactor to provide all management, supervision, personnel, materials and equipment (except materials and equipment provided by the company), plant, consumables, facilities and all other things whether of a temporary or permanent nature, as required under the contract;
- Clause 4.2 requires the contractor to carry out the obligations with due care and diligence and with the skill to be expected of a reputable experienced contractor;
- Clause 6 requires the contractor to inform itself of the extent and nature of the work including the services, personnel, materials and equipment, plant, consumables and facilities for the work, and also the correct rates and prices, etc.

It is important for the contractor and in particular the contract administrator to be well informed about the above since any failure to take account of these matters which affect the work, will not relieve the contractor from its obligations under the contract.

> **Note:** It is important to familiarise yourself with the definitions of company and contractor, company/contractor group and also the definition and role of the company/contractor representative, etc.

Mobilisation

3.335   It is normal for contractors of any size to have one or more business support teams who supply the commercial backup for the management and the operational aspects of the contracts. These teams may have technical input, but they are more often made up of surveyors and accountants for measuring performance and more general administrators who ensure the contract is carried out according to its terms.

3.336   The first issue is mobilising a workforce. In many cases, of course, this is not a problem since the workforce are permanently employed by the contractor; but it is also common for contractors to employ agency staff who they can bring in for the short term and then let go at the end of a contract, or a particular piece of work.

3.337 Note that the contractor has taken on obligations under Clause 9 in relation to the personnel required to carry out the work. The contractor needs to ensure it can meet these obligations and failure to do so may result in termination under Clause 24. Therefore, an estimate of the workforce required is necessary and arrangements will be required for their mobilisation and transport to the worksite. If this is a platform then flights will have to be arranged and offshore safety certificates checked. The contractor will need to plan how long the work will take and will need to co-ordinate this with the operator and/or the employing company, for example to ensure for instance that any work which requires the platform to be shut down is done during a planned shut down if possible.

3.338 The contractor will also need to agree rates with all its own contractors and will need to ensure that it can recover these in full under the contract. The contractor will need to check such cost is covered in the contract and the basis on which it can be recovered. Will it be recovered on a reimbursable basis, will there be an opportunity to build in profit or an overhead contribution? How much will this be? When will the cost be recovered?

3.339 In a call off contract or master service agreement, this activity would be triggered by a Purchase Order (PO) from the company. The business support team must check the PO is covered by the contract; the scope is covered by the contract and nothing has been added to the scope, which changes the work required. The contractor should check what the exposure is under the PO and ensure that it is in line with expectations under the contract. If there is any doubt, insurance cover should be checked.

3.340 The contractor will need to check that the work requested in the PO can be carried out and completed within the timescale requested, or whether an extension or variation is required. The contractor should have already checked that the scope of work is adequately covered by its insurance arrangements, but should also check that any variation to the scope of work is also covered. If, for instance, there is even what seems a small change from, say, carrying out maintenance on foot and using ladders, to carrying out maintenance using rope access, then that would require an extension to the insurance cover of the contractor.

3.341 This may have a considerable effect on margins. For instance if a variation to a contract brings in a design element, this may require the contractor to have professional indemnity (PI) cover. PI is expensive and in low margin contracts the additional premium cost could mean the difference between profit and loss.

3.342   Also, the value of the PO should be checked to ensure it meets the contractor's contractual expectations and also to ensure that the contractor can meet its pricing obligations under the contract. There will need to be a health and safety assessment for the work as well as a commercial assessment. This is important for many reasons. There is the obvious one of ensuring the health and safety of the contractor's employees. But in many cases, the revenue to the contractor from the contract may depend upon a good health and safety performance.

3.343   A similar process is required in dealing with the equipment in the execution of the contractual operations. The equipment required should be identified and located. If it has to be hired then the contract should be checked to ensure it covers the equipment required. The rates should be contained in Section III of the contract and these should include the hire rates if additional equipment has to be hired. The contractor needs to check it has included a charge for the equipment in Section III, and if it has not done so an amendment or variation to the contract should be sought prior to the work being carried out. The contractor should check that the equipment is safe for use offshore, whether personnel are trained to use it, and whether a safety assessment has been carried out.

Again, arrangements will have to be made for transportation of the equipment to the platform if that is necessary.

3.344   Where, on the other hand, the contractor is carrying out an overhaul, let us say, of a major item of equipment such as a gas turbine, then the turbine will have to be decommissioned and transported onshore to the contractor's workshop for overhaul. This process should be timed if possible to coincide with a shut down. What happens if the contract does not cover any of this work?

3.345   Generally a variation can be agreed with the company in terms of Clause 11 of Section II. The variation should be sought at the earliest opportunity. The longer this is delayed then the greater the possibility that this will impact on the timing of the performance of the contractor's obligations. If any variation is sought then the company will require that it be fully costed, so the contractor's commercial team must have the pricing issues fully prepared before the request for a variation is submitted.

3.346   Breach of Clauses 4.1 (contractor to provide all management, supervision, personnel, materials, equipment, etc) and 4.4 (materials to be new and fit for intended purpose) may be the result of any delay caused by a variation request if it is not submitted in a timely manner. The contractor will be aware that if there is a delay in mobilising personnel or equipment due to the contractor's negligence as in the above, then this may result in expense being incurred by the company, which in turn can result in another contractor being instructed. Very few contracts in the North Sea are exclusive. Clause 24.1(a) allows the company to terminate at will. Though rare, there have been occasions when this has been exercised.

> **Note:** Please read Clause 24 to find out the reasons for termination of the contract.

3.347   One of the main obligations on the contractor, which they should maintain as a matter of good practice, is to keep and maintain good records. Clause 25 also gives the company the power to audit the contractor's records. For instance, every variation should be recorded. It is common practice once employees are offshore, for things to be much less formal on the platform. This can cause problems. Many contractual claims arise because extra work carried out by a contractor has not been authorised or, if it has, there are no written records to back up a claim for payment. Once the contract is up and running it is also important to invoice the company on a regular basis.

3.348   Section III of the contract provides the basis for remuneration, and the contractor needs to have sufficient information to enable it to provide sufficient financial information to allow it to produce an invoice. In preparing the invoice the contractor's team need to check the timing of the issue of an invoice: is the company expecting an invoice? Also, is there is a contractual basis for issuing an invoice at this stage? At this stage, the information is gathered, the rates checked and the invoice prepared and sent out.

3.349   In the UKCS, competition has driven down contractors' rates and therefore cash flow is a major consideration, even more so than normal in any business, although recent high oil prices and demand has led to improvement in prices for services. It is, for instance, not uncommon for margins to be as low as 5% in some contracts (as here). This means that cash flow is extremely important and it is therefore essential for the contractor to get its invoices out on time.

3.350   Of course in many contracts, the basis of invoicing is cost reimbursal, so that there is no profit element in the periodic invoices. Instead, the contractor gets its costs reimbursed on the contractually agreed basis, possibly, if lucky, with a fixed overhead cost, and the actual profit is dependent on reaching certain targets.

3.351   It is common practice that on completion of the work, the contractor will be responsible to clear and remove any equipment and materials (provided by the contractor) including debris, leaving the worksite in a clean, tidy and safe condition.

3.352 Finally, it is crucial that the contractor is fully conversant with the entire contract consisting for example of the following important sections:

- Section I: Form of Agreement;
- Section II(a): LOGIC General Conditions of Contract (eg for Services (Onshore and Offshore) Edition 2 – October 2003;
- Section II(b): Special Conditions of Contract;
- Section III: Remuneration;
- Section IV: Scope of Work;
- Section V: HSE;
- Section VI: Subcontractors.

> **Note:** All the sections should be read as one document. In the event of ambiguity or contradiction between the sections, the contents shall be given precedence in the order as listed above, with the exception that the special conditions of contract (ie those in Section II(b)) shall take precedence over the general conditions of contract (ie those in Section II(a)).

Activities

3.353
- What do you consider as essential issues for good contract administration and management?
- As a member of the commercial team for an offshore contractor you are required to advise on the following:
  - (a) the contractor is about to take over the operation of a contract from another contractor. What issues will you need to deal with to ensure a successful transition?
  - (b) the contractor's contract is about to end. What issues should be considered to ensure a successful close out of the contract and handover to the next incumbent?

In both cases most of the work is offshore and there is a considerable amount of equipment offshore which will have to be dealt with one way or another. You will have to suggest ways in which this could be efficiently and cost effectively handled.

Further reading

3.354
- LOGIC General Conditions of Contract for Services (On- and Off-shore) (Edition 2, October 2003): www.logic-oil.com/sites/default/files/documents/Services%20Onshore%20and%20Offshore%20Edition%202.pdf

Useful websites

3.355

- Leading Oil Industry Competiveness (LOGIC): www.logic-oil.com
- Oil and Gas UK (OGUK): www.oilandgas.org.uk
- Industry Mutual Hold Harmless (IMHH): www.logic-oil.com/imhh
- PILOT: http://www.oilandgasuk.co.uk/PILOT.cfm
- Department of Energy & Climate Change (DECC): https://www.gov.uk/government/organisations/department-of-energy-climate-change
- Offshore Contractors Association (OCA): www.ocainternet.com
- International Marine Contractor's Association (IMCA): www.imca-int.com
- International Pipeline and Offshore Contractor's Association (IPLOCA): www.iploca.com/page/content/index.asp?MenuID=49&ID=91&Menu=1&Item=10

J DISPUTE RESOLUTION IN THE OIL AND GAS INDUSTRY

3.356 The oil and gas industry is no stranger to disputes, owing to its international and multifaceted character. In the excitement of seeking to close a contract it is easy to overlook what may occur in the event that a dispute arises. A dispute can be defined as a disagreement concerning a matter of fact, law, or policy, where a claim or assertion of one party is met with refusal, denial or counter-claim by another[1]. When a disagreement involves parties in different parts of the world, the dispute is said to be international. The oil and gas industry has been familiar with disputes ever since the first drilled oil well in 1859 in Pennsylvania, when Colonel Drake fell into dispute with his local suppliers of goods and services.

1 Disputes can involve governments, institutions, juristic persons or private individuals.

3.357 The industry is an international market, as mentioned above, with those involved potentially having assets scattered in many different countries. Many of the contracts made are long term in their nature, involving multiple stakeholders, and can be particularly complex, both technically and legally. Contractual disputes can cost oil and gas companies millions of pounds, not only in their profit but also in terms of both the damage incurred to reputation and the potential for ruining future joint ventures. Both these consequences have more severe, sometimes intangible, impacts which may on their own constitute obstacles which are difficult to overcome. The oil and gas industry is collegiate in its dynamics, where long-lasting relationships are favoured and solutions are sought with minimum disruption to existing relationships and projects. Therefore, disputing parties have no desire to halt or stop their activities, and once the dispute is resolved they would normally wish to continue a commercial relationship.

3.358   Disputes usually arise when an issue occurs which has not been prepared for and agreed on in the principal agreement between the parties, whether this is a delay in the delivery of equipment, maritime boundary issues, a problem with an indigenous community[1] or an unexpected pipeline incident, such as the recent British Petroleum (BP) catastrophe[2]. Oil and gas is one of the most dispute-intensive industries in the world and the types of disputes arising from relevant contracts include disputes among operators, non-operators and joint venturers in property acquisition, exploration developments, supply and marketing arrangements and construction projects, among others. The potential for disputes is also heightened greatly by the decreasing oil reserves in the shallow coastal waters and the need for the industry to seek previously untapped resources further afield, for example in the Arctic. It thus becomes increasingly important to have clear methods of dispute resolution which detail the choice of forum and the choice of law.

1   In 2003 a large group of indigenous people in the Ecuadorian Amazon oil region filed a case against Texaco (now merged into Chevron) for environmental damage. The waste pits, supposedly cleaned up by Texaco, contain varying degrees of pollution at the surface, though Petroecuador itself has had a poor environmental record including a minimum of 800 oil spills since 1990. These indigenous plaintiffs, backed by the Ecuadorian government under President Rafael Correa, demanded $27 billion in added compensation despite the binding nature of the 1998 agreement releasing Texaco from further liability.
2   More details available via www.bp.com/sectiongenericarticle800.do?categoryId=9048915&contentId=7082596.

3.359   In the UKCS, there are two principal mechanisms to resolve contractual disputes: informal dialogue and formal dialogue. The former process occurs when the parties, usually from senior management, meet and seek to address in good faith the issues in dispute with a view to procuring early and informal resolution. This process usually happens in the early stage of a dispute, and so the parties might query the need for a provision in an agreement which recites what they might regard as a self-evident requirement. A provision in the contract to resolve disputes through informal means will rarely recite too much about how the mechanism is to be applied, since to do so would be inconsistent with the nature of such a mechanism. A more formal mechanism is Alternative Dispute Resolution (ADR). This is a mediation-based method within a structured process, involving a third party overseer with or without an imposed outcome, depending on the chosen method. ADR usually does not preclude further resource to arbitration or litigation in the event that no settlement is reached between the parties and for this reason is popular[1]. Although many disputes are nowadays being resolved through negotiation, historically, court litigation has been the medium of choice to settle disputes based on the value of money involved and the assumption that a court judgment would give certainty. Nevertheless, for the reasons outlined below, litigation may not be the most suitable method to serve the needs of the industry players.

1   Some parties prefer to group the dispute resolutions into 'finally determinative' where the outcome is binding (such as arbitration, litigation, and expert determination) as opposed to 'temporarily determinative' (such as negotiation or mediation).

Litigation

3.360   In the event that a dispute arises between those engaged in the oil and gas industry and they have no agreed contractual provision for dispute resolution, it will be referred to the national courts to be resolved by litigation. Due to the international nature of the oil and gas industry, contracting parties are usually domiciled in different countries and usually have most if not all their assets and property in the country of domicile. The main concern for a company facing such a dispute is the prospect of the litigation taking place in the courts of a foreign country, where proceedings will be conducted in a foreign language and in line with a foreign system of laws. For many there is a worry that a foreign court may have a level of xenophobia against a foreign company. To exemplify this point, in 2009 Chevron issued an arbitration claim against the government of Ecuador citing violations of the country's obligations under the United States-Ecuador Bilateral Investment Treaty, investment agreements and international law. The general counsel for Chevron observed that:

> 'Because Ecuador's judicial system is incapable of functioning independently of political influence, Chevron has no choice but to seek relief under the treaty between the United States and Ecuador.'

This case is still pending to date[1]. The only practical way to overcome the xenophobic issue is to insert an arbitration clause in the draft contract.

1   Order on Plaintiff's Motion for a Temporary Restraining Order (09/02/2011) available via www.chevron.com/Ecuador.

3.361   In litigation, the parties involved have no control over the timeline of the process. Therefore, a dispute may not be resolved for a great length of time, during which the expenses involved will continue to spiral higher. As the parties have no control over the appointment of the judge, they will suffer uncertainty and worry that the judge and court involved may lack the necessary expertise to deal with the nature of the dispute. Time may be wasted in conveying the relevant knowledge or by referring the matter to a third party for an expert opinion. In addition, litigation is usually public and all the proceedings and judgments will be recorded publicly. Depending on the nature of the dispute, this could be potentially damaging to the company's reputation and affect their investor relations and market shares. It would allow potential competitors an insight into the company's contract and perhaps give them a competitive edge in future bids. Moreover, the judgment in litigation can usually be appealed at first instance so there may not be immediate closure for a company and consequent greater expense. For the reasons outlined, litigation may not be a promising route to provide a clear jurisdictional path for resolving disputes in the oil and gas industry. However, litigation may be the preferred option available to parties, depending on whether the sums of money involved are considerable or if any other dispute resolution processes have been agreed upon. There have been a number of key cases where litigation has been used. For example, *Amoco (UK) Exploration Co v Teesside Gas Transportation Ltd*[1] where litigation was the preferred choice and resulted in a House of Lords judgment overturning a decision made in favour of the respondent in the Court of Appeal. The case revolved around the commencement date in a capacity reservation and transportation agreement. The significance of the commencement date was that the respondent would at that point become obliged to accept and redeliver the gas and make, send or pay payments at a rate of $8 million per quarter, whether it used the capacity or not. A further example is the judgment in *BHP Billiton Petroleum Ltd v Dalmine SpA*[2] concerning the supply of pipe for a sub-sea gas pipeline from a gas field in Morecambe Bay, near Liverpool, to shore, where part of the pipe was discovered to be metallurgically defective; Dalmine admitted the defects and having submitted fraudulent inspection reports with intent to deceive.

1   [2001] UKHL 18.
2   [2002] EWHC 970 (Comm).

3.362   Nevertheless, choosing ADR over litigation does not mean that litigation will not eventually occur. It is sometimes necessary to have a decision from the court on a point of law, on a protective or injunctive remedy or when an order is necessary[1].

1   See *Regia Autonoma De Electricitate Renel v Gulf Petroleum International Ltd* [1996] 2 All ER 319, (1996) 1 Lloyd's Rep 67.

Arbitration[1]

3.363   In the oil and gas industry, the parties' relationships are characterised by long-term agreements where success is highly dependent on co-operation. Arbitration has become the principal method of dispute resolution in the industry, especially when there is an international contract spanning many countries. However, the decision is not made in a vacuum and there are several major factors, such as the nature of disputes, the identity of the parties, the choice of forum and choice of law, the scope of the arbitration and the location of assets which must be considered while designing the arbitration clause. Arbitration can be defined as the resolution of disputes between two or more parties through a voluntary or a contractually required hearing with determination by an impartial third party. The main attractions for using arbitration are:

- **The underlying principle of party autonomy**: Parties can decide in which country the arbitration will take place, the legal seat (the *lex arbitri*), and the language to be used for the purpose of the dispute hearing. In other words, arbitration provides the parties with neutrality and relative flexibility to resolve the disputes privately outside a national court system, although this flexibility is limited by the extent that it needs to be associated with a legal system. The parties will decide whether to follow an ad hoc arbitration or an institutional arbitration. Institutional arbitration will be administered by an arbitral institute such as the International Chamber of Commerce (ICC) in Paris or the London Court of International Arbitration (LCIA). Ad hoc arbitration gives the parties freedom to decide on every aspect of the procedure. It must be noted that in contracts providing for institutional arbitration, it is likely that the standard arbitration clause will be used. Parties should refrain from any introduction of changes to the institutional rules (although allowed by some institutions); arbitration can be refused if parties alter the rules considered essential for institutional arbitration[2]. For ad hoc arbitration a party can either use the United Nations Commission on International Trade Law (UNCITRAL) model clause in line with the UNCITRAL Rules or write their own. In England, where London is increasingly becoming a popular, preferred arbitration location, arbitration in the LCIA will be subject to the English Arbitration Act 1996. Scotland now has its own Arbitration Act 2010 which it is hoped will contribute to making Scotland an attractive place for dispute resolution by providing a 'modern, impartial and efficient arbitration regime'; whether that will prove to be the case remains to be seen. If parties wish to use ad hoc arbitration and write their own standard clauses, they should take a high level of care and preferably refrain from making changes to institutional rules as the arbiter[3] may refuse to administer the arbitration if the parties have changed the very essence of arbitration to the point that it no longer functions[4].
- **Choice of arbiter**: Arbitration is attractive to those in the oil and gas industry, as the parties can choose a neutral arbiter or tribunal or arbiters based on their specialist knowledge. In litigation there is always the worry that a court will not have the necessary expertise and experience. The tribunal's decision will be binding on the parties and is final, so there is no right of appeal unless otherwise agreed by the parties[5].
- **Privacy and confidentiality**: These are of paramount importance to the industry, not only with respect to the final award, but also in relation to information generated or produced in the course of proceedings. In some cases, parties may wish by the very existence of arbitration to be protected by an obligation of confidentiality[6]. However, identifying and defining the extent of any obligation of confidentiality in arbitral proceedings has proved to be surprisingly controversial. For example, if arbitration is private and litigation is public, how does this private/public dichotomy resolve itself when a party to arbitration seeks to challenge

or to enforce an arbitral decision in court? The status of an arbitral award is something that only the courts can determine. If, therefore, the judge gives a reasoned decision for enforcing or refusing to enforce an arbitrator's award, there is a serious potential for the details of the arbitration to leak out, meaning that confidentiality in those matters can be lost[7]. This is notwithstanding that English courts are distinguished by following a strict confidentiality policy. Irrespective of the fact that no final formulation of the confidentiality obligation can be found in case law, it is generally recognised that under English common law there is an enforceable and implied duty of confidentiality arising out of the nature of arbitration whereby the arbitral proceedings must be privately conducted and subject to the duty of confidentiality[8].

- **Enforceability**: Under the New York Convention on the Recognition and Enforcement of Foreign Arbitral Awards 1958, arbitral awards are enforceable in most trading nations across the world. A national court may, however, refuse to recognise an award if the process or law used to reach the award does not conform to the procedure and law of the seat, in line with Article V, para 1 of the Convention. It is generally seen that an arbitral award is more enforceable for international contracts than a court award, and that courts do not like to interfere with such determinations[9].

1   It is beyond the scope of this book to present the academic debate on whether arbitration should be grouped as a form of ADR or not. This book treats arbitration as a distinctive form of dispute resolution, hence the following discussion on ADR excludes arbitration.
2   For example, in *Iran Aircraft Indus v Avco Corp* 980 F 2d 141, 145 (2d Cir 1992), the ICC refused to administer arbitration proceedings as arbitral clauses.
3   In England, and internationally in the English speaking world (apart from Scotland), an arbiter is known as an 'arbitrator'.
4   This is evident in the US Lower Federal Court in *Iran Aircraft Industries v Avco Corp* 980 F 2d 141 (2d Cir 1992).
5   Arbitration Act 1996, s 58(1).
6   See for example the discussion in *Esso Australia Resources Ltd v Plowman* (1995) 183 CLR 10.
7   See for example the discussion in *Department of Economic Policy and Development of the City of Moscow v Bankers Trust Co* [2004] EWCA Civ 314, [2005] QB 207.
8   *Dolling-Baker v Merrett* [1990] 1 WLR 1205, [1991] 2 All ER 890; *Ali Shipping Corp v Shipyard Trogir* [1999] 1 WLR 314, [1998] 1 Lloyd's Rep 643; *Fraser v Thames Television* [1984] QB 44, [1983] 2 WLR 917.
9   As it was held in *Emmott v Michael Wilson & Partners Ltd* [2008] EWCA Civ 184, [2008] Bus LR 1361 that judicial interference 'should be kept to a minimum and the proper role of the court was to support the arbitral process rather than review it'.

3.364   In addition, arbitration is perceived generally to be faster and less expensive than litigation and can lead to a more tailored and creative conclusion to suit the parties' interests than litigation. Arbitration has been utilised in many high profile oil and gas cases[1] and is also used in industry and company standard contracts and model clauses. For example, under the Model Form International Operating Agreement prepared by the Association of International Petroleum Negotiators, which has become the seminal model for forming JOAs for international development throughout the world, the parties can choose ADR and arbitration for dispute settlement. The litigation option was removed from the model form as it was rarely used.

1 For example, *BP Exploration Co (Libya) Ltd v Government of Libyan Arab Republic* 53 ILR 297 (1979); *Texaco Overseas Petroleum Co and California Asiatic Oil Co v Government of Libyan Arab Republic* 53 ILR 389 (1979); *Kuwait v American Independent Oil Co (Aminoil)* 21 ILM 976 (1982); *Libyan American Oil Co (LIAMCO) v Government of the Libyan Arab Republic* 62 ILR 140 (1977).

3.365 Another example is under the UK Seaward Area Petroleum production module, Clause 43, which states that disputes between the minister and the licensee arising under or by virtue of the licence shall be referred to arbitration comprised of a single arbitrator appointed by Lord Chief Justice of England or the Lord President of the Court of Session (depending on the location of the licensed area)[1].

1 The Petroleum (Current Model Clauses) Order 1999, SI 1999/160, the Petroleum Licensing (Exploration and Production) (Seward and Landward Areas) Regulations 2004, SI 2004/352, Sch 1, para 21, the Petroleum Licensing (Production) (Seaward Areas) Regulations 2008, SI 2008/225, Sch 1, para 43.

3.366 However, large companies who are often involved in joint ventures may be reluctant to engage in arbitration with each other and occasionally prefer a different method to resolve disputes. Moreover, in the event of arbitration against a government, there is a high risk that there will be retaliation and hence arbitration may not be the best option. It is argued that arbitration is time consuming, expensive and can be equally as formal as litigation. It can involve procedural complexity, unpredictability and legal challenges to jurisdiction or competence of proceedings[1]. Dispute resolution clauses may, however, provide for ADR before arbitration is utilised[2].

1 *Petroleos de Portugal and Petrogal SA v BP Oil International* [1999] 1 Lloyd's Rep 854.
2 Arbitration Act 1996, s 12.

Alternative dispute resolution (ADR)

3.367 ADR is a collective term for the range of procedures that serve as alternatives to litigation for the resolution of civil disputes with the assistance of a neutral and impartial third party. The courts recognise the benefits of ADR, and if appropriate, the parties may be referred to ADR. For example, *Emmott v Michael Williams & Partners Ltd*[1] clearly showed the court's support for, and reluctance to intervene in, the arbitral process. *O'Donoghue v Enterprise Inns plc*[2] demonstrated the willingness of the court to uphold the arbitrator's decision provided that there have been no serious irregularities. Further evidence of the court's support is found in the Civil Procedure Rules 1998 (CPR)[3] r 1.4(2):

'Active case management includes … (e) encouraging the parties to use an alternative dispute resolution procedure if the court considers that appropriate and facilitating the use of such procedure'[4].

1   [2008] EWCA Civ 184, [2008] Bus LR 1361.
2   [2008] EWHC 2273 (Ch), [2009] 1 P & CR 14.
3   SI 1998/3132.
4   See also Part 36: both are available in full via www.legislation.gov.uk/uksi/1998/3132/contents/made (accessed 17 January 2013).

3.368   In addition, a party can seek a stay of proceedings for ADR to take place under CPR 26.4(1):

> 'A party may, when filing the completed allocation questionnaire, make a written request for the proceedings to be stayed while the parties try to settle the case by alternative dispute resolution or other means'[1].

1   Also, the Arbitration Act 1996, ss 9 and 12 provide similar rules.

3.369   Furthermore, the Pre-Action Protocols[1] under the CPR 1998 stipulate that:

> 'Starting proceedings should usually be a step of last resort, and proceedings should not normally be started when a settlement is still actively being explored. Although ADR is not compulsory, the parties should consider whether some form of ADR procedure might enable them to settle the matter without starting proceedings. The court may require evidence that the parties considered some form of ADR.'

The LOGIC standard contract has developed clauses for the resolution of disputes and addressing the processes by adopting an escalating approach whereby disputes are initially dealt with by an informal ADR mechanism, for example through negotiation or mediation between representatives from each party, before looking at more formal ADR mechanisms such as expert determination or arbitration[2].

1   Section III (8) available via www.justice.gov.uk/civil/procrules_fin/contents/practice_directions/pd_pre-action_conduct.htm#IDANBFT (accessed 17 January 2013).
2   LOGIC standard contracts are available at www.logic-oil.com/standard-contracts/documents (accessed 16 January 2013).

Expert determination[1]

3.370   This method is widely used in the oil and gas industry as a dispute resolution mechanism where the issue is primarily technical or commercial in nature. In the Unitisation and Unit Operating Agreement (UUOA) in addition to JOAs it has become common industry practice to use expert determination for the resolution of disputes pertaining to redeterminations and field extensions which may impact track participation[2].

1   Arbitration and expert determination both result in binding judgments, and therefore it is arguable whether these should be referred to as ADR methods or not.
2   For example, in *Odebrecht Oil & Gas Services Ltd v North Sea Productions Ltd* [1999] Adj LR 05/10 a performance bond accompanying a conservation contract for a motor tanker indicated expert determination to investigate the alleged breach of the contract and assess the damage.

3.371   When this method is provided for in the contract, there will be other forms of resolution for addressing non-technical issues. The contract should define technical and non-technical issues to ensure that there is no ambiguity at the time of any dispute.

3.372   Expert determination allows for the appointment of an 'expert' to determine the outcome of disputes. The expert is agreed between the parties and is usually selected according to the nature of the dispute. The parties may decide on a method the expert must follow and insist that the reason behind a determination be revealed[1]. A determination may be made in a matter of minutes or a few weeks, but it is generally faster than a dispute going through the national court. The expert's determination is final and binding on the parties unless the contract provides for procedures for appeal to a competent court. In terms of enforceability, as in domestic determinations, it is only binding as a matter of contract. However, in international disputes, unlike an arbitration award for example, expert determinations do not benefit from enforceability under the New York Convention 1958 but may benefit from limited circumstances where bilateral recognition and enforcement treaties exist. Therefore, due to the significant costs of certain operations in the oil and gas industry, expert determination may not be suitable for overseas or highly complex disputes involving very large sums of money.

1   *Halifax Life Ltd v Equitable Life Assurance Society* [2007] EWHC 503 (Comm), [2007] 1 Lloyd's Rep 528.

3.373   Expert determination can be set aside only on limited grounds where there has been fraud or manifest error. There have been numerous cases where the definition of manifest error has been articulated: 'oversights and blunders so obvious as to admit of no difference in the opinion'[1]. Manifest error is restricted to cases where the expert has substantially deviated from his instructions[2], such as using different software from that stipulated in the contract[3] or if the expert has valued machinery himself when the instructions were to employ a separate, independent expert of his choice to value machinery or assets[4].

1   *Conoco (UK) Ltd v Phillips Petroleum* (19 August 1996, unreported).
2   *Jones v Sherwood Computer Services plc* [1992] 1 WLR 277.
3   *Shell UK Ltd v Enterprise Oil plc* [1999] 2 Lloyd's Rep 456.
4   *Jones (M) v Jones (RR)* [1971] 1 WLR 840.

3.374   In general, expert determination is a useful method to resolve oil and gas disputes due to expeditious proceedings, reduced costs, its binding nature and privacy. However, it is always advisable to consider carefully the nature and value of the dispute and the location of the parties before adopting this method.

Negotiation

3.375   This is perhaps the most common and basic dispute resolution approach in the oil and gas industry before any adjudicatory or non-adjudicatory mechanism can be applied. Negotiation is more informal than other forms of ADR and is primarily used where the relationship between the parties is equally as important as the resolution of the dispute. There are essentially three forms of negotiation strategy. The first is hard negotiation, where a commercial position is adopted by leaning on the opponent until they give in, with both sides starting in extreme positions, withholding their true views and making small concessions only to keep the negotiations moving. This strategy is extremely time-consuming, and can often keep both sides from achieving a compromise. The second type is soft negotiation, in which the relationship is valued by giving in to avoid being caught up in a non-negotiable position. Neither is practically suitable for oil and gas disputes.

3.376 A third alternative to these negotiation methods is a model developed by Fisher and Ury[1], which is the principled negotiation, where the main strength lies in the fact that it is hard on problems, but soft on people. Principled negotiation focuses on the merits of the situation rather than the differences that may exist between the two parties involved. This problem-solving approach involves the negotiator trying to resolve the dispute by suggesting resolutions that may be to the advantage of both parties by separating them from the problem, emphasising the importance of dealing with the parties and the need to handle the situation wisely. The negotiator does not take or adopt a position but seeks to overcome what may already be an entrenched position by developing a large range of possible solutions to the dispute. The criteria then used to select the resolution are separate from personal emotions and should be objective and fair[2]. The proposed resolution is described as a wise agreement which should be efficiently reached, and at the very least it should be distinguished by not damaging, but hopefully further advancing, the relationship between the parties. Such an approach seeks to overcome the situation where the negotiating parties become immersed in the positions they have taken to the detriment of focusing on the interest they have in resolving the dispute. Adversarial, inconsiderate and strained situations can thus be avoided or minimised and professional relationships can be revived on the basis of accurate perceptions, good communication and sensible emotions, with a forward looking objective approach. In this approach, the problem encountered would be contained and the greater, more comprehensive benefit of mutual agreement and peaceful resolution would enable parties to sustain their relationship. Many other mutual interests may also be uncovered as a result of this process. The result can be binding if it results in a contract agreement that reflects negotiations, although it is unlikely that the courts will view negotiation as a means to stay proceedings in exercising active case management.

1 Fisher, Ury and Patton, *Getting to Yes: Negotiating an Agreement Without Giving In* (2nd edn, 1991).
2 Fisher, Ury and Patton, *Getting to Yes: Negotiating an Agreement Without Giving In*.

3.377 These approaches are not the only ones. There are degrees of approaches in between, as in fact during the course of a negotiation or series of negotiation the approach may alter, perhaps several times. One side may use one approach, and the other another. The question of which approach to use will vary according to a number of factors including the relative bargaining position of the parties. Many contracts in the oil and gas industry provide for dispute negotiation. For example, within the LOGIC standard form contract[1], a three-level negotiation approach is provided before proceeding to ADR processes. It has an escalated clause approach whereby disputes are initially dealt with by the representatives from each party; if no agreement is reached it then escalates to persons nominated in the form of agreement; then if no resolution is reached it will escalate to more senior negotiation at executive level. Executive negotiation is often used in industry contracts as part of an escalating disputes resolution process. The advantage of this is that it takes the dispute out of the hands of those who work together in the contract activity on a day-to-day basis, thus helping to maintain good working relationships. If the executive negotiation fails then either party can take the dispute to court, but only if the first stages have been completed.

1   Available at www.logic-oil.com/standard-contracts/documents (accessed 16 January 2013).

3.378 The main advantages of negotiation are that disputants remain in control of the process, negotiated resolutions tend to have greater durability, reduced management of time and costs, confidentiality, and since negotiators were not involved in the original conflict, they have sufficient personal and emotional distance which allows impartiality.

3.379 In terms of enforceability, unlike litigation or a foreign arbitral award, the agreement to negotiate has traditionally been unenforceable due to the uncertainty of it having any binding force[1]. In *Walford v Miles*[2] a company agreed to be bound into negotiations with another company and to be bound with negotiations with any third party. However, there was neither indication of how long the two companies were obliged to continue to negotiate for, nor were there indications of what, if anything, would end that obligation. The court held that an agreement to negotiate for an unspecified period was unenforceable.

1   *Courtney & Fairbairn Ltd v Tolaini Brothers (Hotels) Ltd* [1975] 1 WLR 297, CA.
2   [1992] 2 AC 128, HL.

Mediation

3.380 Mediation is an extension of direct negotiation and is also often referred to as a structured negotiation. It is a process where a neutral person is appointed to act as an intermediary between the negotiating parties. Mediation is usually initiated by the parties to the dispute but it can also be initiated by the courts and operated outside the judicial system. The mediator will typically talk to the parties to form an understanding of their respective positions. This will then enable the mediator to try to identify stumbling blocks to a settlement and help to explore solutions. The mediator does not have any power to proscribe a solution. The role is to bring the two parties to an amicable settlement.

3.381 The main advantages of mediation over litigation are the timely proceedings, decreased cost, confidentiality and privacy, flexibility in terms of the degree of control enjoyed by the parties over the process and outcome. Mediation does not set precedents but each case can be treated on its own merit depending on the circumstances and the best solution for the parties, and either party can withdraw at any point whereby settlements cannot be unilaterally imposed. Mediation methods include facilitative and evaluative, transformative, and narrative, allowing advantages over litigation as the parties agree on structure and process. Whereas conciliation is usually more evaluative, mediation is a process which is more consensual in its approach and the mediator does not express an opinion and does not make any recommendations. However, in some instances parties in the oil and gas industry agree on evaluative mediators with specialist knowledge of the industry, in which case recommendations may be made. Although the parties concerned are not bound by any recommendations, such a process does set the scene for both parties to progress with greater understanding towards an agreed outcome. In most cases the mediator is not required to be an expert or to provide a determination on the matter. They will act as a non-adversarial neutral person who helps the parties objectively reach a negotiated agreement.

3.382 In terms of enforceability, traditionally common law courts refused to enforce mediation agreements on the grounds of uncertainty, seeking to oust the jurisdiction of the courts, and provision of inadequate remedies. In order to be enforceable, the contract term must be certain. However, the position of contractual certainty for the parties to refer the dispute to mediation has been upheld: where there was a clear intention of the parties to use litigation as the last resort, an ADR clause was not an agreement to negotiate and public policy supported enforcing the ADR clause[1]. The courts in the UK may grant a stay of proceedings pending the outcome of any mediation process that has been entered into. This has been evidenced in various cases, including *Channel Tunnel Group Ltd v Balfour Beatty Construction Ltd*[2]. The refusal to take part in mediation is also an important legal issue and a number of cases demonstrate this, including the judgment of the Court of Appeal in *Dunnett v Railtrack plc*[3], where it was stated that mediation may sometimes be able to provide a better outcome and solution than is within the power of the courts to provide. In the case of *Hurst v Leeming*[4] a clearer line was drawn, defining the application of *Dunnett* principle in that the courts will not be willing to permit matters to proceed to arbitration or litigation if mediation is seen as a reasonable means of dispute resolution. What may appear to be outside the boundaries of being resolved by mediation has often proved otherwise if the parties concerned choose to enter into ADR and mediation in particular. That said, there is also case law to demonstrate that the courts will not support the use of ADR in a non-discriminatory fashion as was demonstrated by *Halsey v Milton Keynes General NHS Trust*[5]. In terms of enforceability, unlike foreign arbitral awards, mediation lacks international enforceability. Therefore, those engaged in the oil and gas business prefer to use mediation as part of a multi-tiered dispute resolution clause rather than as a primary method for resolving disputes.

1   *Cable & Wireless plc v IBM United Kingdom Ltd* [2002] EWHC 2059 (Comm).
2   [1993] AC 334, [1993] 2 WLR 262, HL.
3   [2002] EWCA Civ 303, [2002] 1 WLR 2434.
4   [2002] EWHC 1051 (Ch), [2003] 1 Lloyd's Rep 379.
5   [2004] EWCA Civ 576, [2004] 1 WLR 3002.

Multi-tiered dispute resolution clauses

3.383   The current trend in the oil and gas industry indicates an increased use of multi-tiered dispute resolution processes, especially in international contracts. The process involves resolving disputes through clauses which provide different dispute resolution processes at distinct and escalating stages. The multi-tiered dispute resolution clause may take various forms. For example, in *Thames Valley Power Ltd v Total Gas & Power Ltd*[1] a long-term gas supply agreement provided a three-tiered dispute resolution clause. After service of written notice of dispute, the parties agreed to meet and use all reasonable endeavours to resolve that dispute or difference in good faith. In the event that a dispute between the parties was not resolved it would be referred for decision to an independent expert. Finally, in the event that no expert could be appointed or procedures could not be implemented the dispute could be referred by either party to arbitration pursuant to the Arbitration Act 1996.

1   [2005] EWHC 2208 (Comm), [2006] 1 Lloyd's Rep 441.

3.384   Moreover, the LOGIC General Conditions of Contract (including guidance note) for Services (On-and-Off-shore)[1] Clause 30 and the Supply of Major Items of Plant and Equipment[2] Clause 36 provide examples of tiered dispute resolution clauses. In brief, the process is to refer the dispute initially to company representatives for discussion and reasonable efforts to reach an agreement. If no agreement is reached, the dispute is then referred to the two persons named in the appendix to the contract. If, again, no agreement is reached, the dispute is referred to executive negotiation consisting of the managing directors of the companies. The court is the final dispute resolution recourse. However, the parties have freedom to agree to use arbitration as an ADR method, especially in cases where an international marine element is involved.

1   2003, Edition 2, available via www.logic-oil.com/standard-contracts/documents.
2   2005, Edition 2, available via www.logic-oil.com/standard-contracts/documents.

3.385   A further example is a contract for the provision of a Floating Production, Storage and Offloading (FPSO) installation in the North Sea. It was originally signed in 1996 and included a chapter on the resolution of disputes. The procedure was designed to solve disputes without the use of any form of arbitration or litigation. Instead, the contract called for disputes to be resolved by a hybrid, escalating process of negotiation, followed by executive negotiation and culminating in the use of expert determination. Under the relevant clause of the contract, disputes were first to be discussed by the client and contractor representatives. These positions were defined in the contract and persons duly appointed in writing. If they were unable to resolve the issue then it would be passed to the next level of management, senior or director level, and they would attempt to negotiate a settlement. If this subsequently failed to produce a resolution, then the two sides would jointly appoint an expert to decide the dispute. The process was laid out in 14-day blocks with that period being the time each stage had to carry out its function. However, the stumbling block for the whole process was that there was no agreement in the contract for the parties to be bound by the findings of the expert (ie 'the company was not duty bound to accept the determination and, if this was the case the contractor could resort to litigation'). The latter position could defeat the whole process as it allowed the client, but not the contractor, to disregard the whole process as laid down in the contract. This particular contract illustrates the need to ensure that the agreed process, whatever that might be, also includes an agreement, binding on both parties, to accept the end result, whatever that might be.

3.386   In terms of enforceability, whether the parties are only entitled to comply with the sequence of dispute resolution methods set out in the clause or whether they are also under a legal obligation to do so, is initially dependent on the wording of such clause. The effect of failure to comply with pre-arbitral requirements under the multi-tiered process may be that jurisdiction over the dispute does not pass to the arbitral tribunal. If a party raises an objection to this effect, the arbitral tribunal will decide the jurisdictional question, relying on authorities under the competence-competence principle[1].

1   Doug Jones, 'Dealing with Multi-tiered Dispute Resolution Process' (2009) 75(2) Arbitration 188.

3.387   The oil and gas industry seeks fast and cost-effective resolution of disputes with the least amount of impact on operations and relationships between the industry participants. A preferred conflict management strategy would employ lower cost processes where the disputants have greater control, such as negotiation or mediation, before turning to more costly processes such as arbitration or litigation. Adopting litigious proceedings is potentially very expensive, adversarial and lengthy and all parties involved lose their right to confidentiality. In addition, in terms of enforcing the judgment overseas this option may not be suitable unless bilateral recognition and enforcement treaties exist between the parties' countries of dispute. Therefore, oil and gas players tend to opt for an agreed dispute resolution method other than litigation. Arbitration is often less expensive than litigation but this is not always the case. Its advantages over litigation are that proceedings are not public and the enforceability of a foreign arbitral award under the New York Convention 1958 is allowed. Despite its disadvantages, arbitration remains a popular choice for dispute resolution in the industry.

3.388   The current trend of the industry indicates that arbitration and litigation are used as a last resort after exhausting more informal and/or formal ADR options. It is more common to opt for an agreed dispute resolution process in the form of multi-tiered choice of methods which usually include negotiation, mediation, expert determination and finally arbitration. The primary benefits of using a multi-tiered process are to improve efficiency and lower the cost of the dispute resolution process. This acts as a filtering process, where only serious and complex disputes are resolved by arbitration and less complicated disputes are addressed at a lower level, therefore saving time, energy and money. By shifting the resolution of disputes to adopting a sequence of ADR proceedings aimed at co-operation, future relationships between the parties are preserved.

3.389   However, there may be a limit to the extent to which industry players can design their own models of dispute resolution, especially in international contracts. For example, if a foreign legal system regulates a specific type of business, the law there will dictate the type of dispute resolution process to be used. In addition, dispute resolution clauses, except agreement to negotiate, can be enforced and the courts would grant stay of proceedings if the process has not been followed. However, it is important to draft unambiguous and certain clauses in order to ensure they are enforceable.

Part 4

The future of UKCS

4.1   The UKCS is that area of the North Sea (the North Sea is shared with Netherlands, Norway and Denmark) in which the UK exercises its sovereign rights over natural resources

'The UKCS has the potential to satisfy close to 50 per cent of the UK's oil and gas demand in 2020 if the current rate of investment is sustained'[1].

1   Oil and Gas UK 2012 Economic Report.

4.2   A state which possesses hydrocarbons within its continental shelf will no doubt want to exercise control over how these resources are depleted, for a number of reasons including the security of its energy supplies, the revenue to be accrued from such exploitation and the employment opportunities for its citizens associated with such exploration and exploitation. Since the UK was the third largest gas and second largest oil producer in Europe, and 19th largest in the world for both oil and gas[1], this chapter considers the extent of the advantages available to the UK over the next few years/decades and how this should be sustained in the long run.

1   BP Statistical Review of World Energy 2012.

A   OVERVIEW OF THE UKCS

4.3   The business environment in which a company or an industry operates is no doubt very important, the oil and gas industry being no exception. In assessing the UKCS one would have to consider the political, economic, social, technological, environmental and legal factors.

4.4   It is no news that the UKCS is a mature or maturing province[1], irrespective of the parameters used. As production and exploration of a province continues, so its proven and probable reserves decline. The UK, it is estimated, has over the last 45 years produced a cumulative amount of more than 41 billion barrels of oil equivalent (boe) of oil and gas and is estimated[2] to still have recoverable hydrocarbons between 15 and 24 billion boe of oil and gas, most of which is located offshore, ie on the UKCS. Oil production peaked in 1999, with gas a year later. Since then, UK production has been in steady decline. It was 1.3 billion boe in 2005, but in 2011 the UK produced 656 million boe (a reduction of almost 50% from 2005). That is 19.2% from the 812 million boe produced in 2010, which is the biggest year-on-year reduction ever recorded. The effect of this reduction has been felt by the UK economy as a whole. The government was forced to reduce its forecast of tax receipts from the UKCS by £2.2 billion in 2011, despite oil prices being higher than anticipated. Output of oil and natural gas liquids (NGLs) fell by 17.5%. This shortfall is the biggest year-on-year drop since the Piper Alpha disaster in 1988. Gas production also suffered, falling by an unprecedented 21.6%. As stated above, the UKCS is a mature basin, but these reductions are much larger than economists expected[3].

1   A mature province is one which has developed its hydrocarbon regime extensively, with a profile that is usually characterised by declining production, declining average new field size and increasing costs.
2   Oil and Gas UK *2012 Economic Report*.
3   Considering that between 2004 and 2010, the average year-on-year decline in production was 7.5% (6.6% for oil and NGLs and 8.6% for gas), see Oil and Gas UK *2012 Economic Report*.

4.5   This decline is largely based on the fact that several of the oil and gas fields discovered in the 1970s, like Brent, Forties and Ninian, which have consistently produced large quantities of oil and gas[1] in addition to the other producing fields on the UKCS are now mature with new discoveries[2] being typically a tenth to a hundredth of the mature fields[3]. Moreover, according to Oil and Gas UK, a variety of other factors contributed to the production decline in 2011, some of which were force majeure. These are outlined below.

1   Having average reserves of 500mmboe.
2   Having average reserves of 26mmboe although the Buzzard, Lochnager and Jasmine fields it is estimated have reserves totalling more than 1 billion boe.
3   Oil and Gas UK *2012 Economic Report*.

Health and safety

4.6   In February 2011 the Gryphon FPSO broke anchor chains and was docked for the remainder of the year for repairs. Gryphon and its satellite fields (Tullich and Maclure) are both subsea tie-backs were therefore unable to produce the 1.2% of the UK's oil and gas production that they contributed in 2010. The combined production of Brent Alpha, Bravo and Charlie in 2011 was 72% below the 28.7 thousand boepd seen a year earlier. These depressed production figures followed a shutdown in February after a platform fender was found on the seabed near the main export pipeline. The extended shutdown of Brent Charlie also had ramifications for the Penguins cluster, a collection of subsea developments that in 2010 sent 9.2 thousand boepd to Brent Charlie for processing. The Penguins cluster has been shut since January 2011.

Political

4.7   The Rhum field has substantial recoverable reserves in place and in 2010 it accounted for 1.8% of domestic gas production. The two participants in the field, BP and the Iranian National Oil Company, each have a 50% equity share. Due to EU sanctions against Iran, the government mandated the shutdown of the field in November 2010 and the field remains closed.

Fiscal regime

4.8   Due to the current over-supply in the world market, it is expected that the oil price will remain unstable during the next few years. It is also opined that these price fluctuations will make it more difficult to access new investment, with investors adopting cautious behaviour in such unstable and unpredictable market conditions. Against these considerations, the ultimate effect is that it will also make it harder for the UKCS to compete internationally in attracting new investment, given the high cost of operating in this mature oil and gas province, combined with the small size of new field developments, something which needs to be addressed through the fiscal regime and accommodated by the government. However, the 2006 supplementary tax charge increased to 20% projects approved in 2008 and 2009 should now be contributing to production, but the reserves associated with 2008 and 2009 were much smaller than previous and subsequent years which has left 2011 production rates exposed. The impact of fiscal change on future investment decisions is not instantaneous. There is invariably a time lag before any consequences for field approvals are seen. The 2006 tax change is likely to be a factor behind the low volumes approved for development in 2008 and 2009, which is now manifesting itself in lower production in 2011. Furthermore, Centrica cited the 2011 Budget[1] as a reason for keeping the South Morecambe field closed following summer maintenance in 2011. South Morecambe is an important field which accounted for almost 6% of domestic gas production in 2010.

1   When the supplementary charge increased to 32%.

Increased maintenance activity

4.9   The Budget in March 2011 coincided with warmer than normal weather which continued through April, causing gas demand to fall by 17.8% and affecting gas prices. These factors will have encouraged gas producers to reduce output, or bring maintenance forward where possible.

Reliance upon ageing infrastructure

4.10   The use of existing infrastructure to transport a constant, reliable flow of hydrocarbons to shore will be a key issue for the industry in the years ahead. Around 60% of new field developments in 2011 were subsea tie-backs to existing infrastructure, and a significant amount of infrastructure in the UKCS is over 30 years old. In July 2010 the Health and Safety Executive

(HSE) launched its KP45 programme, focusing inspection effort on ageing assets. It is possible that this, allied with the need for constant vigilance with maintenance work, could have adversely affected production rates.

An increase in the number of planned and unplanned shutdowns

4.11 Generally, oil and gas asset maintenance programmes are planned for the summer months when the weather is better and demand, at least for gas, is lower. There is an inverse correlation between production and the number of fields not producing in a given month. As the number of shutdowns per month increases, production of oil and gas decreases.

4.12 Following from the above, the number of new developments regularly required to replace and replenish the depleted oil and gas reserves of the older fields is much lower as smaller fields generally require a significant amount of managerial effort when compared to the anticipated rewards of such fields[1]. Where such new fields are located near existing infrastructure, the costs of producing oil and gas will be considerably reduced although this is not always the case, for example a few gas fields on the west of Shetland where such field is described as economically and geographically stranded[2].

1 AG Kemp, 'Current Economic Issues in the Maturing UKCS' in G Gordon and J Paterson (eds) *Oil and Gas Law: Current Practice and Emerging Trends* (2007).
2 DECC, Oil and gas: infrastructure at www.gov.uk/oil-and-gas-infrastructure. For a further discussion please see U Vass, 'Access to Infrastructure' in G Gordon and J Paterson (eds) *Oil and Gas Law: Current Practice and Emerging Trends* (2007).

B CURRENT OUTLOOK OF THE UK OFFSHORE OIL AND GAS INDUSTRY

4.13 Over the last 45 years oil and gas production has contributed considerably to tax revenues for the government. During the 2011–12 fiscal year the amount of tax accruing to the government was £11.2 billion, no less than 25% of all corporate taxes. This provides significant economic benefits to the local economies across the UK which are stimulated as a consequence of the economic activity, as well as making a major contribution to national tax revenues[1].

1 Oil and Gas UK 2012 Economic Report.

4.14 But the oil markets and the price of oil cannot be ignored when considering the viability of the UKCS. A stable oil price of over $100 per barrel was a key factor in enabling smaller companies to have the capacity to purchase more assets. However, the maturing nature of the UKCS makes it less appealing for large companies who may have more profitable opportunities in emerging regions elsewhere in the world and will thus tend to want to concentrate on the larger remaining opportunities in the UKCS[1].

1 Oil and Gas UK 2012 Economic Report.

4.15 The upstream oil and gas industry in 2011, according to Oil & Gas UK's figures, continued to invest heavily; a total expenditure of £17 billion was spent overall in the UKCS. This expenditure covered the cost of operating existing assets, the cost of E&A drilling and capital investment in new production. This was around £3 billion more than was spent in 2010 and around £0.5 billion more than Oil & Gas UK's forecast for 2011. Growth in capital investment accounted for most of the increase, having risen to £8.5 billion in 2011 from £6.0 billion in 2010. The cost of operating existing assets stayed broadly similar to 2010, increasing by less than 2%. Despite 30% fewer E&A wells being drilled in 2011, the amount of money spent in this area increased from £1.1 billion to £1.4 billion. This was because of a combination of a tight market causing higher rates for rigs, and more technically demanding wells being drilled, at higher costs as the UKCS matures[1].

1 Oil and Gas UK 2012 Economic Report.

4.16 The average number of active fields not producing in 2011 was 64 fields (each month without production). Occasionally, sudden fall in production such as the one in August 2011 can be explained, especially when one considers that 86 fields produced nothing during the month. For example, Buzzard, as the largest field currently in production on the UKCS, undertook key planned upgrades and unscheduled maintenance during the summer of 2011 which resulted in a 22% fall.

4.17 From the above, it is clear that investment has slowed and the number of large new finds on the UKCS is declining. In fact, as a result of the reserves base being almost the same and the relatively low production in 2011, it is expected that the number of fields in the UKCS will be in operation post-2040 and even until 2050[1]. That is another 30 more years or so, but this also is due to the various government initiatives[2] to spur continuous exploration and production activities, the large scale of decommissioning activities, and the technically and commercially experienced skill and supply chain that have developed over the past four decades. It is opined that much is still to be learnt from the UK offshore oil and gas industry in the near future.

1 Oil and Gas UK 2012 Economic Report.
2 Promote and Frontier Licences; PILOT Vision 2010 and initiatives; voluntary industry Code of Practice on Access to Infrastructure etc.

Guidance on Disputes over Third Party Access to Upstream Oil and Gas Infrastructure

INTRODUCTION

1. Access for developers of offshore oil and gas fields to upstream infrastructure for the purpose of transporting and processing hydrocarbons is a key element in the process of extracting the UK's petroleum resources (see paragraph 9 below). Companies seeking access for their hydrocarbons to such infrastructure must apply in the first instance to the relevant owner[1] of the infrastructure in question.

1 In the rest of this document, "owner" should where the context permits be taken to include owners.

2. There is a voluntary industry *Code of Practice on Access to Upstream Oil and Gas Infrastructure on the UK Continental Shelf* (the "Infrastructure Code of Practice") which sets out principles and procedures to guide all those involved in negotiating third party access to oil and gas infrastructure on the UK Continental Shelf (UKCS). The Department encourages all parties to follow the Infrastructure Code of Practice including the related guidance notes which describe informal escalation procedures.

3. If a third party is unable to agree satisfactory terms of access with the owner of upstream oil and gas infrastructure, the third party seeking such access ("the applicant") can make an application to the Secretary of State to require access to be granted and to determine the terms on which it is to be granted.[1]

1 The relevant legislation is contained in sections 82 to 91 of the Energy Act 2011. The scope of the legislation extends to access to services used for operating upstream petroleum pipelines – for example, metering or allocation services and the provision by the host facility of fuel or power needed to operate third party equipment on or from such a facility. It does not extend "downstream" so, for example, while the Mossmorran Natural Gas Liquids plant and Braefoot Bay *are* covered, the Fife Ethylene Plant is *not*.

4. The Department encourages and expects most issues related to infrastructure access to be resolved in timely commercial negotiation and believes the potential use of the Secretary of State's powers will act as an

183

incentive to such an outcome. Nevertheless, those powers are there to be used in the overall national interest if a commercial solution can genuinely not be found within a reasonable time frame.

5.   This document describes how the Department proposes to handle formal applications under the Energy Act 2011.[1] **It sets out the requirements and obligations on all parties; the approach the Department would take in handling applications; and the principles it would expect to be guided by in determining terms of access.**[2] If the Secretary of State decides that access should be granted he may serve a notice to that effect on the parties. This may allow for connections to be made to the owner's infrastructure; authorise the owner to recover any necessary payments from the applicant; and set out the terms of access.[3]

1   In addition to the informal escalation procedures described in the guidance notes to the Infrastructure Code of Practice, DECC officials are available to play an informal role, at the request of a party, as a mediator/facilitator in disputes to see whether the issues can be resolved by agreement without recourse to the formal regulatory powers available under the relevant legislation.
2   This Guidance is compliant with the eight rules of good guidance in the *Code of Practice on Guidance on Regulation* (BIS, October 2009).
3   In the rest of this document, "terms" should where the context permits be taken to mean "terms and conditions".

6.   In deciding the terms on which access should be granted, the main issue is the need to identify the relevant costs and risks and to decide on fair and appropriate terms. These will have to be decided on a case by case basis.

7.   In circumstances where an application relates to a pipeline which crosses national boundaries, the Secretary of State has a duty to consult the relevant authorities of the other Government before considering an application for dispute settlement himself and to honour any obligations resulting from any treaty covering operational and jurisdictional matters relevant to that pipeline.[1] Where companies are considering an application to settle a dispute regarding access to a particular transboundary pipeline, they are therefore advised to seek early guidance from the Department on the precise nature of the access provisions in the relevant inter-Governmental agreement.

1   Disputes about the various transboundary pipelines are subject to different arrangements according to the respective treaties. In particular, access to a controlled petroleum pipeline subject to the Norwegian access system by virtue of the Framework Agreement concerning cross-boundary petroleum co-operation dated 4th April 2005 and made between the government of the United Kingdom and the government of the Kingdom of Norway is regulated by sections 17GA and 17GB of the Petroleum Act 1998. In some circumstances, a treaty may provide for the Secretary of State to settle a dispute in consultation with the other Government. In others, it may fall to the authorities of the other Government, rather than the Secretary of State, to address any dispute over access to the pipeline.

8.   This document describes the approach the Department expects to take to applications for access to existing pipelines and facilities. Variations to pipeline works authorisations provide a means of seeking access to a pipeline that has not yet been built.

CONTEXT

9. The Government's main objective in operating its petroleum legislation is to ensure the recovery of all economic hydrocarbon reserves taking into account the environmental impact of hydrocarbon development and the need to ensure secure, diverse and sustainable supplies of energy for business and consumers at competitive prices (see paragraphs 44–45 below for more detail). Access to infrastructure and associated services on fair and reasonable terms is crucial to maximising the economic recovery of the UK's oil and, particularly, gas because many fields on the UKCS do not contain sufficient reserves to justify their own infrastructure but are economic as satellite developments utilising existing infrastructure.

10. The investment required to build the infrastructure needed to transport oil and gas from offshore oil and gas fields is characterised by significant costs, significant economies of scale and irreversibility. This can lead to conflict between the efficient use of resources and the wish for greater competition. The efficient use of resources requires no unnecessary duplication of infrastructure while greater competition requires alternative offtake routes to be available to producers. Effective regulatory action may be necessary to prevent the exploitation of local monopoly positions where competition does not exist.

11. The evolution of offshore infrastructure on the UKCS has been characterised by field owners developing pipelines for sole usage, followed by ullage (i.e. spare capacity) progressively being made more available for use by third parties on payment of a tariff (i.e. a payment for transportation and processing services). Field-dedicated lines are economically viable when fields are relatively large but become less viable as fields get smaller. As a consequence, there is scope for gains by all parties if the development of small fields is made viable by the owners allowing access to their existing infrastructure on fair and reasonable terms, with the infrastructure owners gaining additional revenue from the new users. Some of these gains would be lost if monopolistic behaviour were to deter the timely exploration for and development of new small fields.

12. In principle, the more mature areas of the Southern North Sea, with large amounts of part-empty infrastructure, offer good opportunities for pipe on pipe competition, though in practice this is limited by the small size of most new fields. In other regions, notably the Central North Sea, there is less spare capacity and the additional complication of relatively small gas volumes associated with oil production. Throughout the UKCS there is, therefore, the potential for commercial tension between the owners of infrastructure and the owners of third party fields seeking access to that infrastructure.

COMPETITION LEGISLATION

13. General competition law applies to activities on the UK Continental Shelf. European Community competition rules apply to activities which may have an appreciable effect on trade between Member States of the European Union. The same rules have also been extended to trade within the European Economic Area, which includes Norway and Iceland. The opening of the gas interconnectors to Ireland and Belgium means there is now considerable inter-state trade in this area. Article 81 of the Treaty establishing the European Community prohibits anti-competitive agreements, decisions and concerted practices. Article 82 prohibits abuse of a dominant position.

14. The Competition Act 1998 has now introduced into UK law similar prohibitions modelled on those in Articles 81 and 82 (the "Chapter I" and "Chapter II" prohibitions). These concern similar agreements etc. and conduct that may affect trade within the UK (subject in certain cases to transitional arrangements). In applying those provisions of the Competition Act 1998, both the courts and the Office of Fair Trading (OFT) are required to follow the relevant jurisprudence of the European Court of Justice and to have regard to decisions of the European Commission.

15. Both EU and UK competition law prohibit abuse of a dominant position. Broad categories of business behaviour within which abusive conduct is most likely to be found include:

(a) directly or indirectly imposing unfair purchase or selling prices or other unfair trading conditions;

(b) limiting production, markets or technical development to the prejudice of consumers;

(c) applying dissimilar conditions to equivalent transactions with other trading parties, thereby placing them at a competitive disadvantage;

(d) making the conclusion of contracts subject to acceptance by the other parties of supplementary obligations which, by their nature or according to commercial usage, have no connection with the subject of the contracts.

16. In determining whether or not a business is in a dominant position, the OFT will look first at its market share. Generally, a business is unlikely to be considered dominant if it has a market share of less than 40 per cent. But this does not exclude the possibility that an undertaking with a lower market share may be considered dominant if, for example, the structure of the market enables it to act independently of its competitors. In looking at market structure the OFT will consider the number and size of existing competitors as well as the potential for new competitors to enter the market. **A dominant position essentially means that the business is able to behave independently of competitive pressures, such as other competitors, on that market**. Market power exists where a business can consistently charge higher prices, or supply a service of a lower quality, than they would if they faced effective competition.

17. The OFT has published, in a series of guidelines, guides as to how they and the sector regulators intend to enforce the Competition Act 1998 and to deal with particular matters. Although the OFT has not issued specific guidance on the application of the Act to upstream oil and gas infrastructure (including on the definition of the relevant market), it considers that **infrastructure owners are unlikely to have breached the Chapter II prohibition on abuse of a dominant position where they have had due regard to the Secretary of State's principles for setting terms** (as set out in paragraphs 47–59 below) **in arriving at the terms that they offer to, and agree with, third parties**.

18. If a third party applicant for a right to use a third party's infrastructure covered by the relevant legislation[1] is dissatisfied with the outcome and/or progress of a negotiation with the infrastructure owner, he may as described here apply to the Secretary of State to require access and to set appropriate terms. (If the procedures of the Infrastructure Code of Practice are being followed, the third party will have undertaken to do this at a pre-determined point in accordance with the Automatic Referral Notice provisions of that Code.) If the applicant considers that there may have been abuse of a dominant position, he may make a complaint to the OFT. However, the OFT may conduct a formal investigation only if it has reasonable grounds to suspect an infringement; simply receiving a complaint does not automatically trigger an investigation. Even then, investigation is at the OFT's discretion and would be subject to resource constraints and priorities. Recourse to the sector specific legislation therefore provides a more certain process and is likely to give a speedier outcome.

1 See sections 82 to 91 of the Energy Act 2011.

GENERAL APPROACH OF THE DEPARTMENT TO APPLICATIONS UNDER THE PETROLEUM LEGISLATION

19. The Department's approach is intended to ensure that:

- the procedure is fair;
- the procedure is transparent, subject to appropriate regard to commercial confidentiality; and
- applications are dealt with consistently, effectively and expeditiously, avoiding unnecessary expense.

Making an application to the Secretary of State

20. There is no standard format for an application. It should, however, normally take the form of a letter with supporting annexes. Fuller guidance on submitting an application, including the essential information which should be included, is given in Annex 2. To ensure efficient management of the application and to facilitate communication between the parties and the

Department, a case manager will be assigned to each application. This single point of contact will be advised to both parties – i.e. applicant and owner – on receipt of an application. Should an applicant wish to withdraw their application at any time they should contact the case manager advised to them in the initial acknowledgement letter.

Departmental consideration of an application

21. Annex 1 sets out the expected milestones in the consideration of an application. The Secretary of State must first establish that there is a case to consider. In deciding whether the parties have had a reasonable time in which to reach agreement, the Department will have regard to:

- Whether the minimum information set out in the legislative provisions[1] was provided by the applicant to the owner and, if so, when it was provided.
- Whether the parties have negotiated in good faith – a lack of good faith might be evidenced by either the applicant or the owner drawing out the negotiations with no real intention of bringing them to a conclusion; and
- Whether all parties have followed the Infrastructure Code of Practice.

22. If, having considered the factors above, it is clear that the parties have not had a reasonable time to reach agreement, the Secretary of State cannot consider the case for dispute resolution. While in general an application made after the parties have followed all the prior provisions of the Infrastructure Code of Practice, including the Automatic Referral Notice (ARN) procedure and possible extensions of the timetable under that procedure, is likely to qualify for consideration, it cannot be guaranteed to do so. Equally, an application not triggered by the ARN procedure may qualify for consideration. The Secretary of State has a further option to adjourn consideration of the case to allow the parties to negotiate further.

1   See sections 82 to 91 of the Energy Act 2011.

Modifications to infrastructure

23. When considering an application, the Secretary of State will assess whether the pipeline or facility needs to be modified so as to increase its capacity or to install a junction or other apparatus through which a pipeline of the applicant's can be connected. Should such modifications appear to be necessary, the Secretary of State will inform the parties of his intention to issue a notice in due course that will describe the required work to be carried out. This would be a separate notice to that required to secure rights to the applicant to use the infrastructure in question.

24. The notice describing the required work must specify the sums or the method of determining the sums which the Secretary of State considers should be paid to the owner by the applicant for the purpose of defraying the costs of the modifications. It would also specify the period in which the modifications are to be carried out. It is anticipated that the sums to be paid would reflect the actual cost of the modifications including appropriate overhead costs but with a ceiling to limit the exposure of the applicant to cost overruns over which they have little or no control.

Inviting the owner to provide information

25.   Where the Secretary of State concludes there *is* a case to consider, he will invite the owner of the infrastructure to provide information which will assist him in considering the application. Annex 3 describes the type of information the Department anticipates will be required. While the Department will endeavour to identify at this stage all additional information it will need to conclude the case, it may be necessary to require the provision of supplementary information from the applicant at this stage and from both parties as the case is being considered.

Agreeing the facts

26.   To maintain transparency in the consideration of cases and to provide an opportunity for both parties to agree as many of the facts as possible or, where appropriate, provide their own view of the negotiations, the Department expects each party to copy to the other party its submissions to the Department unless there is good reason not to do so. The Department encourages the parties to agree the facts of the case and, as far as possible, to focus on the issue(s) for determination by the Secretary of State.

Meetings with officials

27.   Given the complexity of the issues, the Department may consider that it would be effective to hold one or more meetings or presentations to clarify and explore aspects of the information provided to it. If such meetings or presentations occur, the Department will encourage both parties to agree to the other being present.

Sharing information with the Health and Safety Executive

28.   The Secretary of State is under a statutory obligation to take relevant advice from the Health and Safety Executive (HSE). This ensures that safety is safeguarded in disputes which focus on financial matters. The Secretary of State will also wish to seek advice from the HSE in the case of applications where safety, for example pipeline integrity or the composition of fluids, is an element of the dispute.

Interaction with Field Development Plan approval

29. Were the Secretary of State to conclude that there is a case to consider for access to be granted, applicants should be aware that any determination in relation to access for a proposed field would separately be subject to the necessary development approval for that field and that obtaining a determination would not guarantee field development approval.

30. Where an application was being considered prior to field development approval, work could normally continue on the sub-surface elements of the field development plan but discussions on development options that may have a bearing on the determination outcome would be deferred until the determination process was complete.

31. Although the Secretary of State would not decline to make a determination solely on the grounds that the proposed development would not be one which the Department would be likely to approve, the Department would strongly encourage developers with a choice of export routes to consider carefully whether to make an application for a determination where approval of a field development plan including that route would be unlikely.

Timetable

32. Annex 1 describes the expected stages in handling an application and gives indicative timings of actions to be followed by all parties; meeting this timetable would require full co-operation of all the parties. The Department would wish to agree a timetable with the applicant and the infrastructure owner. With limited practical experience of applications to date, it is difficult to be sure how long the process would take. The Department hopes that the majority of determinations could be completed in 16 weeks but it may well be necessary to extend this period, possibly significantly depending on the complexity of the case; in such cases the Department would discuss and seek to agree an alternative timetable with the parties as the need arises.

Form of a determination

33. In all cases, a determination requiring access to be provided is expected to comprise a comprehensive and detailed set of terms and conditions specified by the Secretary of State. Although the main issue in a particular case in practice is likely to be the financial terms including the tariff and risk apportionment (e.g. liabilities and indemnities), there may, of course, also be other (non-financial) aspects which the Secretary of State may need to settle.

34. It is envisaged that the applicant and owner will be provided with an indication of the likely outcome of the determination, in the form of terms that the Secretary of State is minded to set and/or draft notice(s). This step will allow the parties to review the completeness of the proposed terms and to identify possible difficulties with their implementation, prior to finalising notices. The legislation allows either party to apply to the Secretary of State to vary a notice after it has been issued; this is discussed later.

Implementation of a determination

35. The Secretary of State would normally specify a short period of time following a determination of terms for access during which the applicant may confirm their willingness to obtain access on those terms. If the applicant were to decline to accept the terms during that period, the owners would not be required to provide access to the applicant on those terms.

Publication of outcomes of applications

36. Section 86 of the Energy Act 2011 allows the Secretary of State to publish part or all of a notice, or to publish a summary of the effect of a notice or any part of it. Before publishing anything, the Secretary of State must give an opportunity to be heard to the persons to whom the notice was given and to anyone else that he considers to be appropriate. In practice, it is expected that a summary would be prepared in the same format required for completed negotiations by Annex H of the Infrastructure Code of Practice, unless there are good reasons to the contrary. The summary would be published on the DECC web site.

Power of Secretary of State to give notices on own initiative

37. Section 83 of the Energy Act 2011 provides for the Secretary of State to act on his own initiative to give a notice to secure rights to an applicant. In deciding to use this power, the Secretary of State must not only be satisfied that the parties have had sufficient time to reach agreement, but must also be satisfied that there is no realistic prospect of their doing so.

38. This power would be used in only very limited circumstances, as it would override the right of a prospective user to make an application to the Secretary of State at the time that they see fit. Circumstances where it might be used include when the Secretary of State believes that the prospective user is deterred from making an application by fear of upsetting the infrastructure owner, or where the infrastructure owner is believed to be drawing out negotiations without any intention of reaching a conclusion.

39. Before using this power, the Secretary of State would inform the parties that he was minded to act. This would take the form of a letter that would explain the reasons for his view and the timescale in which he proposed to act. The parties would be given time to make representations regarding the proposed action, and the Secretary of State would give careful consideration to any views they expressed. The Secretary of State would need to gather evidence to support any decision to act; this may involve use of the power in section 87 to request information from any party.

40. If this power is invoked, the process described in paragraphs 23–36 above will be followed.

Applications to vary notices

41. Section 85 of the Energy Act 2011 allows either party to whom a notice is given to apply for that notice to be varied. The legislation requires that the Secretary of State may vary a notice only in order to resolve a dispute that has arisen in connection with the notice. It is expected that requests for variations would be relevant only where the notice is incomplete or deficient in some significant aspect. It is not expected that this would extend to challenging the terms of a notice that are clearly stated without room for reasonable misunderstanding. The legislation requires that the Secretary of State give all relevant persons the opportunity to be heard. Section 86 of the Energy Act 2011 allows the Secretary of State to publish a variation or a summary of the effect of it, or the notice as varied.

RELEVANT FACTORS TO BE CONSIDERED IN AN APPLICATION

42. The Secretary of State is statutorily required to (so far as relevant) take into account:

(a) capacity which is or can reasonably be made available in the pipeline or facility in question;[1]

(b) any incompatibilities of technical specification which cannot reasonably be overcome;[2]

(c) difficulties which cannot reasonably be overcome and which could prejudice the efficient, current and planned future production of petroleum;[2]

(d) the reasonable needs of the owner and any associate of the owner for the conveying and processing of petroleum;[1]

(e) the interests of all users and operators of the pipeline or facility;[3]

(f) the need to maintain security and regularity of supplies of petroleum; and

(g) the number of parties involved in the dispute.

1 The Department considers that owners of infrastructure are entitled to make reasonable provision of capacity for their own future use. "Reasonable" in this context is not capable of exhaustive definition and is therefore illustrated here by example. It includes:
 – realistically anticipated upsides or plateau extensions from fields currently using the infrastructure

- new field developments where there is a firm plan or which are expected to be developed within a reasonable time frame or which were foreseen and were part of the reason for the original decision to install the infrastructure.

Reasonable provision would not include, for example, deliberately refusing access in order to deny market access to a competitor or to gain some other market advantage. Nor would it seem reasonable for an infrastructure owner to refuse access on the basis that the owner will have a requirement for it in time for some as yet unidentified purpose.

2   The Department considers that this includes, for example, sterilising capacity to provide other services within the system (in addition to the capacity actually requested) as a result of accepting the particular request for service. Examples might be:
- where taking in a small field could reduce the ullage to the extent that a current negotiation with a large field could not be completed;
- in circumstances where a particular small field consumes all of the, say, de-propanising capacity at an oil treating facility thus preventing the use of upstream capacity which would otherwise be available;
- where a sour gas field would, by coming in, preclude the owners from a future opportunity to operate the system sweet.

However, the Department emphasises that the primary consideration when determinations are required to consider these issues will be the facts of a particular case.

3   The Department considers that this includes the need to honour all existing contractual commitments – since it is essential for business that an environment in which contracts which were freely entered into are respected – and to take account of the effect on existing users; for example, accommodating a new user may cause compression suction pressure to rise which would have a material detrimental impact on the deliverability of the existing fields.

43.   This is not an exhaustive list and the Secretary of State will also take into account any other material considerations, including financial information, relevant to the dispute. Existing users are given further protection by sections 82(9) and (10) of the Energy Act 2011, which require that the reasonable expectations of owners and the rights of other users are not prejudiced unless they are compensated.

THE GOVERNMENT'S OBJECTIVES

44.   As stated in paragraph 9 above, the Department's main objective in operating its petroleum legislation is to ensure the recovery of all economic hydrocarbon reserves. The Government has sought to avoid the unnecessary proliferation of pipelines and other infrastructure. Access to existing infrastructure on fair and reasonable terms is therefore important for third parties. It is also important that the integrity of that existing infrastructure is maintained. More generally, the Government is committed to promoting greater competitiveness in energy markets. In determining the basis for access, it is therefore necessary to balance a variety of different interests and objectives.

45.   The maturity of the UKCS means that an increasing proportion of production comes from new fields which are too small to support their own infrastructure to shore. Access to infrastructure services on a fair basis is necessary for their development. At the same time, more production is coming from incremental investment in older fields. Such fields can rely on ageing infrastructure which may be economic to maintain only with the income from transportation of third party production. There is also some new investment in pipelines which may be used in future for third party production.

46. The Department seeks to ensure that the development option chosen by the prospective developer of a new field does not lead to the permanent loss of reserves which could otherwise be recovered economically. This might, for example, happen if gas produced in association with oil from a new field would be flared although its market value exceeded the resource cost of bringing it to market. That might be the result if the least cost export option for the gas was to use ullage (i.e. spare capacity) in an existing pipeline, but – perhaps in the absence of pressure from pipe-on-pipe (or pipe-within-pipe) competition – the pipeline owner were to abuse a position of market power and seek too high a tariff to justify the new field owner paying for a connection. In such circumstances, the new field owner might ask the Secretary of State to set a lower, cost-reflective tariff, which would bring the best commercial option into line with the best economic option.

THE DEPARTMENT'S GUIDING PRINCIPLES ON SETTING TRANSPORTATION AND PROCESSING TERMS

47. While acknowledging that it is reasonable for owners to safeguard capacity for their own reasonably anticipated production, the Department supports the principle of non-discriminatory negotiated access to upstream infrastructure on the UKCS, encourages transparency and promotes fairness for all parties concerned since it is important that prospective users have fair access to infrastructure at competitive prices. At the same time, the Department is of the view that any terms determined by the Secretary of State should reflect a fair payment to the owner for real costs and risks faced and for opportunities forgone. It recognises that, for example, spare pipeline capacity has a commercial value and that the owner, having borne the cost and risks of installing, operating and maintaining the pipeline system, should be entitled to derive a fair commercial consideration for that value.

48. Where, as in upstream oil and gas processing and transportation, there are so many technical, economic and commercial variables, any attempt to be too prescriptive in setting out guidance on whether to grant a third party access to an owner's processing facilities or pipeline infrastructure and on what terms is likely either to overlook an important factor or to introduce a factor which, in some circumstances, might be entirely inappropriate. There is, for example, a balance to be struck between setting terms which reward past investment in infrastructure (to maintain the attractiveness of the UKCS for continued investment) and allow owners to take on risks which a field developer may not be able to bear alone, while ensuring that the terms set by the Secretary of State are attractive enough to encourage exploration for, and development of, new fields. The relative weight to place on these factors would vary from case to case. This guidance is therefore, of necessity, in general terms.

49. In a Lords Committee debate on 15 October 1975,[1] the Government of the day gave the following assurances on the use of the Secretary of State's powers to require access and to set a tariff (which were seen very much as a long stop):

- it was not the intention that, in those cases where the Secretary of State was called upon to intervene, the owner of a pipeline would be financially worse off ("in any way out of pocket") through the admission of a third party;[2]
- accordingly, pipeline owners would have all costs reimbursed, including direct additional capital costs arising from a third party's entry and indirect costs (e.g. the cost of interruption to the owner's throughput while a line is modified to enable third party use);
- the tariff would be set so that the third party would bear a fair share of the total running costs incurred after his entry;[3]
- unless the supply in question were marginal or the pipeline owner had already made other sufficient arrangements to recover the full capital costs, the financial arrangements proposed would normally be expected to take account of the basic capital costs as well as the costs arising from the entry of the third party.

1 See the debate from 5.20pm onwards as reported at http://hansard.millbanksystems.com/lords/1975/oct/15/petroleum-and-submarine-pipe-lines-bill-1.
2 While this was seen as a fundamental, basic safeguard in such cases, the Department now takes the view that it should be seen on an *ex ante* (forward-looking) not an *ex post* (backward-looking) basis and would thus not prevent determinations from including an apportionment of overall risk to the owner in return for an appropriate level of reward.
3 See paragraph 52.

50. If called on to resolve a dispute over access to infrastructure on the UKCS, it should be assumed that the Secretary of State would normally adopt an approach which continues to reflect the assurances given in the Lords debate in 1975.[1] **The main issue in this approach is the need to identify the relevant costs and risks and to decide on fair and appropriate terms. These will have to be decided on a case by case basis.**

1 It was noted during the Lords debate that assurances "can be given fully only in terms of the Government who make them. It is a commitment by the Government. One hopes that the spirit of the legislation will be followed through by subsequent successive Secretaries of State; but it cannot, of course, be fully binding. I can only say in this case that laws also can be repealed." While the assurances do not have the force of law they are helpful guidance and, as with any guidance, need to be reviewed in the circumstances pertaining at the time. For example, we would not see the assurances as binding the Secretary of State so as to produce an outcome that was not fair and appropriate.

51. The Department recognises that infrastructure owners have a key role to play in ensuring maximum economic recovery of the UK's petroleum resources and that too narrow a focus on setting terms on a cost-reflective basis would reduce the incentive for them to bear risk, keep their infrastructure in operation and available, invest in innovative solutions and offer added value services. It anticipates that the Secretary of State would consider these factors in making a determination.

52. Although the Secretary of State's discretion to use the powers in sections 82 to 91 of the Energy Act 2011 cannot be constrained by published guidance, he would in general be guided by the principles set out below, which amplify the general principles set out above, for what are thought to be the four most likely (not mutually exclusive) scenarios:

- **Terms for infrastructure built as part of an integrated field development project**

  When spare capacity can be made available to a third party applicant in infrastructure for which provision has already been made for its capital costs (including ongoing costs) to be recovered (including a reasonable return taking account of the risks incurred and expected and acknowledging that it may in practice not be easy to determine whether provision has already been made for the capital costs of a specific piece of infrastructure to be recovered), it is anticipated that the Secretary of State would normally set terms reflecting the incremental costs and risks imposed on the infrastructure owner.

- **Terms for infrastructure built, oversized or maintained with a view to taking third party business**

  On equity grounds and in order to retain an incentive for further such investment, in infrastructure constructed, oversized or maintained with a view to taking third party business, the terms set by the Secretary of State would normally provide for recovery of capital costs incurred in the expectation of third party business. This would be achieved by setting the tariff at a level just sufficient, taking into account the risks involved, to earn the owner a reasonable return on costs incurred by him in the anticipation of third party use if the tariff were applied to the third party throughput expected at the time of the decision to invest, recognising the uncertainty inherent in projections of future third party usage. This tariff may well be higher than the level that the owner would offer if prospective users have alternative export options available in infrastructure with sufficient capacity for the hydrocarbons in question and would, in general, be above the level required simply to reflect incremental costs and risks.

- **Terms for infrastructure associated with a field at or near the end of its economic life**

  In the case of infrastructure associated with a field at or near the end of its economic life, the prospective tariff for third party access may need to be set above incremental costs to ensure that it is maintained and remains available for third party use. The terms set by the Secretary of State would need to provide for appropriate cost sharing or recovery arrangements in such circumstances including a mechanism for determining the date from when or circumstances in which they should operate.[1]

- **Terms where there is competition for limited capacity**

  On occasion, prospective third party users may be competing for access to the same limited capacity in infrastructure. In such circumstances, the Secretary of State is unlikely to require the owner to make the capacity available to an applicant who values the capacity less than other prospective users – for example as evidenced by the tariffs they are willing to pay – and thus does not offer a better deal for the owner.

- **Terms set to cover costs of displacement of own production or contractual commitments**

  For infrastructure with insufficient ullage to accommodate a third party's requirements, given the owner's rights and existing contractual commitments, the Secretary of State is unlikely to require access to be provided. If he were to do so, the terms would need to reflect at least the cost to the infrastructure owner of backing off their own production and/ or another party's contracted usage to accommodate the third party's (i.e. be based on the concept of opportunity cost).

---

1 At some point it may be appropriate to switch from a tariff per unit of throughput to a cost sharing arrangement. If it is expected that such a point will be reached during the period for which a determination is made, the Secretary of State will determine a mechanism for deciding a date from which cost sharing will be effective. If an operating cost share arrangement applies, the applicant would normally pay a throughput-based share of the operating costs of the facilities used to transport and process his hydrocarbons. Operating costs would normally include, for example, costs of replacing outdated metering equipment with new equipment necessary to maintain the services required by existing users of the host facility but would not include any capital expenditure that the infrastructure owners elect to spend to attract/win future third party business or future equity production. Cost sharing may be on an individual facilities basis (e.g. water injection, gas conditioning, oil production) or it could be based on the cost of the total facilities. The cost sharing arrangement would take account of all operating and maintenance modes e.g. extended shutdowns when there is no throughput. Owners' overheads and risks e.g. in relation to ongoing liabilities would be captured as identified element of cost rather than as an uplift on costs. The determined cost sharing arrangements would normally include a provision for the infrastructure owner to provide regular projections of unit costs to aid decision making by users. If costs escalate beyond those anticipated at the time of a determination the determination would allow for the applicant to terminate his use of the facilities having given a reasonable notice period.

53. Accordingly, in most cases the terms that would be determined by the Secretary of State are likely to be in line with those that would be offered by infrastructure owners were they to face *effective* competition from other infrastructure owners who also have sufficient spare capacity to accommodate the hydrocarbons in question. That does ***not*** mean that where there has been competition between infrastructure owners the Secretary of State will refrain from making a determination or be guided by the terms already offered. There are practical limitations on the extent to which in practice competition between UKCS infrastructure owners can be effective.

Compensation, Liabilities and Indemnities during the construction and tie-in phase

54. In the case of periods of shut-downs required for the sole purposes of the tie-in or modification, the applicant would be required to pay a reasonable level of liquidated damages to cover losses arising from loss or deferral of production. These damages may be calculated on an hourly or daily basis and would normally be subject to a reasonable cap. In deciding how much should be paid to the owner by the applicant for the purpose of defraying the cost of the modifications, the Secretary of State would thus make provision for the cost of interruption to the owner's throughput while a pipeline is modified to enable third party use. That requires an assessment of whether the owner's production would be lost or deferred and, in the latter case, the difference in timing and price. Allowance may also need to be made for any incremental benefit from the modification accruing to the owner for his own or third party production.

55. Except in cases of wilful misconduct of the infrastructure owner, the Secretary of State would normally require applicants to indemnify owners against liabilities and losses arising out of tie-in or modification activity but with caps on their maximum liability exposure. These caps would be reasonable and have regard to the realistic exposure of the infrastructure owners and the risk/reward balance of the overall determination. The Secretary of State would be as specific as possible as to the types and categories of non-physical loss recoverable under any indemnity with a view to avoiding subsequent disputes on the extent of recovery under the indemnity and helping the placement of any insurance for the risk. In general, the Secretary of State would require that specific insurance arrangements be put in place to cover tie- in or modification activity.

Liabilities and Indemnities during the transportation and processing phase

56. The liability and indemnity (L&I) regime forms an important part of the overall risk/reward balance with consequent impact on reward levels. It is the intention of the Department that in the determination the applicant and the owner should each bear appropriate risks having regard for the respective rewards which each is expected to enjoy. A fundamental presumption is that the applicant and owner will both mitigate their losses when seeking recovery from each other. The L&I terms that would be determined by the Secretary of State would have regard to the terms prevailing with existing users of a system and by the specific circumstances of each case: every deal is different, as is the overall risk/reward balance and the final liability and indemnity regime.

57. The Department would normally expect there to be a mutual hold harmless regime in respect of losses of property, death or injury to people and pollution from the respective facilities and consequential losses, usually subject to exclusions in the case of wilful misconduct by the party seeking to rely on the indemnity. This regime would typically extend to contractors.

Off-specification deliveries during the transportation and processing phase

58. The terms determined by the Secretary of State would normally make provision during the production period (i.e. post completion of the tie-in phase) for recovery by the infrastructure owner from the applicant of documented incremental costs and/or expenses incurred as a result of the delivery by the applicant, whether or not accepted by the owner, of off-specification hydrocarbons. The applicant would be expected to indemnify and hold the owner harmless from and against direct losses, costs, damages and/or expenses caused as a result of such off-specification delivery of hydrocarbons.

59. In determining the appropriate liability and indemnity regime to apply to off-specification deliveries, the Secretary of State would consider, *inter alia*:

i. whether the indemnities given by the applicant to the owner are to be capped;

ii. what were the consequences to the owner and the other users of the system, and whether the nature of the service being offered should have a bearing on which party retains liability for off-specification contamination for various events;

iii. whether blending arrangements are included, and which party retains liability for blending failure leading to off-specification contamination;

iv. whether the off-specification event was a previously known occurrence or was unexpected, whether the user was aware of an event, and whether the owner was aware and had given consent in advance;

v. the quality and availability of the data input stream to the infrastructure owners and the owners' ability to control the system;

vi. that the identity of the off-specification user in a multi-user system may never be satisfactorily proved;

vii. whether an existing Cross–User Liability Agreement (or other inter–user agreement) regulates inter–user liabilities and is applicable; the Secretary of State would usually require the applicant to adhere to any existing inter–user agreement; and

viii. whether the applicant is proposing to deliver a contaminant into a commingled stream on a planned, long term basis (on the proposition that a downstream processor will clean up the commingled stream).

ANNEX 1

Minimum timetable

Milestones	The Department will endeavour to ...	Applicant and owner
Receipt of an application	assign and notify to the parties contact details of an official who will be responsible for managing consideration of the application	**Applicant** provides information set out in **Annex 2** to enable the Secretary of State to establish if there is a case to consider. This information will also inform consideration of the case.
Establishing there is a case to consider	advise the parties of receipt of the application and of whether the case will be considered or, whether the case will be adjourned or rejected **within 5 working days of receipt of the application**	
Submitting information to inform consideration of the case	allow **at least 10 working days** for full submissions to be made, where the case is to be considered	**Owner** should submit information to the Secretary of State within the deadline requested which will be **at least 10 working days but unlikely to be more than 20 working days. Applicant** may be asked to supplement their initial submission to assist the Secretary of State's consideration.
During consideration of the case	allow **at least 5 working days** for companies to respond to requests for further information	**Owner** and **applicant** should submit supplementary information to the Secretary of State within the deadline requested which will be **at least 5 working days but not likely to be more than 10 working days.**

Milestones	The Department will endeavour to …	Applicant and owner
Meetings with officials during consideration of the case	give **at least 5 working days'** notice of any meeting with officials to explore the information provided and at the same time notify companies of the issues for discussion. Several meetings may be needed for complex cases.	
Provide the parties with an indication of the likely terms of the determination		Respond with comments on completeness and ease of implementation within 10 working days.
Advising the parties of the determination	advise both parties of the determination within 16 weeks of receipt of the application	
Applicant to make decision		Within the time period specified by the Secretary of State, the **applicant** will decide whether or not to proceed to obtain access under the determined terms.

ANNEX 2

Submitting an application to the Secretary of State

1. There is no standard format for an application. It should, however, normally take the form of a letter with supporting annexes. Applicants should send 2 hard copies of written applications and an electronic version (preferably in Word, PowerPoint and/or Excel) to:

Robert White   email:
Infrastructure Manager   robert.a.white@decc.gsi.gov.uk
Department of Energy and Climate Change
3 Whitehall Place   Telephone:
London SW1A 2AW   +44 (0)3000 686056

2. Applications must be signed and dated by the applicant or their legal representative. Where the application is made on behalf of a group of companies acting under a joint venture agreement, the application should be submitted by the lead negotiator and include contact details of representatives of all other participants in the joint venture.

3. Applicants should include the following information in their request:

- the legislative provision(s) under which the application is made;
- the applicant's name and address and, if different, an address for service in the UK;
- details (name, location) of the infrastructure which is the subject of the dispute;
- the name and address of the owner of the infrastructure which is the subject of the dispute;
- details of the negotiation to date including:
  - i) the request to the owner of the infrastructure
  - ii) details (including dates) of the negotiations to date including any indicative information provided by the owner.
- all specific information on the service requested, to include but not be limited to:
  - i) broad outline of the service requested (e.g. firm or reasonable endeavours) and a description of the field development
  - ii) the range of production profiles that have been the subject of the request for processing and transportation
  - iii) the range of compositions of the fluids that have been the subject of the request for processing and transportation
  - iv) period for which service has been requested
  - v) any additional services requested e.g. blending
  - vi) any additional terms requested e.g. priority in the case of capacity restrictions, special terms for transport, incremental production, flexibility in nominations

4. Applications should include details of the composition and quantity of products to be processed or conveyed and the period during which the service is to be provided. This information will have already been provided to the owner as part of the initial request for access.

5. It is expected that this information will enable the Secretary of State to establish there is a case to consider and inform his consideration of the case. The Secretary of State will not solely base his decision on information provided as part of this process. It may also be necessary to seek supplementary information from the applicant during consideration of the case.

ANNEX 3

Information required from owners

1. Where the Secretary of State concludes there is a case to consider under the dispute resolution provisions, the Department will invite the owner of the infrastructure in question to provide information to assist him in considering the case.

2. Owners will be asked to confirm their ownership or joint ownership of the infrastructure in question and where applicable the details of other joint owners. In the case of jointly owned infrastructure the representative responding to the Secretary of State's request should confirm that he has the agreement of all owners to act on their behalf. Owners will also be asked to provide details of existing third party users.

3. Owners should expect to provide, as appropriate, a demonstration of the technical and commercial issues that led them to calculate the tariff and arrive at the terms that they have offered or the reasons for refusing to provide a service. These may include but are not limited to:

i   A summary of the technical reviews or studies that were undertaken for the proposed service, including any incompatibilities of specification or other difficulties that could prejudice the efficient current and planned future use of the infrastructure

ii   A statement of the capacity that is or can reasonably be made available, including a forecast of available capacity in the relevant period in processing facilities and pipelines, detailing current and future committed throughput from third party users or equity production and future equity production that may reasonably expect to use the infrastructure, identifying individual field profiles within the overall profile

iii   Details of the feasibility of and costs for any incremental capacity e.g. whether additional equipment or processing facilities would be required to meet the services requested by the applicant

iv   Where the owner considers that there is insufficient capacity to take the applicant's production without backing out any other production, a description of the associated opportunity cost and any incremental costs

v   Details of any interests or contractual constraints that could affect the access and services requested by the applicant, e.g. the rights of existing users to increase production nominations

vi   Estimates of the incremental costs on an annual basis of accommodating the applicant's production, including separately any one-off costs (e.g. of tying-in)

vii   Estimates of the business risks associated with accommodating the applicant's production, including separately any one-off risks (e.g. of tying-in) viii If the infrastructure was built or oversized to take third party throughput, an indication of the incremental capital costs and of the owner's expectations of such throughput at the time of the decision to invest, giving an indication of the risks then associated with different projections of throughput.

4. The Secretary of State will not base his decision solely on information provided as part of this process and may wish to seek supplementary information as the case is considered. This could include a detailed assessment of the costs and risks caused by the applicant's production over the lifetime of the infrastructure in question, as well as consideration of any benefits that may accrue to the applicant or owner. Information may also be sought about the possible impact of unplanned future events or performance or regulatory changes on all users of the infrastructure, along with the likelihood of such occurrences.

Appendix 2

Oil & Gas UK 2012 Economic Report – Summary and Key Facts

Reproduced with the kind permission of Oil & Gas UK.

SUMMARY

By Chief Executive, Malcolm Webb

With the publication of the latest edition of Oil & Gas UK's annual economic report on the offshore oil and gas industry, I encourage you to take a fresh look at this truly remarkable British industrial success story. It is something of which we can all be proud.

The report discloses the immense scale of the sector's contribution to the wealth and well-being of this country. The industry is not only a key provider of long-term jobs, but it is also by far the most important supplier of primary energy and the country's biggest payer of corporate taxes. Furthermore, it is a world-leading centre of excellence in engineering, manufacturing and applied technology. A major export earner and the UK's largest industrial investor, the oil and gas industry is a powerful engine for renewed growth in the economy.

Unfortunately, research we have conducted shows that many people seem to be unaware that the UK still produces the bulk of its needs for oil and gas from its own reserves, and that we have sufficient resources to keep producing for at least another 40 years. Much concern was expressed recently at the temporary suspension of Libyan oil and gas production; however, only a few of the commentators seemed to appreciate that our own daily production is larger than that of Libya.

With continued investment in exploration and production, the significant economic benefits this country reaps from oil and gas activities will flow for a long time to come. The right fiscal environment, however, is crucial and so the industry welcomed the improvements announced by the Chancellor of the Exchequer in his Budget for 2012, especially those which will bring certainty and predictability to the tax regime. Oil & Gas UK is keen to continue to work closely and openly with Government in pursuit of our shared and common purpose of maximising the recovery of Britain's offshore oil and gas reserves. Challenges remain. We will need to address the decline in production which accelerated unexpectedly last year as well as the fall in exploration drilling.

However, we will not be assisted in achieving this important national goal by ill-conceived legislation such as the offshore safety regulation proposed by the EU Commission. If enacted, this new law would be a serious backward step for safety in the UK's offshore oil and gas areas and for our industry as a whole. We cannot stand back and simply let that happen. So we have objected to and will continue to oppose this damaging proposal. We are grateful to both the British and Scottish Governments for their clear support in this, along with, very importantly, that of colleagues in the trade union movement and other parts of the industry in this country and abroad, including all of the other significant European offshore oil and gas producing nations. It is time for the EU Commission to think again.

Britain's offshore oil and gas industry is well worth supporting. Take another look at its achievements highlighted overleaf and the overwhelmingly positive benefits this industry provides to all of us in this country. It makes a hugely important contribution to our living standards even in the best of times for the economy. Right now that contribution is vital. Without our oil and gas today, the deficit on the country's balance of trade would double, half a million or more jobs would be lost from the economy and there would be a £17 billion hole in the Government's tax and national insurance receipts for this year alone. We would also be wholly dependent on imported oil and gas for three quarters of our total primary energy supply. Happily, thanks to this industry, these are some challenges we do not face today.

KEY FACTS

The following summarises the key findings of Oil & Gas UK's 2012 Economic Report. Figures below refer to 2011, unless otherwise stated.

Security of Supply

- Currently, oil and gas provides some 73 per cent of the UK's total primary energy
- Production from the UK's Continental Shelf (UKCS) satisfied 49 per cent of the country's primary energy demand:
  - 68 per cent of oil demand and 58 per cent of gas demand
- In 2020, 70 per cent of primary energy in the UK will still come from oil and gas, even if the 15 per cent target for renewable energy is met
- The UKCS has the potential to satisfy close to 50 per cent of the UK's oil and gas demand in 2020 if the current rate of investment is sustained

Economic Contribution

- Production of oil and gas boosted the balance of payments by some £40 billion
- The supply chain added another £6 billion in exports of goods and services
- The UKCS remained the largest investor and the largest contributor to national gross value added (GVA) among the industrial sectors of the economy

Oil and Gas Prices

- The price for Brent crude oil averaged $111 a barrel (bbl), peaking at $127 in May during the Arab uprisings from a low of $93 in January
- In early June 2012, the price of Brent oil had fallen by 25 per cent compared with its peak earlier in the year and was under $100/bbl
- Day-ahead gas prices averaged 56 pence per therm (p/th), peaking at 66 p/th in March when the Fukishima disaster in Japan caused some diversion of LNG supplies away from Europe
- Gas traded at a discount to oil throughout 2011, at around 50 per cent in energy equivalent terms
- The combined oil and gas price for UKCS production was $90 per barrel of oil equivalent (boe)

Production

- Production was 656 million boe, or 1.8 million boepd, a decline of around 19 per cent from 2010
- The UK was the third largest gas and second largest oil producer in Europe, and 19th largest in the world for both oil and gas (ref. BP's Statistical Review of World Energy 2012)

Total Expenditure

- Total expenditure reached almost £17 billion on exploration, developments and operations
- In more than 40 years to 2011, the industry has spent £486 billion (in 2011 money) by:
  - investing £310 billion in exploration drilling and field developments and
  - spending £176 billion on production operations

Taxation

- The industry paid £11.2 billion in corporate taxes on production in 2011–12, almost 25 per cent of total corporation taxes received by the Exchequer
- This is expected to fall to £9.6 billion in 2012–13, but will still provide over 20 per cent of total corporation taxes
- The wider supply chain is estimated to have contributed another £6 billion in corporation and payroll taxes
- Over £300 billion in production related corporate taxes have been paid to the Exchequer in over 40 years since production began

Capital Investment

- With a number of large developments receiving field approval in recent years, capital investment rose to £8.5 billion. This represented a 40 per cent increase on 2010
- Investment is expected to rise in 2012, possibly reaching £11.5 billion
- Sixteen new fields and major field redevelopments secured approval, together requiring £13 billion of capital investment and expected to deliver 1.5 billion boe of reserves over time
- Total investment committed or already in progress was £31 billion at the end of 2011, £7 billion higher than 12 months earlier

Operating Costs

- Total operating expenditure remained similar to 2010 at £7 billion
- This is expected to increase slightly, roughly in line with inflation, to £7.5 billion in 2012
- Unit operating costs rose sharply to $17/boe because of poor production. The cost per barrel is expected to rise further to around $18/boe in 2012

Reserves

- A total of 41 billion boe has so far been recovered from the UKCS
- Further overall recovery is estimated at 15–24 billion boe
- Current investment plans have the potential to deliver around 12 billion boe in total:
  - 7.1 billion boe from existing fields and ongoing investment plus
  - 5 billion boe from incremental and new field developments
- The aggregated portfolio for the UKCS contains around 20 per cent more reserves than a year ago

New Developments

- Five new fields came on-stream, bringing 30 million boe of reserves into production
- DECC approved 12 new projects, as well as four major incremental redevelopments
- 60 per cent of all new fields are subsea tie-backs to existing infrastructure

Drilling Activity

- The total number of wells drilled (incl. side-tracks) was lower than 2010 with:
  - 122 development wells (down 6 per cent)
  - 14 exploration wells (down 50 per cent)
  - 28 appraisal wells (down 18 per cent)
- Part of the fall in drilling activity can be attributed to the unexpected increase in the Supplementary Charge on Corporation Tax from 20 per cent to 32 per cent in 2011's Budget
- Exploration drilling is expected to pick up in 2012 with 64 exploration and appraisal (E&A) wells forecast, although only 40 of those are firmly committed

Employment

- The industry supported at least 440,000* jobs across the UK with:
  - 32,000 directly employed by oil and gas companies and major contractors
  - 207,000 in the wider supply chain
  - 100,000 in jobs induced by the economic activity of employees and
  - 100,000 in jobs exporting goods and services
- Employment is spread across the UK comprising:
  - Scotland – 45 per cent
  - South East England – 21 per cent
  - North West England – 6 per cent
  - West Midlands – 5 per cent
- Each £ billion expended on the UKCS provides 15–20,000 jobs

* Numbers are based on analysis commissioned in 2010; this work is currently being updated and will be reported on later in 2012.

Decommissioning

- Some 470 installations, 10,000km of pipelines, 15 onshore terminals and 5,000 wells will eventually have to be decommissioned

- From 2012 onwards, decommissioning expenditure is projected to be £28.7 billion (2011 money) by 2040 for existing facilities
- New investment in probable developments could add £4.3 billion to this total
- High oil prices and sustained investment in asset integrity mean that decommissioning expenditure over the next decade is expected to be around £10.3 billion, some 10 per cent below last year's forecast

The full report is available at
www.oilandgasuk.co.uk/2012economic_report.cfm

Contact Oil & Gas UK

Oil & Gas UK Aberdeen
3rd Floor
The Exchange 2
62 Market Street
Aberdeen AB11 5PJ
Tel: +44 (0)1224 577250
Fax: +44 (0)1224 577251

Oil & Gas UK London
6th Floor East
Portland House
Bressenden Place
London SW1E 5BH
Tel: +44 (0)20 7802 2400
Fax: +44 (0)20 7802 2401

Email: info@oilandgasuk.co.uk
Website: www.oilandgasuk.co.uk
Twitter: follow us @oilandgasuk

Editorial note: the drafting of the Economic Report was undertaken during May and early June 2012.

Appendix 3

Framework Agreement

Norway No. 1 (2006)

between the Government of the United Kingdom of Great Britain and Northern Ireland and the Government of the Kingdom of Norway concerning Cross-Boundary Petroleum Co-operation

Oslo, 4 April 2005

The Government of the United Kingdom of Great Britain and Northern Ireland (hereinafter referred to as "the United Kingdom Government") and the Government of the Kingdom of Norway (hereinafter referred to as "the Norwegian Government");

Referring to the Agreement of 10 March 1965[1] between the two Governments relating to the Delimitation of the Continental Shelf between the two Countries and the Protocol supplementary to it of 22 December 1978[2];

1 Treaty Series No. 71 (1965) Cmnd 2757.
2 Treaty Series No. 31 (1980) Cmnd 7853.

Having regard to Article 4 of the said Agreement under which the two Governments have undertaken, in consultation with the licensees, to seek to reach agreement as to the manner in which trans-boundary reservoirs shall be most effectively exploited and the manner in which the proceeds deriving therefrom shall be apportioned;

Having regard also to the existing Agreements entered into between the two Governments relating to the joint exploitation of trans-boundary reservoirs and to the laying and operation of pipelines for transportation of petroleum produced from one side of the Delimitation Line to a destination on the other side of that line, listed in Annex E;

Mindful that submarine pipelines may be subject to special arrangements which may or may not contain provisions identical with relevant rules of general international law;

Affirming that the provisions of this Agreement will not prejudice the views of the Parties in the negotiation and conclusion of any future treaty;

Mindful of the initiative taken by Energy Ministers at the end of 2001 and the Pilot-Konkraft recommendations made in August 2002 in their report 'Unlocking Value Through Closer Relationships' to strengthen co-operation between the Kingdom of Norway and the United Kingdom in petroleum developments across the continental shelves appertaining to the two States;

Recognising that neither Government will impede the transportation of petroleum from one side of the Delimitation Line to the market on the other side of the Delimitation Line by means of any unfair, non transparent or discriminatory charge or in any other way, nor impose any requirements which have the practical effect of hampering such transportation;

Desiring to deepen further their co-operation with respect to petroleum cross-boundary projects and to achieve optimal exploitation of the petroleum resources on the continental shelves appertaining to the two States;

Recognising that to this end there is a need to secure proper sharing of information between the two Governments;

Have agreed as follows:

CHAPTER 1
GENERAL PRINCIPLES

Article 1.1

Scope

This Agreement shall apply to cross-boundary co-operation between the United Kingdom Government and the Norwegian Government with regard to Petroleum activities.

Article 1.2

Definitions

For the purposes of this Agreement:

"Authorisation" means any authorisation, consent, approval, Licence or permit issued under the law of either State, relating to the exploration and/or the Exploitation of Petroleum and/or the Construction and Operation of Installations and/or Pipelines;

"Construction and Operation" includes the design, fabrication, installation, laying, use, maintenance, repair and decommissioning of Installations and/or

Pipelines but does not include access to Pipelines in accordance with Articles 2.4 to 2.7;

"Cross-Boundary Pipeline" means:

(a)   a Pipeline crossing the Delimitation Line transporting Petroleum from the continental shelf of one State to the continental shelf or the territory of the other State; or

(b)   a Pipeline transporting Petroleum and which is associated with a Trans-Boundary Reservoir, whether crossing the Delimitation Line or not, and where Licensees of both States of that Trans-Boundary Reservoir have a participating interest in that Pipeline;

but shall not include a Pipeline covered by an Agreement listed in Annex E;

"Cross-Boundary Project" means any of the following projects which are not covered by an Agreement listed in Annex E:

(a)   the Construction and Operation of a Cross-Boundary Pipeline;

(b)   the exploration for and/or the Exploitation of a Trans-Boundary Reservoir, including the Construction and Operation of an Installation for that purpose; and

(c)   a project making use of a Host Facility;

"Delimitation Line" means the line defined in the Agreement of 10 March 1965 between the two Governments relating to the Delimitation of the Continental Shelf between the two Countries and the Protocol supplementary to that Agreement of 22 December 1978;

"Exploitation" includes the appraisal, production, treatment and processing of gas or liquids from a reservoir and/or the injection, reinjection or storage of any substance used for or derived from the appraisal, production, treatment and processing of those gases or liquids;

"First Dry Gas Link" means the Pipeline which is the first one authorised to be constructed after the date of signature of this Agreement and which transports dry gas originating from the Norwegian regulated dry gas system into United Kingdom offshore Infrastructure, whether or not that Pipeline is an "interconnecting pipeline" under the Framework Agreement signed at Stavanger on 25 August 1998;[1]

1   Treaty Series No. 9 (2003) Cm 5762.

"Host Facility" means:

(a)   an Installation on one side of the Delimitation Line used for the exploration and/or Exploitation of a reservoir which is wholly on the other side of the Delimitation Line; and/or

(b)   an Installation used for the exploration and/or Exploitation of a Trans-Boundary Reservoir if the Installation is placed outside the Unit Area of that Trans-Boundary Reservoir; and/or

(c)   an Installation within a Unit Area which is used for the exploration and/or Exploitation of a reservoir outside that Unit Area;

"Infrastructure" means Installations and Pipelines;

"Inspector" means any person authorised by the competent authority of either State to carry out inspection activities relating to:

(a)   the Construction and Operation of any Infrastructure relating to a Cross-Boundary Project; or

(b)   any metering system relating to a Cross-Boundary Project;

"Installation" means any artificial island, structure or other facility for Petroleum activity, including drilling rigs, floating production units, storage units, flotels, well heads, intrafield Pipelines and intrafield cables, but excluding supply and support vessels, ships that transport Petroleum in bulk, other Pipelines and cables;

"Langeled South" means the part of the Langeled Pipeline starting at the downstream tie-in weld on the downstream expansion spool connected to the Langeled sub-sea valve station located at the Sleipner field on the Norwegian continental shelf and terminating immediately downstream of the Langeled pig receiving facilities at the terminal at Easington in Yorkshire in the United Kingdom;

"Licence" means a permit issued by one of the Governments to carry out exploration for and/or Exploitation of Petroleum in a given area or, if applicable, for the Construction and Operation of a Pipeline;

"Licensee" means the individual or body corporate, holding a Licence;

"Licensees' Agreement" means an agreement between the Licensees of the United Kingdom Government and the Licensees of the Norwegian Government, entered into in accordance with this Agreement, relating to a Cross-Boundary Project, and any supplementary agreement to such agreement, including any amendment or modification to or any waiver of or departure from any provision of such agreement;

"Petroleum" means all liquid and gaseous hydrocarbons existing in or derived from natural strata, as well as other substances produced in association with such hydrocarbons;

"Pipeline" includes any connection point and/ or associated valve or pig trap to that Pipeline;

"Trans-Boundary Reservoir" means any single geological Petroleum structure or Petroleum field which extends across the Delimitation Line; and

"Unit Area" means the area for joint exploration and/or Exploitation of a Trans-Boundary Reservoir, as set out in the Licensees' Agreement as approved by the two Governments.

Article 1.3

Jurisdiction

(1)   Nothing in this Agreement shall be interpreted as affecting the sovereign rights and the jurisdiction which each State has under international law over the continental shelf which appertains to it.

(2)   All Installations on the continental shelf appertaining to the United Kingdom shall be under the jurisdiction of the United Kingdom and all Installations on the continental shelf appertaining to the Kingdom of Norway shall be under the jurisdiction of the Kingdom of Norway.

Article 1.4

Authorisation

(1)   The two Governments shall use their best efforts to facilitate Cross-Boundary Projects and shall not prevent or impede such projects by unreasonably withholding Authorisations.

(2)   The two Governments shall co-ordinate their relevant Authorisation procedures and where both Governments issue Authorisations they shall be given simultaneously, unless agreed otherwise, and shall be compatible with each other.

(3)   A Government shall not alter or modify any Authorisation for Cross-Boundary Projects nor grant the like rights to any other person nor consent to any assignment of any rights or obligations under such Authorisation where such changes are likely to affect materially the interests of the other Government, without prior consultation with that Government and having taken due account of all relevant matters raised by it.

(4)   In particular, a Government shall not grant any Authorisation or alter or modify an Authorisation for a Pipeline referred to in Chapter 2, so as to prevent there being joint or unified ownership of the whole length of the Pipeline, unless the two Governments agree otherwise.

(5)   A copy of an Authorisation granted by one of the Governments shall be made available on request to the other Government.

Article 1.5

Health, Safety and Environment: Standards

(1) The health, safety and environmental standards and/or requirements of the Government issuing the Authorisations relating to Cross-Boundary Projects shall be met. Both Governments recognise that, where there is an agreement pursuant to Article 2.4(5), that agreement shall not affect the application by the receiving coastal State of its own health, safety, environmental and other requirements for the Pipeline in question.

(2) To facilitate Cross-Boundary Projects, the two Governments shall encourage, where possible, the adoption of common health, safety and environmental standards and requirements. In any event, the two Governments shall seek to ensure that their respective standards and requirements are compatible. There shall be full consultation between the two Governments to this end.

(3) Having regard to the fact that:

(a) the Government with responsibility for the Host Facility may have an interest in health, safety and environmental issues concerning the reservoir being exploited and any associated facilities on the other State's continental shelf, and

(b) the Government with responsibility for the reservoir being exploited and any associated facilities may have a similar interest in such issues concerning the Host Facility,

the competent authorities of the two Governments shall consult with a view to putting in place appropriate procedures to safeguard the said interests of each Government.

(4) The two Governments undertake to make every endeavour, jointly and severally, after consultations, to ensure that:

(a) the Construction and Operation of any Installation or Pipeline shall not cause pollution of the marine environment or damage by pollution to the coastline, shore facilities or amenities, or damage to sensitive habitats or damage to vessels or fishing gear of any country; and

(b) appropriate procedures are in place for the safety and health of personnel.

(5) The competent authorities of the two Governments shall develop procedures for the implementation of this Article, including measures to be taken in an emergency.

Article 1.6

Health, Safety and Environment: Physical Access and Inspection

(1)   To enable Inspectors from each State to safeguard the interests of their Government in respect of health, safety and environmental matters, the competent authorities of the two Governments shall consult in order to agree on procedures for:

(a)   consultation;
(b)   access to all relevant information;
(c)   physical access, at all stages, to any Infrastructure relating to a Cross-Boundary Project; and
(d)   physical access in the territory of either State to terminals which are relevant to a Cross-Boundary Project.

(2)   The Inspectors of each Government shall act in co-operation and consult with Inspectors of the other Government with a view to achieving compliance with the health, safety and environmental standards and/or requirements applicable to a Cross-Boundary Project.

(3)   An Inspector of one Government may, with regard to Installations located on the continental shelf appertaining to the other State, request an Inspector of the other Government to exercise his powers to ensure compliance with the standards and/or requirements referred to in paragraph (2) whenever it appears that circumstances so warrant. In the event of any disagreement between the Inspectors of the two Governments or the refusal of the Inspector of the one Government to take action at the request of the Inspector of the other Government, the matter shall be referred to the competent authorities of the two Governments.

(4)   If it appears to an Inspector of either Government to be necessary or expedient for the purpose of averting an incident involving risk to life or serious personal injury, whether the danger is immediate or not, or minimising the consequences of such an incident, and time and circumstances do not permit consultation between the Inspectors of the two Governments, that Inspector may order the immediate cessation of any or all operations in relation to a Cross-Boundary Project. Immediately thereafter, the fact of such an order and the reason therefore shall be reported to the competent authorities of the two Governments who shall then consult to consider the actions necessary for the safe and speedy resumption of operations.

Article 1.7

Metering Systems and Inspection

(1)   Both Governments shall approve any metering system which is related to a Cross-Boundary Project and which is of common interest. The competent

authorities of the two Governments shall establish procedures for early approval of such a system.

(2)   When adopting standards for such metering systems, the two Governments shall pay particular regard to the economic impact of such standards on the Cross-Boundary Project in question, and shall ensure that the adoption of such standards shall not unfairly or unduly burden the economics of that Project. In the case of a Cross-Boundary Project making use of a Host Facility, the two Governments shall pay due regard to the prevailing standards for metering systems on that Host Facility. The two Governments shall also give due consideration as to whether new metering systems are appropriate in the light of metering arrangements already in place elsewhere on the continental shelf or in the territory of either State.

(3)   The competent authorities of the two Governments shall establish arrangements so that Inspectors of both Governments have access to relevant metering systems on the continental shelf or in the territory of either State to ensure that their interests are safeguarded.

Article 1.8

Physical Security

The competent authorities of the two Governments shall consult one another with a view to concluding such mutual arrangements as they consider appropriate in relation to the physical protection of Infrastructure.

Article 1.9

National and International Emergency

Nothing in this Agreement shall prejudice the exercise by each Government of its powers in the case of national or international emergency. Consultations shall be held at the earliest opportunity in order that the two Governments may agree on appropriate joint measures to reconcile the urgency of the situation with their common interest in the most effective Exploitation of reservoirs or the use of Infrastructure.

Article 1.10

Exchange of Information

(1)   Subject to lawful restrictions as to disclosure and use, both Governments will ensure the proper exchange of information between them relating to Cross-Boundary Projects.

(2) Recognising that the United Kingdom and Norwegian offshore pipeline and production systems will increasingly become interlinked, there is a need for increased information flows about upstream operations which affect downstream operations, and vice versa, and for information sharing, in particular between the Governments, other regulatory authorities and the relevant system operators. The two Governments recognise that such considerations apply also to existing pipeline connections between the two States.

(3) Where one Government, in order to ensure safe, effective and stable operations of the systems, places obligations on its field, pipeline, terminal or system operators to provide information about forecast or actual production from or through their facilities, or seeks to establish voluntary arrangements for the provision of that information, the other Government will not put obstacles in the way of the provision of such information by those field, pipeline, terminal or system operators about production crossing the Delimitation Line and being landed in the territory of the first Government. Both Governments will encourage the fullest exchange of information to meet these requirements.

(4) This Article applies to Cross-Boundary Projects, as well as to any installation and/or pipeline covered by any of the Agreements listed in Annex E.

Article 1.11

Tax

Profits arising from the use of Infrastructure relating to Cross-Boundary Projects, capital represented by such Infrastructure and capital gains arising from the disposal of such Infrastructure or an interest therein shall be taxed in accordance with the laws of the United Kingdom and the Kingdom of Norway respectively, including the Convention for the Avoidance of Double Taxation and the Prevention of Fiscal Evasion with respect to Taxes on Income and Capital signed at London on 12 October 2000[1] and any Protocol or Protocols to that Convention or any Convention replacing that Convention as may be signed in the future.

1   Treaty Series No. 26 (2001) Cm 5136.

Article 1.12

Construction of Pipelines and Use of Existing Infrastructure

(1) The two Governments shall seek to facilitate the use of existing Infrastructure capacity on fair, transparent and non-discriminatory terms including, where appropriate, the installation of connection points and/or any necessary associated valves during the construction of Pipelines to facilitate the process for subsequent tie-ins.

(2)   In furtherance of paragraph (1), should the two Governments receive a proposal for the Construction and Operation of a Pipeline (additional to Langeled South) to land Norwegian dry gas directly in the United Kingdom in circumstances where adequate spare capacity is available in United Kingdom offshore Infrastructure, the two Governments shall consult with a view to satisfying themselves that the process for selecting the transportation solution has been open and transparent and that the best economic solution has been selected. The determination of the need for and selection of transport capacity shall follow broadly the Work Process set out in Annex A.

Article 1.13

Continued Use and Termination

(1)   Where an Authorisation which has a direct effect on a Cross-Boundary Project is about to expire, and the holder of the Authorisation seeks its renewal, the Government responsible for that Authorisation shall, subject to its law, renew it.

(2)   Where an Authorisation which has a direct effect on a Cross-Boundary Project:

(a)   is likely to be or has been revoked; or
(b)   is due to expire or has expired without a renewal of that Authorisation being sought; or
(c)   is likely to be or has been surrendered,

the Government responsible for that Authorisation shall, in consultation with the other Government, consider the economic and practical options for continued use. Provided that economic and practical options for continued use are established, the Government responsible for that Authorisation shall, in accordance with its law, issue a new Authorisation to enable the Cross-Boundary Project to continue.

Article 1.14

Decommissioning

(1)   In respect of Installations associated with Cross-Boundary Projects, decommissioning plans are subject to the approval of the Government on whose continental shelf or in whose territorial waters the Installation is situated, after full consultation with the other Government. The aim of both Governments shall be to seek to reach agreement on decommissioning methods and standards and both Governments shall approve the timing of any such decommissioning.

(2) In respect of Cross-Boundary Pipelines:

(a) both Governments shall approve the timing of the decommissioning of a Cross-Boundary Pipeline;

(b) both Governments shall seek to reach agreement on decommissioning methods and standards; and

(c) in respect of the decommissioning of Langeled South, the two Governments shall approve the timing, methods and standards of such decommissioning.

(3) Decommissioning plans shall include:

(a) an estimate of the cost of the measures proposed in it; and

(b) details of the times at or within which the measures proposed in it are to be taken or make provision as to how those times are to be determined.

(4) In making decisions on decommissioning plans, the Government or Governments responsible shall address fully and take proper account of:

(a) applicable international requirements, standards or guidelines;

(b) safety hazards associated with decommissioning, including where relevant transport and disposal;

(c) safety of navigation;

(d) the environmental impact of the measures proposed;

(e) the impact of the measures proposed on other users of the sea;

(f) best available cost-effective techniques;

(g) economic factors;

(h) the timetable for decommissioning;

(i) the impact of the measures proposed on the continued operation or decommissioning of the Infrastructure not covered by the decommissioning plan;

(j) the views expressed by other persons having an interest; and

(k) other relevant matters raised by either Government.

(5) The Government or Governments responsible for the approval of the decommissioning plan may approve the plan with or without modifications or conditions. Before approving the plan with modifications or subject to conditions, the Government or Governments responsible for the approval of the decommissioning plan shall give the person (whether or not a Licensee) who submitted the plan an opportunity to make representations about the proposed modifications or conditions.

(6) The Government or Governments responsible for the approval of the decommissioning plan shall act without unreasonable delay in reaching a decision as to whether to approve or reject the plan and shall require the implementation of any plan so approved.

(7) If the decommissioning plan is rejected, the Government or Governments responsible for the approval of the plan shall inform the person who submitted the plan of the reasons for doing so. That person shall, in such circumstances,

223

be required to submit a revised plan within a specific time limit acceptable to the Government or Governments.

Article 1.15

Framework Forum

The two Governments hereby establish a Framework Forum to facilitate the implementation of this Agreement. The Framework Forum shall include representatives of each Government. The two Governments may agree to other parties attending when appropriate. The Framework Forum shall provide a means for ensuring continuous consultation and exchange of information between the two Governments and a means for resolving issues without the need to invoke the dispute settlement procedures set out in Chapter 5. The Framework Forum shall meet twice yearly or at other intervals agreed by the two Governments, and shall be subject to such further arrangements as may be agreed by the two Governments from time to time.

CHAPTER 2
CONSTRUCTION AND OPERATION OF AND ACCESS TO PIPELINES

Article 2.1

Authorisations

(1)   Where the two Governments agree to the Construction and Operation of a Cross-Boundary Pipeline, they shall individually grant the Authorisations required by their respective national law.

(2)   When an Authorisation referred to in paragraph (1) is required by only one Government, that Government shall consult with the other Government before granting such Authorisation.

Article 2.2

Agreement between Pipeline Owners

(1)   In respect of a Cross-Boundary Pipeline which is associated with a Trans-Boundary Reservoir and where Licensees of both States of that Trans-Boundary Reservoir have a participating interest in that Pipeline, each Government shall require its Licensees and/or its holders of an Authorisation to enter into a Licensees' Agreement. The Licensees' Agreement shall incorporate provisions

to ensure that, in the event of a conflict between the Licensees' Agreement and this Agreement, the provisions of this Agreement shall prevail.

(2) The Licensees' Agreement shall be submitted to the two Governments for their approval. Such approval shall be deemed to have been granted unless the Licensees and/or the holders of an Authorisation have been notified to the contrary, by either Government, within 60 days of its receipt of the document in question.

Article 2.3

Pipeline Operator

The appointment and any change of operator of a Cross-Boundary Pipeline shall be subject to agreement by the two Governments.

Article 2.4

Access System: Terms and Conditions

(1) The terms and conditions for access to a Cross-Boundary Pipeline, including the setting of entry and exit tariffs, shall be in accordance with applicable European Union law. The principles of fairness, non-discrimination, transparency and open access to spare capacity and avoidance of any abuse of a dominant position or other anti-competitive behaviour shall apply.

(2) Access to a Cross-Boundary Pipeline shall include physical access to capacity and, where appropriate, to facilities supplying technical services incidental to such access.

(3) Where a Government determines the financial terms for access to Pipelines related to a Cross-Boundary Project, those terms shall be such that they promote the optimal use of existing Pipelines and do not inhibit alternative options for using United Kingdom and Norwegian Pipelines and Pipeline systems, in whole or in part, for the transportation of Petroleum from one State to the other State.

(4) Where there are proposed changes to the regulations or guidelines relating to access to Pipelines of one State which may affect the commercial parties of the other State, there shall be the fullest consultation between the two Governments before any changes are made and due account shall be taken of any representations made.

(5) The two Governments may agree, on a case-by-case basis, to apply the access regime applicable to a Cross-Boundary Pipeline on the continental shelf of one State to the same Pipeline whilst on the continental shelf of the other State, but not in the coastal State's territorial waters.

(6)   The two Governments have agreed, in conformity with paragraph (5), that the Norwegian regulated access system shall apply to Langeled South and that the Norwegian Government shall set the exit tariffs, onshore, for that Pipeline.

Article 2.5

Access System: Entry Points and Tariffs

(1)   This Article applies to the setting of regulated entry points on either continental shelf and entry tariffs for Langeled South for Petroleum produced from a reservoir wholly or in part on the continental shelf appertaining to the United Kingdom.

(2)   Entry points and tariffs referred to in paragraph (1) shall be agreed jointly by the two Governments. Such entry tariffs shall normally be set at zero, subject to adjustments for positive or negative effects on the throughput and provided that all costs related to the tie-in are otherwise covered.

(3)   The two Governments shall, upon request, supply commercial parties with relevant information regarding the setting of new entry tariffs in such a manner as to provide predictability prior to investment decisions. Such information shall be supplied without undue delay, and, if possible, within sixteen weeks of such request. Such tariffs shall be formally determined simultaneously with the approval of the relevant project.

(4)   The conditions set out in this Article may also apply to other Cross-Boundary Pipelines if so agreed by the two Governments.

Article 2.6

Access System: Exit Points and Tariffs

(1)   This Article applies to the setting of regulated exit points and exit tariffs, offshore, in connection with the establishment of the First Dry Gas Link between United Kingdom and Norwegian offshore Infrastructure.

(2)   Exit points and tariffs referred to in paragraph (1) shall be set by the Norwegian Government in accordance with the principles set out in Annex B, and after full consultation with the United Kingdom Government.

(3)   The Norwegian Government shall provide sufficient information to the United Kingdom Government to enable that Government properly to satisfy itself that the decision fully and properly takes into account the principles set out in Annex B.

(4)   The conditions set out in this Article may also apply to other Cross-Boundary Pipelines if so agreed by the two Governments.

Article 2.7

Access System: Dispute Settlement

(1) This Article shall apply to:

(a) any dispute between the owner or operator of Langeled South and a shipper of Petroleum originating from the continental shelf appertaining to the United Kingdom as to whether or not the owner or operator of Langeled South has fully and properly complied with the terms and conditions laid down in the applicable regulated access system;

(b) any dispute concerning a tariff between the owner or operator of a United Kingdom Pipeline to which the First Dry Gas Link is to be connected and a shipper of Petroleum originating from the Norwegian continental shelf; and

(c) any dispute with regard to access to any other Cross-Boundary Pipeline, not covered by sub-paragraph (a) or (b) above, to the extent agreed by the two Governments.

(2) As regards a dispute covered by paragraph (1)(a), the dispute shall be submitted simultaneously to both Governments who shall jointly resolve the dispute within a reasonable time frame, taking into account the need for a speedy resolution. The principles underlying the determination of the dispute by the two Governments shall be transparent and non-discriminatory and wholly in accordance with Article 2.4(1). The decision of the two Governments shall be binding on all the parties involved.

(3) As regards a dispute covered by paragraph (1)(b), the dispute shall be resolved by the United Kingdom Government in accordance with the principles set out in Annex C, after fully consulting the Norwegian Government. The United Kingdom Government shall provide sufficient information to the Norwegian Government to enable the latter Government properly to satisfy itself that the decision fully and properly takes into account the principles set out in Annex C.

CHAPTER 3
JOINT EXPLOITATION OF TRANS-BOUNDARY
RESERVOIRS AS A UNIT

Article 3.1

Unitisation and Authorisations

(1) Where the two Governments, after consultation with their respective Licensees, agree that a Petroleum reservoir is a Trans-Boundary Reservoir which should be exploited, it shall be exploited as a single unit in accordance

with the terms of this Agreement, unless otherwise agreed by the two Governments.

(2)   Subject to paragraph (1), the two Governments shall individually grant the Authorisations required by their respective national law.

(3)   In the event that a Trans-Boundary Reservoir is to be exploited as a single unit by making use of a Host Facility, the two Governments shall agree the most appropriate procedures to exploit that Trans-Boundary Reservoir.

Article 3.2

Agreement between the Licensees

(1)   Each Government shall require its Licensees to enter into a Licensees' Agreement to regulate the Exploitation of a Trans-Boundary Reservoir in accordance with this Agreement. The Licensees' Agreement shall incorporate provisions to ensure that in the event of a conflict between the Licensees' Agreement and this Agreement, the provisions of this Agreement shall prevail.

(2)   The Licensees' Agreement shall be submitted to the two Governments for their approval. Such approval shall be deemed to have been granted unless the Licensees have been notified to the contrary, by either Government, within 60 days of its receipt of the Licensees' Agreement.

Article 3.3

Determination and Apportionment of Reserves

(1)   The Licensees' Agreement shall define the Trans-Boundary Reservoir to be exploited and include proposals for the determination of:

(a)   the geographical and geological characteristics of the Trans-Boundary Reservoir;
(b)   the total amount of the reserves and the methodology used for the calculation; and
(c)   the apportionment of the reserves as between the Licensees of each Government.

(2)   The Licensees' Agreement shall also specify:

(a)   either the arrangements for the outcome of a determination to apply for all time to all activities connected with the Exploitation of the Trans-Boundary Reservoir, or the procedures, including a timetable, for any redetermination of the matters referred to in paragraph (1), to be carried out by the unit operator, at the request of the Licensees or of either Government; and

(b)   the procedures, including a timetable, for the resolution of any dispute between the Licensees about any of the matters referred to in paragraph (1).

Article 3.4

Determination and Expert Procedure

(1)   If either Government is unable to agree to a proposal for the determination or redetermination of any of the matters referred to in Article 3.3(1), it shall so notify the other Government and the unit operator within the period provided for in Article 3.2(2).

(2)   The two Governments, having regard to the desire to reach an early resolution, shall use their best endeavours to resolve the matter in question. The unit operator may submit alternative proposals for this purpose.

(3)   If, within 60 days of the notification referred to in paragraph (1) or such other period as the two Governments may agree, the two Governments remain unable to resolve the matter in question, a single expert shall be appointed to reach a timely and independent determination of that matter. The expert shall be appointed and act in accordance with the terms of Annex D.

Article 3.5

Inclusion of Additional Licensed Area

(1)   If, after a Licensees' Agreement has been approved by the two Governments, the Governments agree that the limits of the Trans-Boundary Reservoir extend into an area of the continental shelf in respect of which another party holds a production Licence, the two Governments shall require all their respective Licensees with a participating interest in the Trans-Boundary Reservoir to agree arrangements for the effective Exploitation of the Petroleum in the area.

Any such arrangements shall be made within the time limit stipulated by the two Governments, be consistent with the provisions of this Agreement and be subject to the approval of the two Governments. The provisions of Article 3.2 shall apply to any such arrangements which take the form of a Licensees' Agreement.

(2)   In the event that arrangements are not made within the stipulated time limit, any further action to be taken shall be decided jointly by the two Governments.

Article 3.6

Inclusion of Non-Licensed Area

(1) If, after a Licensees' Agreement has been approved by the two Governments, the two Governments agree that the Trans-Boundary Reservoir extends into an area of the continental shelf which is not covered by a production Licence, the Government, to which the area of the continental shelf appertains, shall, without unreasonable delay, seek to remedy the situation by offering the said area for Licence.

(2) In the event that a production Licence is granted covering the area referred to in paragraph (1), the two Governments shall require all their respective Licensees with a participating interest in the Trans-Boundary Reservoir to agree arrangements for the effective Exploitation of the Petroleum in the area. Any such arrangements shall be made within the time limit stipulated by the two Governments, be consistent with the provisions of this Agreement and shall be subject to the approval of the two Governments. The provisions of Article 3.2 shall apply to any such arrangements which take the form of a Licensees' Agreement.

(3) If a production Licence is not granted or if a production Licence is granted but arrangements are not made within the stipulated time limit, any further action to be taken shall be decided jointly by the two Governments.

Article 3.7

Unit Operator

A unit operator shall be appointed by agreement between the Licensees of the two Governments as their joint agent for the purpose of exploiting a Trans-Boundary Reservoir in accordance with this Agreement. The appointment of, and any change of, the unit operator shall be subject to prior approval by the two Governments.

Article 3.8

Appraisal Wells

Subject to its law, neither Government shall withhold a permit for the drilling of wells by, or on account of, its Licensees for purposes related to the determination of any of the issues referred to in Article 3.3.

Article 3.9

Development Plan: Exploitation of a Trans-Boundary Reservoir

(1) The unit operator shall submit to the two Governments for their approval a development plan for the effective Exploitation of a Trans-Boundary Reservoir and for the transportation of Petroleum therefrom.

(2) In the event that a Trans-Boundary Reservoir is to be exploited by making use of a Host Facility, the development plan referred to in paragraph (1) shall include a description of those modifications to and operations on the Host Facility which are directly linked to the Exploitation of the Trans-Boundary Reservoir.

(3) The unit operator may at any time submit amendments to the development plan to the two Governments and may also be required to do so at the request of the two Governments. All amendments to the development plan are subject to approval by the two Governments.

Article 3.10

Commencement of Production

Unless otherwise agreed by the two Governments, neither Government shall permit the commencement of production from a Trans-Boundary Reservoir unless the two Governments have jointly approved, in accordance with this Agreement:

(a)   the Licensees' Agreement;
(b)   the unit operator referred to in Article 3.7; and
(c)   the development plan referred to in Article 3.9;

and have each granted any other necessary Authorisations.

Article 3.11

Use of an Installation within a Unit Area for the Exploitation of another Reservoir

In the event that an Installation, which is located within a Unit Area, is to be used for the exploration and/or Exploitation of a Petroleum reservoir outside that Unit Area, any necessary amendments required to the development plan referred to in Article 3.9 shall be submitted to the two Governments for approval. Such approval shall not be granted if such use would adversely affect the Exploitation of the Trans-Boundary Reservoir in accordance with this Agreement, unless the two Governments agree otherwise.

Article 3.12

Cessation of Production

The two Governments shall agree on the timing of the cessation of the production from a Trans-Boundary Reservoir.

CHAPTER 4
PROJECT USING A HOST FACILITY

Article 4.1

Authorisations

Where the two Governments and their respective Licensees agree to a project using a Host Facility, each Government shall, in addition to giving any approvals for the purposes of Articles 3.9 and 3.11, individually grant any Authorisations required by its respective national law.

Article 4.2

Development Plan

Subject to Articles 3.9 and 3.11, each Government shall require its Licensees to submit to it for its approval a development plan or a modification to an existing development plan, covering matters relevant to a project referred to in Article 4.1.

Article 4.3

Governmental Decision

Subject to Chapter 3, any Governmental decision:

(a) which relates to an Installation outside a Unit Area and which is relevant to its use as a Host Facility for a reservoir on the other side of the Delimitation Line or a Trans-Boundary Reservoir; or

(b) which relates to a reservoir on one side of the Delimitation Line making use of a Host Facility on the other side of the Delimitation Line, and which is relevant to that use;

shall be made by the Government on whose side of the Delimitation Line the Host Facility is placed or the reservoir lies, in close consultation with the other Government, taking due account of all matters raised by that Government.

An example of such a decision is the timing of the cessation of the relevant activities.

Article 4.5

Operator

Subject to Article 3.7, the appointment or change of operator of the reservoir and/or the Host Facility shall be subject to the approval of the Government on whose continental shelf the reservoir or Host Facility lies after consultation with the other Government.

CHAPTER 5
DISPUTE SETTLEMENT

Article 5

Conciliation Board

(1) Subject to paragraph (2), should the two Governments fail to reach agreement on the interpretation or application of this Agreement, including any matter to be resolved under it, the following dispute settlement procedure shall apply, unless the dispute falls within the procedures agreed under Article 3.4, or unless the two Governments agree otherwise:

(i)   either Government may request that the disputed matter be submitted to a Conciliation Board;

(ii)   the Conciliation Board shall consist of five members. Each Government shall designate two members, and the four members so designated shall designate the fifth (who shall not be a national of or habitually reside in the United Kingdom or in the Kingdom of Norway) who will act as the Chairman of the Conciliation Board;

(iii) if either Government fails to designate one or more members of the Conciliation Board within one month of a request to do so, either Government may request the President of the International Court of Justice to designate the required number of members;

(iv)   the same procedure shall apply *mutatis mutandis* if the four Conciliation Board members fail to designate a fifth member to act as Chairman within one month of the designation of the fourth member;

(v)   the Conciliation Board shall be entitled to all relevant information and may carry out any necessary consultations;

(vi)   the Conciliation Board shall be required to reach a decision within a reasonable time limit (taking into account the need for a speedy resolution);

(vii) decisions of the Conciliation Board shall be taken by simple majority and shall be binding on the two Governments; and

(viii) further rules of procedure relating to decisions of the Conciliation Board may be agreed by the two Governments.

(2) Where it falls to one Government, in accordance with Article 2.6 or Article 2.7(3) to determine an exit tariff, offshore, in a regulated access system or to settle a dispute over a tariff in a negotiated access system and the Framework Forum has been unable to resolve a disagreement between the two Governments on the matter in question, the Conciliation Board shall consider, at the request of either Government, whether:

(a) the information, which the Government taking the decision has provided to the other Government, was sufficient to enable that other Government properly to satisfy itself that the decision fully and properly took into account the principles in Annex B or Annex C; and

(b) the decision fully and properly took account of the relevant principles in Annex B or Annex C.

CHAPTER 6
FINAL CLAUSES

Article 6.1

Amendments and Termination

The two Governments may amend or terminate this Agreement at any time by agreement. Either Government may at any time request that consultations are initiated with a view to considering amendments to this Agreement. Such consultations shall commence within two months of the request, and shall be conducted expeditiously. In such consultations the two Governments shall consider fully and take proper account of the proposals for amendment with the aim of reaching a mutually acceptable solution within the shortest possible time.

Article 6.2

Other Petroleum Agreements

Without prejudice to Articles 1.10 and 2.6, this Agreement shall not affect the continued operation of the other Petroleum Agreements listed in Annex E, which shall prevail as long as they remain in force. Consequently, where the development of a Trans-Boundary Reservoir or of a project making use of a Host Facility is subject to this Agreement, a Pipeline, which is associated with such a development and which falls within the provisions of the Framework

Agreement signed at Stavanger on 25 August 1998, shall be subject to the latter Agreement.

Article 6.3

Entry into Force

This Agreement shall enter into force on the date on which the two Governments shall have informed each other that all necessary internal requirements have been fulfilled.

In witness whereof the undersigned, duly authorised by their respective Governments, have signed this Agreement.

Done in duplicate at Oslo this 4th day of April 2005 in the English and Norwegian languages, both texts being equally authoritative.

For the Government of the United
Kingdom of Great Britain and
Northern Ireland:

For the Government of
the Kingdom of Norway

MIKE O'BRIEN

THORHILD WIDVEY

ANNEX A

Work process to determine the need for and selection of additional transport capacity for dry gas from the kingdom of Norway to the United Kingdom

(1)   The following describes the process for establishing additional capacity for dry gas transport from the Gassled dry gas system to the United Kingdom, i.e. capacity in excess of the Vesterled and the Langeled South pipelines. This work process will involve Gassco (operator of the Norwegian continental shelf dry gas infrastructure), the owners of gas infrastructure in the Kingdom of Norway and the United Kingdom, gas shippers and the authorities in both countries (the Ministry of Petroleum and Energy and the Petroleum Directorate in Norway and the Department of Trade and Industry in the United Kingdom).

(2)   The annual Shipping and Transportation Plan prepared and maintained by Gassco registers the bookings and requests for future transport capacity by all companies (i.e. shippers) on the Norwegian continental shelf. The requested capacities in the Shipping and Transportation Plan are based on indicative volumes. The information provided by the shippers identifies both the entry and exit points for the different Gassled Areas (e.g. Area D – dry gas system) in the Norwegian continental shelf gas transportation system. The annual Shipping and Transportation Plan published in the second quarter of each year identifies the need for possible new transportation capacity and will determine the need for a new, dry gas connection from the Norwegian continental shelf to the United Kingdom. Timing (i.e. start up year) and the alternative Norwegian continental shelf node points to be assessed (e.g. Draupner, Sleipner, Heimdal etc.) will be included.

(3)   For example, the Shipping and Transportation Plan for 2003, presented to the User Forum on 12 June 2003 showed a requirement for an aggregated future capacity for shipments of dry gas to the United Kingdom from 2008 of 120 Million Sm3/d. Based on data from the Shipping and Transportation Plan in 2003, planned capacity at that time (Vesterled + Langeled South pipelines) was 105 Million Sm3/d, indicating a need for possible new transport solutions from the Norwegian continental shelf to the United Kingdom from 2008 of up to 15 Million Sm3/d.

(4)   Financing of any new transportation connection will require, on the one hand a group of gas shippers with an interest in transporting gas from the Norwegian continental shelf, and on the other, groups of investors (United Kingdom, Norwegian or others) putting forward proposals to build new transportation capacity. These groups may, therefore, have common members. United Kingdom infrastructure owners may also be part of the investor group.

(5)   Gassco will publish a Shipping and Transportation Plan every year. If such plan concludes that additional transport capacity is required and the shippers are prepared to take forward a project then they will open commercial discussions with United Kingdom infrastructure owners and potential investor groups. At the same time, the shippers and investors will initiate the commercial process with Gassco, on behalf of Gassled, for a tie-in to the Norwegian Gassled dry gas system. Exit tariffs will be determined by the Norwegian Government in accordance with Annex B. It is recognised that the potential investors and shippers must have early information on the cost of transportation in both the new and existing transportation systems to provide a basis for their investment and booking decisions.

(6) The shipper group and the potential investors, working with Gassco, will consider the technical and commercial proposals and carry out the concept selection process for the most appropriate new transportation connection. If a new connection is needed at least two years will be needed in preparation, to allow for the commercial and contractual discussions and for construction.

(7) All reasonable options for gas transportation will be developed to a similar level of technical and commercial maturity before concept selection to ensure a fair and open competition. Cost estimates and corresponding technical documentation will be open and accessible to all relevant parties.

(8) The process will be transparent but will also need to recognise the need to maintain effective competition between the proposals. To aid transparency, the mechanism for measuring and assessing proposals against the selection criteria will also be published in advance of the evaluation. The decision on the best option, including the route, for transporting gas to the United Kingdom, should be based on clear economic principles and provide the best economic solution for the shippers. The process will be fully transparent to the Framework Forum and that body will be the final arbiter in verifying that the concept selection process is being carried out in an open, fair and non-discriminatory manner and in accordance with the predetermined process. The Framework Forum will also be responsible for keeping development of new transport infrastructure under review and for encouraging a timely commercial process.

(9) If it is agreed that the link pipeline is incorporated into Gassled then Gassco will chair the process for establishing or amending the Participants' Agreement (ownership agreement) for the new infrastructure, including decisions on the investment shares and capacity rights, and will become the operator of the connection.

(10) The two Governments recognise that changes to the way in which the offshore industry in either the United Kingdom or the Kingdom of Norway is organised and/or regulated could result in a need to revise the Work Process set out in this Annex. In such event, the two Governments will, through the Framework Forum, revise this Annex so that it continues to reflect the process for establishing additional capacity to transport Norwegian dry gas to the United Kingdom. In drawing up any revision of this Annex, the two Governments will seek to satisfy themselves that the work process for selecting the best option, including the route, for transporting gas to the United Kingdom is fair and transparent, based on clear economic principles and provides the best economic solution for the shippers.

ANNEX B

The principles for determining exit points and tariffs offshore for the Norwegian dry gas system

(1) When an application to connect a Norwegian upstream system into a United Kingdom upstream system, or vice versa, is made and an exit tariff is to be determined, the Norwegian Government stipulating the tariff shall fully consult the United Kingdom Government before establishing a new exit point from the regulated system and the related tariff at such exit point.

(2) The two Governments shall apply the principles of non-discrimination, transparency and fairness for all parties concerned. The two Governments will aim to ensure optimal development and use of existing United Kingdom and Norwegian upstream transportation systems to ensure economically sound solutions and encourage the cost-efficient use of existing systems. The tariffs shall be cost- reflective.

(3) The Norwegian Government shall, when establishing an exit point and the related tariff, address fully and take proper account of the following factors:

(a) system effects in one system (capacities, pressures, temperatures, quality, etc.) as a result of offshore connection to another system. Such effects could be positive or negative;

(b) as a general principle all relevant investment costs arising from the new connection, including, where appropriate, a fair expected return to owners, shall be reimbursed by the users. Due account shall be taken of any wider benefits or costs to that system as a result of that connection;

(c) fair sharing of operating costs. The exit tariff from the Gassled system will include a fair share of the operating cost of the Gassled system;

(d) a fair expected return to owners on all basic (historic) capital costs of existing systems used to transport gas to the new exit point. This element will be well below the exit tariff at landing points.

(4) The Norwegian Government shall upon request supply commercial parties or the United Kingdom Government with relevant information regarding the stipulation of new tariffs in such a manner as to provide predictability prior to investment decisions and in any event, if possible, within sixteen weeks of such a request being made.

(5) Exit tariffs shall be formally determined simultaneously with the approval of the relevant project.

ANNEX C

Third party access to upstream infrastructure on the United Kingdom continental shelf

Tariff setting principles

(1) The United Kingdom Government supports the principle of non-discriminatory negotiated access to upstream infrastructure on the United Kingdom continental shelf, encourages transparency and promotes fairness for all parties concerned since it is important that prospective users have fair access to infrastructure at competitive prices whilst recognising that spare capacity in upstream infrastructure has a commercial value and that, having borne the cost and risk of installing it, the owner should be entitled to derive a fair commercial consideration for that value. Any tariff imposed by the Secretary of State would, accordingly, reflect a fair payment to the owner for real costs and for opportunities forgone.

(2) If the Secretary of State's powers to require access and to set a tariff were to be used:

(i)   infrastructure owners would have their consequential costs reimbursed, including indirect ones (e.g. the cost of interruption to the owner's throughput while a pipeline is modified to enable third party use);

(ii)   the tariff would be set so that the third party would bear a fair share of the total running costs incurred after his entry;

(iii) unless the supply in question were marginal or the infrastructure owner had already made other sufficient arrangements to recover the full capital costs, the financial arrangements proposed would normally take account of the basic capital costs[1] as well as the costs arising from the entry of the third party.

1   In newer infrastructure or infrastructure constructed or oversized with a view to taking third party business, the tariff set by the Secretary of State would normally include an allowance for recovery of capital costs incurred in the expectation of third party business. This allowance in the tariff would be set at a level sufficient to earn the owner a reasonable return on these costs if that allowance were applied to throughput expected at the time of the decision to invest – recognising the uncertainty inherent in projections of future use.

(3) On occasion, prospective third party users may be competing for access to the same limited capacity in infrastructure. In such circumstances, the Secretary of State is unlikely to require the owner to make the capacity available to a prospective user who values the capacity less than other prospective users and thus does not offer a better deal for the owner.

(4) For infrastructure with insufficient ullage to accommodate a third party's requirements, given the owner's rights and existing contractual commitments, the Secretary of State is unlikely to require access to be provided. If he were to do so, the tariff would need to reflect at least the cost to the infrastructure owner of backing off their own production and/or another party's contracted usage to accommodate the third party's (i.e. be based on the concept of opportunity cost).

ANNEX D

Expert procedure

(1) This Annex shall apply where a matter is to be determined by an expert pursuant to Article 3.4 of this Framework Agreement.

(2) The expert shall be chosen and his mandate and employment terms settled by agreement between the two Governments. The expert shall be chosen from amongst persons or organisations who or which are recognised as experts in the relevant field and who or which can provide undertakings in respect of any conflict of interests which shall be in the form set out in the Appendix, unless otherwise agreed by the two Governments. Any contractors that the expert may employ to assist in reaching his decision must also provide undertakings in substantially similar terms. The expert and any contractor so employed will be required to safeguard the confidentiality of any information supplied to him.

(3) If no agreement has been reached on the choice of expert, the mandate and/or his employment terms within 6 weeks from the date on which either Government initiates the process provided for in this Annex, the two Governments shall ask the President of the Institut français du pétrole, or such other person or organisation if so agreed by the two Governments, to choose an expert from between two candidates, one nominated by each Government, and/or to determine the mandate and/or the terms of employment. If only one Government has nominated an expert, that expert shall be chosen.

(4) Each Government shall ensure that all information requested by the expert in order to reach a decision shall be provided promptly. The expert may only meet with one Government jointly with the other Government. All communications between one Government and the expert outside such meetings shall be conducted in writing and any such communication shall be copied to the other Government.

(5) Within 12 weeks of his appointment, the expert shall provide a preliminary decision to the two Governments together with a fully detailed explanation of how that decision has been reached. Thereafter there will be a period of 8 weeks (or such other period as the two Governments may agree) from the date that the preliminary decision is communicated to the two Governments so that they may seek clarification of that decision and/or make submissions to the expert for his consideration. The final decision of the expert along with a fully detailed explanation for that decision shall be communicated in writing to the two Governments within 4 weeks of the end of this period. Save in the event of fraud or manifest error, the decision of the expert shall be final and binding on the two Governments who shall ensure that the decision is implemented by the unit operator acting on behalf of the relevant licensees.

(6) The expert shall apportion liability for his fees and costs between the two Governments in a way that seems to him to be just and reasonable in all the circumstances. Either Government may recover from the unit operator any amounts payable under this paragraph.

APPENDIX TO ANNEX D

Model conflict of interest undertakings

(1) [Name of expert] hereby warrants that he has not performed since [date], and will not perform during the course of his resolution of the matters in question, any work for either the Government of the United Kingdom or the Government of the Kingdom of Norway, or any Licensee of the [ ] Field or a Licensee of any other Field on the continental shelf appertaining to the United Kingdom or the Kingdom of Norway, which could influence his performance of, or conflict with his duties in relation to his resolution of the aforesaid matters in question. In particular, he warrants that he has not undertaken any work relating to the [ ] Field or for any of the [ ] Field Licensees within the last two years.

(2) [Name of contractor] hereby warrants that he has not performed since [date], and will not perform during the period for which he has been engaged by [name of expert] in connection with the Framework Agreement of 4 April 2005 concerning Cross-Boundary Petroleum Co-operation, any work for either the Government of the United Kingdom or the Government of the Kingdom of Norway, or any [ ] Field Licensee or a Licensee of any other Field on the continental shelves appertaining to the United Kingdom or the Kingdom of Norway, which could influence his performance of, or conflict with his duties under his contract with [name of expert]. In particular, he warrants that he has not undertaken any work relating to the [ ] Field or for any of the [ ] Field Licensees within the last two years.

ANNEX E

Existing petroleum agreements

Agreement of 22 May 1973,[1] as amended by the Exchange of Notes dated 27 July 1994[2], relating to the transmission of petroleum by pipeline from the Ekofisk field and neighbouring areas to the United Kingdom

1 Treaty Series No. 101 (1973) Cmnd 5423.
2 Treaty Series No. 1 (1995) Cm 2721.

Framework Agreement

Agreement of 10 May 1976[1], as amended by the Agreement of 25 August 1998[2] and the Exchange of Notes dated 21 June 2001[3] relating to the exploitation of the Frigg Field Reservoir and the transmission of gas therefrom to the United Kingdom; and the use of the installations and pipelines for the exploitation and transmission of Hydrocarbons

1   Treaty Series No. 113 (1977) Cmnd 7043.
2   Treaty Series No. 21 (2002) Cm 5513.
3   Treaty Series No. 43 (2001) Cm 5258.

Agreement of 16 October 1979[1], as amended by the Exchange of Notes dated 24 March 1995[2], relating to the exploitation of the Statfjord Field Reservoirs and the offtake of petroleum therefrom

1   Treaty Series No. 44 (1981) Cmnd 8282.
2   Treaty Series No. 57 (1995) Cm 2941.

Agreement of 16 October 1979[1] and Supplementary Agreements of 22 October 1981[2] and 22 June 1983[3], as amended by the Exchange of Notes dated 9 August 1999[4], relating to the exploitation of the Murchison Field Reservoir and the offtake of petroleum therefrom

1   Treaty Series No. 39 (1981) Cmnd 8270.
2   Treaty Series No. 25 (1982) Cmnd 8577.
3   Treaty Series No. 71 (1983) Cmnd 9083.
4   Treaty Series No. 110 (2000) Cm 4857.

Agreement of 21 November 1985[1], amended by the Agreement of 1 November 2004, between the two Governments relating to the transmission by pipeline of Heimdal Liquids to the United Kingdom

1   Treaty Series No. 39 (1987) Cm 201.

Framework Agreement of 25 August 1998[1] relating to the laying, operation and jurisdiction of inter-connecting submarine pipelines

1   Treaty Series No. 9 (2003) Cm 5762.

Index

[All references are to paragraph number]